Palgrave Studies in Classical Liberalism

Series Editors
David F. Hardwick, Department of Pathology and Laboratory Medicine, The University of British Columbia, Vancouver, BC, Canada
Leslie Marsh, Department of Pathology and Laboratory Medicine, The University of British Columbia, Vancouver, BC, Canada

This series offers a forum to writers concerned that the central presuppositions of the liberal tradition have been severely corroded, neglected, or misappropriated by overly rationalistic and constructivist approaches.

The hardest-won achievement of the liberal tradition has been the wrestling of epistemic independence from overwhelming concentrations of power, monopolies and capricious zealotries. The very precondition of knowledge is the exploitation of the epistemic virtues accorded by society's situated and distributed manifold of spontaneous orders, the DNA of the modern civil condition.

With the confluence of interest in situated and distributed liberalism emanating from the Scottish tradition, Austrian and behavioral economics, non-Cartesian philosophy and moral psychology, the editors are soliciting proposals that speak to this multidisciplinary constituency. Sole or joint authorship submissions are welcome as are edited collections, broadly theoretical or topical in nature.

More information about this series at
https://link.springer.com/bookseries/15722

Geoffrey C. Kellow

The Wisdom of the Commons

The Education of Citizens from Plato's Republic to The Wealth of Nations

Geoffrey C. Kellow
The College of the Humanities
Carleton University
Ottawa, ON, Canada

ISSN 2662-6470   ISSN 2662-6489 (electronic)
Palgrave Studies in Classical Liberalism
ISBN 978-3-030-95871-8   ISBN 978-3-030-95872-5 (eBook)
https://doi.org/10.1007/978-3-030-95872-5

© The Editor(s) (if applicable) and The Author(s), under exclusive license to Springer Nature Switzerland AG 2022

This work is subject to copyright. All rights are solely and exclusively licensed by the Publisher, whether the whole or part of the material is concerned, specifically the rights of translation, reprinting, reuse of illustrations, recitation, broadcasting, reproduction on microfilms or in any other physical way, and transmission or information storage and retrieval, electronic adaptation, computer software, or by similar or dissimilar methodology now known or hereafter developed.

The use of general descriptive names, registered names, trademarks, service marks, etc. in this publication does not imply, even in the absence of a specific statement, that such names are exempt from the relevant protective laws and regulations and therefore free for general use.

The publisher, the authors and the editors are safe to assume that the advice and information in this book are believed to be true and accurate at the date of publication. Neither the publisher nor the authors or the editors give a warranty, expressed or implied, with respect to the material contained herein or for any errors or omissions that may have been made. The publisher remains neutral with regard to jurisdictional claims in published maps and institutional affiliations.

This Palgrave Macmillan imprint is published by the registered company Springer Nature Switzerland AG

The registered company address is: Gewerbestrasse 11, 6330 Cham, Switzerland

For Aidan and Jamieson, who never cease to teach me about virtue.

Acknowledgments

The author thanks the University of Toronto Press for permission to reprint sections of an earlier essay, "A Shortage of Men: Wealth, Rank, and Recognition in Cicero's Civic Education," from *On Oligarchy: Ancient Lessons for Global Politics*, edited by David Edward Tabachnick and Toivo Koivukoski © University of Toronto Press 2011.

This project started out as a Doctoral dissertation. While it has grown and changed a great deal from that original effort, I remain indebted to the members of my Doctoral Committee for their insights and criticisms of the original work. I am particularly grateful to the members of that committee who in time became my colleagues and friends, W. R. Newell, Tom Darby, and Farhang Rajaee. W. R. Newell, who served as my supervisor, has long been a vital resource and prudent counsellor not only regarding political theory but academic life and politics more generally. Some of his insights appear explicitly in this book, his wisdom can be found throughout. I am grateful to two other colleagues I am fortunate to count as friends. Jarrett Carty and John Colman have encouraged my research and challenged my thinking ever since graduate school.

I must finally acknowledge the tireless support and encouragement of Kelly Walker, she was this work's first reader, from beginning to end, from title to index, as in all things, her advice has been invaluable.

Contents

1	**Introduction**	1
2	**Plato's Journey from the Cave to the City**	9
	Introduction	9
	Athenian Education and Politics	13
	Socrates and Plato as Teachers	20
	Education and Diaresis	23
	The Civic Education of the Non-Philosophic in Plato's *Republic*	26
	Education and Socialization	29
	True Opinion and Civic Education	34
	The Laws	42
	Education and Habituation	44
	Reason and Calculation, Logos and Logismos	48
	Consonance	51
	Plato's Civic Prescription	56
	An End and an Invitation	64

3	**Cicero's Civic Education at the Dawn of Empire**	65
	Introduction	66
	The Athenian Capture of Rome	67
	Roman History and Greek Philosophy	74
	Innovation and Transformation	80
	The Decline of Roman Education	89
	The Status of the Student	95
	Statesmen and Teachers	98
	A Shortage of Men	102
4	**Locke's Education for Ordinary Life and Liberal Citizenship**	107
	Introduction	108
	The Teaching of the Tabula Rasa	113
	The Reintroduction of Nature and the Philosophic Student	117
	Civic Education and the Non-Philosophic Citizen	126
	The Non-Philosophic Student and the Uniform Pedagogy	130
	Habit and Custom: The Civic Education of Gentlemen	137
5	**Rousseau and the Redefinition of Nature and Education**	147
	Introduction	147
	Duty and Inclination: Nature at the Crossroads	152
	A Savage for the City: The Education of Emile	157
	After Locke: Rousseau's Education in Sense and Experience	161
	The Lesson of Necessity	170
	Politics, Citizenship, and Philo-Sophie	175
	Rousseau's Revolution	184
6	**Adam Smith's Sentimental Education**	187
	Introduction	187
	A Civic Reading of the *Wealth of Nations*	190
	The Division of Labor	193
	Civic Character and the Division of Labor	195

    The Theory of Moral Sentiments: Sympathy
    as the "Essential Part"   199
    Sympathy, Variety of Experience, and Civic Character   209
    "Things Familiar to the Mind"   214

7   **The Future of Character and Education**   219
    Recovering the Lost Legacy of Liberal Learning and Civic
    Virtue   223

Selected Bibliography   229

Index   237

1

Introduction

Less than two-thirds of Canadians voted in the last federal election. Over the last fifty years, voter participation has trended steadily (if not quite exclusively) downward. Political scientists, the press and policy analysts attribute a portion of this incremental retreat of Canadians from the public life of their country to "voter fatigue." Similar symptoms and similar diagnoses can be found across the liberal and democratic world. A peculiarly modern malaise, voter fatigue apparently presents as an increased sense of political apathy and a withdrawal from civil society brought on by being asked to vote too often.[1] The diagnosis of voter fatigue constitutes one of those rare moments when the suggestion of a possible diagnosis, in and of itself, indicates a more severe underlying malaise afflicting both doctor and patient. Like the diagnosis of bourgeois tendencies, demonic possession, or imbalanced humors, the very

---

[1] Arend Lijphart, "Unequal Participation: Democracy's Unresolved Dilemma," *American Political Science Review* 91, no. 1 (1997): 8.

act of diagnosing voter fatigue itself presents as a far more dismaying social symptomatology. A public worn out and emptied of its reserves of civic duty by the occasional act of voting and semi-regular attention to public events must be morally and politically enfeebled to a degree unforeseen by both ancient and modern advocates *and* critics of popular government. More worrying still, a populace so enfeebled, threatens free government in a manner all too often seized upon by its enemies.

In what follows I plan to consider a question pointedly put to the emerging British democracy by Adam Smith. Smith, all too rarely recognized as an advocate for the ordinary citizen, in contemplating the industrial immiseration of the poor suggested

> In free countries, where the safety of government depends very much upon the favourable judgment which the people may form of its conduct, it must surely be of the highest importance that they should not be disposed to judge rashly or capriciously concerning it.[2]

Voter fatigue, the listless avoidance of the mildest of civic duties, surely constitutes the rashest of judgments, the most capricious approach to matters of highest import and ultimately a grave threat to the safety of government. Nonetheless this book does not directly concern itself with this lamentable malaise. Instead, it focusses on the whole patient: the ordinary citizen. It seeks to uncover, in a study of five of the most influential political thinkers in the Western tradition, a common concern for the education of the ordinary citizen. It seeks to locate, within a tradition that stretches from Pericles' Funeral Oration to the deep wells of democracy described in the Letter from the Birmingham Jail, the educational sources of civic virtue. From Plato's *Republic* to the *Wealth of Nations* I aim to identify the means by which liberal education sustains the combination of conviction, custom, and character upon which liberal democracies depend.

In examining Plato, Cicero, John Locke, Jean-Jacques Rousseau, and Adam Smith I intend to establish the existence and illuminate the essence of a common concern with civic education civic virtue and citizenship

---

[2] Adam Smith, *An Inquiry into the Nature and Causes of the Wealth of Nations* (Indianapolis: Liberty Fund, 1981), V.i.g.

stretching from Athens to America. Fundamental to this connection my account implies a second more immediate contention: that a full understanding of these earlier philosophers enriches both the context and the content of the present debates surrounding liberal education and offers powerful arguments, beyond those found in that debate currently, for a reinvigoration of civic virtues and a recovery of civil society through a robust liberal civic education. I hope to uncover a long-overlooked strand of the tradition of liberal education: the education of the ordinary citizen. I further seek to demonstrate that there exists a continuous, specific, and discrete concern for the civic education of the student for whom civic education constitutes the apex of possibility. Moreover, I will argue that such an education provides a pedagogic, political, and moral foundation upon which rests the fate of the entire community.

Speaking about liberal education the philosopher Leo Strauss once (in)famously commended that education as "the ladder by which we try to ascend from mass democracy to democracy as originally meant. Liberal education is the necessary endeavour to found an aristocracy within democratic mass society."[3] At its core this book addresses the education of that democratic mass society, those out of whom Leo Strauss' aristocracy might emerge. Liberal education may have been concerned historically with founding an aristocracy, but it also maintained, over nearly the entirety of its tradition, an equal regard for the education of the demos. The tradition of liberal education, defined, debated, and constructed by the authors examined, always understood that general society, in its civic capacities, to be foundational. Each of the philosophers I will discuss endorses a bicameral (at least) vision of liberal education, each accepts the inextricable connection between the education and the existence of both the philosophic and the civic pupil.

For at least a quarter century now, dating back to the publication of Allan Bloom's *The Closing of the American Mind*, a renewed debate, accompanied by an ever-expanding literature, has explored the relationship between liberal education and citizenship. Much of this literature has been of a decidedly popular character, clearly written in the hope

---

[3] Leo Strauss, *Liberalism Ancient and Modern* (New York: Basic Books, 1968), 5.

of engaging a readership beyond the usual ambit of scholarly composition. This popular approach suggests the already widespread and growing conviction that the decline of liberal education presents a threat to the health of modern political community. This conviction contains an urgency and range of concern that goes far beyond the traditional interests or preferred issues of right or left. Indeed authors as diverse as Allan Bloom, Christopher Lasch, Martha Nussbaum, and Todd Gitlin have published highly accessible, and more remarkably, mutually sympathetic books addressing liberal education's relationship to politics.

I don't plan to contribute directly to this debate in its current incarnation. Instead, I hope that by discussing five philosophical treatments of the relationship of liberal education to citizenship and civic virtue I can draw out the historical lineage of both liberal civic education and the debate surrounding it. In examining Plato, Cicero, John Locke, Jean-Jacques Rousseau, and Adam Smith I hope to illustrate the existence and essence of a common concern for civic education that connects all five philosophers' discussions of civic virtue and citizenship. Fundamental to this connection my account implies a second more immediate contention: that a full understanding of these earlier philosophers informs both the context and the content of the present debates surrounding liberal education and offers powerful arguments, beyond those found in the present debate, for a reinvigoration of civic virtues and a recovery of civil society through a robust and liberal civic education.

I use the somewhat adjectivally awkward formula "liberal civic education" advisedly. I want to draw out the specific civic vision of liberal education. I want to argue that the distinction between civic and philosophic education is central to the tradition of liberal education. It is a distinction not only in degree but in kind. Indubitably, philosophic education and its intended pupil enjoy a pedagogically and indeed an epistemologically privileged status in the tradition I am considering. However, their privileged education and access to knowledge do not translate into a commensurate primacy of concern in the treatment of education offered by Plato, Cicero, Locke, Rousseau, and Smith. Each philosopher offers a full account of education and therefore each philosopher offers an account not only of the ultimate but also the penultimate liberal education.

In recognizing two distinct educations this tradition explicitly recognizes two distinct pupils definitively divided by the facts of their respective natures. Even Rousseau, the most reluctant of my pedagogic bicameralists, rejects a monolithic account of liberal education because those it seeks to educate are not monolithic in nature. A differentiated conception of liberal education is the necessary consequence of the natural differentiation of ability among students. All five of the philosophers I treat conclude that difference among students does not provide an argument only for an exclusive and elite education for the few but instead insists upon a nuanced acknowledgment of the necessity of an ontologically appropriate education for the many. This complex and multifaceted understanding of liberal education is sensitive to the diverse and multivariate character of its intended. This sense is the second common thread that connects these philosophers as deeply as the recognition of the inextricable character of the civic and philosophic. These thinkers all divide the population of potential pupils in to two groups on fundamentally epistemic grounds. All five thinkers seek to educate those who are not destined for philosophic knowledge, for whom the truths of the civil order must remain as true opinions. They seek to settle these truths in the characters of their charges by using non-rational means, most especially exercise, habit, and custom. In all five thinkers the philosopher stands apart from the citizen. This intellectual and epistemic sorting, with its assumptions about how the truth is encountered, separates these five philosophers out from the central assumptions of both the Christian tradition in liberal education as commonly propounded and the Enlightenment's hope for a widespread and rational escape from reason's regency.

That this bicameral and ontologically differentiated understanding of liberal education needs recovering testifies to the success of liberal education's critics and the failure of its supporters to understand and defend its true nature. This failure presents most obviously and egregiously in the intemperate debates around the "The Western Canon." While attention invariably focuses on clashes over curricula, the real challenge and the fundamental necessity of liberal education gets lost and the truly existential crises it faces are ignored. By far the most pressing consequence of the misapprehension of liberal education as the rote learning of the normative, epistemological, and cultural assumptions of the West has been the reinvigoration of two powerful streams of criticism of liberal education. Neither is new. Both have persisted since the beginnings of liberal education; both have grown stronger in recent decades. In place of a liberal education the first stream of criticism advocates an education that is narrowly utilitarian and increasingly technological. This line of argument contends that inasmuch as an education in "the canon" ill equips students for success in the modern marketplace it has become unprofitable and anachronistic. The second stream of criticism is cultural and contends that liberal education, also understood as an education in "the canon," amounts to an assertion of cultural superiority that it is intolerant of difference and harmful to non-Western students. To each of these critiques, from Plato to Smith, the tradition of liberal civic education has provided convincing rejoinders rooted in the close connection between pedagogy and ontology, between civic education and the nature of its intended, and between philosophic and political life.

There can be little doubt that the idea of democratic citizenship changed dramatically between its origins in the Athenian polis to its early modern re-emergence. Much of this transformation presents as progress toward ever-increasing inclusion in the institutions of citizenship combined with a commensurate impoverishment of the substantive content of those institutions. This double movement is tragically self-reinforcing. As it occludes from view the deep connection between liberal education and citizenship the purview and import of the latter diminishes and the perceived necessity of the former, the only possible curative, also disappears from view. Liberal education, an education meant to prepare the student for the meaningful exercise of liberty understood as the informed participation in political life, is both dependent on and generative of robust citizenship.

Liberal education aims at a very particular sort of citizen. A citizen who is fitted for both governing and being governed, educated to participate in meaningful deliberation about the good life to the extent the institutions of citizenship and his nature permits and to both implement and abide by the outcome of those deliberations. This definition of the citizen, in its essence, has been present since liberal education's beginnings. His deliberations and their results are the consequence of the right education of his character and not the mere expression of the prejudices of his time or place. Such a citizen, so educated, escapes both the cultural critique's derision and the consequences of transforming liberal education along the utilitarian lines. To the philosophers to be discussed and the tradition I aim to describe genuine liberal civic education aims at a full realization of citizenship, that unique dual noun, both virtue and institution. Civic education teaches neither praxis nor values, civic education is a revelatory act, it ushers into the world its citizens.

Recalling the cultural critique need not suggest that such an education is or must be explicitly hostile to culture or for that matter to the idea of multiculturalism. Nothing of the philosophers here to be discussed precludes the possibility, indeed the reality that various cultures have over time contributed to our understanding of the world and our place in it. What this conception of education and citizenship rejects is the notion that human nature and the structure of human society is something purely conventional, contingent, and specific to each political community. In an undeniably multicultural era this teaching has gained new significance. What this model of education and citizenship offers is an alternative to the parlor Nietzscheanisms propounded by of cultural relativists, that all too often serve as little more than a festive mask over an unserious nihilism. This vision of the liberal education of citizens, far from being anachronistic, addresses the modern cultural condition wherein the unquestioning acceptance of the truth of a given culture's worldview is effectively ruled out by the ready availability of alternatives. A condition in which, in the absence of a forceful defense of liberal education, crass cultural relativism has won by default. This vision of liberal education and citizenship also offers an alternative to a Pyrrhic approach to diversity which struggles vainly (and all too often vitriolically) to assimilate and sublimate all difference into a highly dubious monoculture described simply as "The Western Tradition." Liberal education is, for the philosophers discussed herein, an education directed at liberty, in particular liberty that gains its fullest expression in the lived virtues of the institution.

In seeking to understand the education of the ordinary citizen what emerges, in place of a belief in a broad potential for philosophic enlightenment, is a belief in a broad potential for civic virtue. The education of the ordinary citizen is based on a fundamental supposition about his nature beyond the quotidian, it is based on a belief in the common possibility on the part of ordinary individuals, to participate fully in virtue. Virtue, and specifically civic virtue, is the democratic quality of humanity, distributed by nature much more broadly and on much more generous terms than philosophic reasoning. To posit the suitability of most citizens for a non-philosophic education is to place them in the penultimate position, but for none of the philosophers discussed below does this ordination imply derision.

2

Plato's Journey from the Cave to the City

> Just as Socrates felt that it was necessary to create a tension in the mind so that individuals could rise from the bondage of myths and half-truths to the unfettered realm of creative analysis and objective appraisal, so must we see the need for nonviolent gadflies to create the kind of tension in society that will help men rise from the dark depths of prejudice and racism to the majestic heights of understanding and brotherhood.
>
> Martin Luther King, Letter from Birmingham Jail, April 16, 1963[1]

Introduction

Plato's dialogues contain no more famous image than that of the Cave in Book Seven of the *Republic*. The Myth of the Cave, moving between metaphor and allegory in a fluid chiaroscuro of ascent, illumination, descent, and darkening marks the starting point for any understanding of

---

[1] Martin Luther King, "Letter from Birmingham Jail, April 16, 1963. http://mlk-kpp01.stanford.edu/index.php/resources/article/annotated_letter_from_birmingham/.

Plato's theory of education. Plato's master metaphor illuminates not only in its imagery but also in the context in which it is found, deep within a discussion of the ideal city. Significantly, Plato places his philosophic and lyrical account of the ascent to wisdom in the center of a philosophic account of politics and the limits of its wisdom. The *Republic* presents a vision of education bracketed and bounded by politics. The allegory of the cave, its illuminating fire and the path upward to daylight are immersed in the story of the city.

While the *Republic* centers on a Cave Plato's other dialogue of the city, *Laws,* concludes at the mouth of another cave, the Cretan shrine to Zeus. Plato ties the dialogues together with journeys, toward and out of caves. Moreover, in both instances Plato's caves serve as metaphors for classroom and city, a subterranean venue for the schooling of citizens in the civic as opposed to the super mundane virtues. The *Republic* explores this distinction and boundary by placing education, the ideal education to be precise, in a context and a conflict with a politics that defines the realm of the pedagogically possible. In the *Laws* Plato treats the natural correlate to the philosophic education delimited by politics: the political education delimited by philosophy. Like philosophy and politics, Plato's two greatest dialogues engage one another in conversation, they complement and imply one another, all the while drawing attention to the essential tension between philosophy and politics, philosopher, and citizen.

Of course, this only partially explains the relationship between Plato's two most expansive and thematically diverse dialogues. Indeed, it does not even exhaust the educational relationship between the two. However, it suffices for my purposes, namely unpacking the specifically civic education that Plato presents. Setting aside the focus of my own inquiry, my interest in Plato's account of a specifically civic education, much remains to suggest that the *Republic* surrounds but does not overwhelm the substance of the *Laws*. More than anything else, the dramatic action of the *Laws* seems to justify treating the *Republic* as both prelude and postscript.

In the *Laws* three men set out on a day's journey. The three men, an Athenian Stranger, a Spartan named Megillos, and Kleinias the sole native of Crete, travel across the island to a shrine to Zeus, a sacred cave. On the way they discuss the founding of a new city to be established in

Crete, a task charged to Kleinias. They debate laws, discuss education, and compare governing institutions and forms. In discussing the education of rulers and citizens the Athenian outlines the civic education of the latter and hints at the philosophic education of the former. As their journey nears its end the three begin to discuss the highest ruling institution, the Nocturnal Council. Of all the Cretan city's citizens these ruling councilors alone will receive a philosophic education. Placing it alongside the account of civic education discussed on their daylong sojourn, the Athenian promises to describe this higher philosophic education (*Laws* 965b).[2] The Athenian Stranger does not keep his promise, but Plato does. At journey's end the Stranger pauses, assesses his two pupils and realizes that he has taken the civic-minded Kleinias and Megillos as far as they can go. The Athenian Stranger takes them up to the entrance of the cave and no further. The journey into philosophy and ultimately out of the cave is left to another Athenian and another dialogue, to Socrates and to the *Republic*.

In the *Republic* the philosopher stands, albeit ever so briefly, above but also outside the Cave. Then, inevitably, he returns. Journeying into the cave the account of education offered inverts the order, the thematic substance, and the silences of the *Laws*. In the Cave of the *Republic,* Plato admits the necessity of educating its subterranean denizens but never fully illuminates what such an education entails. Plato acknowledges that the philosopher who returns must rule, and by implication, educate the cave dwellers, as Socrates reminds Glaucon

> My friend, you have again forgotten," I said, "it's not the concern of law that any one class in the city fare exceptionally well, but it contrives to bring this about in the city as a whole, harmonizing the citizens, by persuasion and compulsion, making them share with one another the benefit that each is able to bring to the commonwealth. (*Republic* 519e–520a)[3]

How precisely Socrates plans to effect this harmonization remains radically under-explained in the *Republic*. For an adequate account Plato's

---

[2] Plato, *The Laws of Plato*, trans. Thomas Pangle (Chicago: University of Chicago Press, 1988).
[3] Plato, *The Republic of Plato*, trans. Allan Bloom (Basic Books, 1991).

readers must turn back to the *Laws*. As Glenn Morrow noted in his scrupulous *Plato's Cretan City*, Plato's cavernous contrapuntal movement, with the civic and the philosophic ever approaching and retreating from one another, mimics the mutually prefacing and post-scripting relationship between *Laws* and *Republic*.[4]

The *Laws* and *Republic*, treating philosophy and politics, are strung together by the cord of character. Character, both of citizen and statesman reveals itself in two distinct but not discrete elements of the Platonic dialogue: the argument and the action. Examining the question of civic education in Plato's *Republic* and *Laws* entails examining the action and then the argument as intertwined aspects of that education. The dramatic portrayal of Socrates as a teacher alone suggests volumes about Plato's views on education.[5] As much as the dramatic character of Socrates reveals about Plato's ideas of civic education those ideas gain further nuance in the nature of the dialogues themselves. The complex interplay of argument, admonition, and aporia on the page serves to cultivate an equally complex interplay between reader and text. The dialogue, in the act of its careful study, teaches in a way connected and yet still distinct from the teaching presented by the characters of Socrates and the Athenian Stranger.

Moving on from a discussion of the action to the argument in Plato's *Republic* and *Laws* to the substance of Plato's teaching involves exploring the explicit imagery of approach and ascent common to both dialogues. Such an approach suggests a fruitful application of Plato's schematic teaching in *Republic* to an interpretation of the pedagogic methods in the *Laws*. The detailed and specific pedagogic content of the *Laws,* most especially the full significance of its recommendations regarding civic education, surface only when drawn out alongside the account of education and soul craft offered in the *Republic*. Reading the *Laws* before,

---

[4] Glenn Morrow, *Plato's Cretan City* (Princeton: Princeton University Press, 1966), 507.

[5] I am convinced by the Aristotelian contention that the Athenian Stranger in the *Laws* is a dramatic rendering of Socrates had he visited Crete instead of remaining in Athens until the events that lead to his trial and execution. For more on this see Aristotle (*Politics* 1265b, 18) and Leo Strauss, *What Is Political Philosophy?* (Chicago: University of Chicago Press, 1988), 32–33.

through, and after the *Republic* illuminates elements much more important than any one of the specific civic provisions. Read this way the *Laws* reveals a teaching about the character and *nous* of the non-philosophic citizen and the implications for education. The *Laws* ultimately illuminates *how* Plato hoped to educate the non-philosophic for political life more than *what* they are to be taught.[6] In the civic pedagogy they reveal both dialogues reveal and replicate the persistent Platonic dyad of epistemology and ontology. Addressed to the citizen, Plato's central ethical and educational pairing ties together both what he knows and who he is.

Athenian Education and Politics

Plato's dialogues appeared in an Athens that was the most politicized community the West had ever seen. They were written and disseminated to a population that participated in politics to a degree unthinkable today. They moved into a body politic with a keen sense of its self-identity as citizen and a healthy appreciation and broad conception of the role of the state. Any accurate understanding of Plato's teaching on civic education in the *Republic* and *Laws* requires a picture of the politics they were written into. Of particular importance is an understanding of the nature of Athenian political identity, the degree to which that identity was shaped by political involvement and the popular perception of the state. For my purposes and to some extent by necessity, my account must be provisional but hopefully adequate to show how particular aspects of Athenian democratic politics led to both the increasing presence of "teachers for hire" and of "schools" in fifth and fourth century Athens. Most especially, the context of a vigorous conception of citizenship and a citizenry eager and available to be "schooled" constitutes the dramatic and informative background for many of Plato's dialogues not least of all the two to be examined here.[7]

---

[6] This is not to suggest that the two can or should be fully separated, indeed any discussion of the one demands some discussion of the other.

[7] Of course the *Laws* like the *Phaedrus* occurs outside of Athens but in both dialogues the striking absence of the traditional background constitutes a powerful reminder of the force of its existence.

It is difficult for the modern liberal citizen to imagine the degree to which the political institutions of democratic Athens informed the identity of its citizens. As early as the late sixth century the citizens of Athens began to construct a series of legal provisions and prohibitions that eventually evolved into robust institutions of citizenship and a comprehensive civic ethos.[8] It seemed obvious and unproblematic to Athenian citizens that the term "citizenship" connoted both an institution and a virtue. In the famous Funeral Oration from *History of the Peloponnesian War* Thucydides' Pericles frames this semantic duality elegantly.

> Here each individual is interested not only in his own affairs but in the affairs of the state as well: even those who are mostly occupied with their own business are extremely well-informed on general politics-this is a peculiarity of ours: we do not say that a man who takes no interest in politics is a man who minds his own business, we say that he has no business at all.[9]

For Pericles viewing citizenship in purely procedural or institutional terms meant confusing means with ends and interests with identities. Unlike modern liberal citizenship, the Greek *politiea* provided no citizen's charter, no list of rights, prohibitions, and entitlements. The *politiea* involved neither position nor procedure, instead it defined itself in terms of participation. To be an Athenian citizen was "to be someone who *metechei tes poleos:* someone who shares in the polis."[10] Of course a citizen of Athens also possessed a list of rights and entitlements. But these rights and entitlements were positive not negative in character, best embodied in the ruddle soaked rope drawn through the market marking

---

[8] As early as 510/9 B.C. Athenian citizens were protected against torture and were entitled to some extremely limited protections while traveling to other Greek cities. As Alan L. Boegehold points out, such protection necessarily implies *some definition* of citizenship if only to determine who is and isn't entitled to them. See Alan L. Boegehold "Perikles Citizenship Law of 451/0 B.C.," in *Athenian Identity and Civic Ideology*, eds. Alan L. Boegehold and Adele C. Scafuro (Baltimore: The Johns Hopkins Press, 1994), 58.

[9] Thucydides, *History of the Peloponnesian War*, trans. Rex Warner (London: Penguin Books, 1972), 148.

[10] Phillip Brook Manville, *The Origins of Citizenship in Ancient Athens* (Princeton: Princeton University Press, 1990), 5.

those who failed to appear, as duty demanded, in the Agora. The foremost right of the Athenian citizen was the right to hold public office, to participate, to have a share in politics.[11] Moreover, ideally at least, this right was not contingent on material concerns. Instead, the Athenian's share rested primarily on the ability of the citizen to prove his legitimate place on the deme register, the *lexiarkhikon grammateion*.[12] Proof of Athenian ancestry established political ability. Thucydides also valorized this principle in *The Peloponnesian War*, having Pericles declare "No one, so long as he has it in him to be of service to the state, is kept in political obscurity because of poverty."[13]

The principle of universal participation of citizens (not to be confused with universal suffrage!) was not only a matter of the Athenian public ethos it was a matter of necessity, both military and political. In an irony not lost on Plato and treated with acerbity in *Gorgias*, Athens demanded greater civic participation as it slowly moved from city to empire. The remarkable military successes of Athens in the fifth and fourth centuries played a crucial and counter-intuitive role in creating a demotic political identity. As the Athenian military transformed from an aristocratic land army of *hoplites* into a naval power dominated by the demotic *thetes* this new and numerous class became increasingly aware of its significance to Athens' new power and influence among the Hellenes. As Pseudo-Xenophon writes

> My first point is that it is right that the poor and the ordinary people there should have more power than the noble and the rich, because it is the ordinary people who man the fleet and bring the city her power: they provide the helmsman, the boatswains, the junior officers, the look-outs and the shipwrights: it is these people who make the city powerful much more than the hoplites and the noble and respectable citizens.[14]

---

[11] Boegold, "Perikles," 60.
[12] Frank J. Frost, "Aspects of Early Athenian Citizenship," in *Athenian Identity and Civic Ideology*, eds. Alan Boegehold and Adele C. Scafuro (Baltimore: The Johns Hopkins Press, 1994), 45.
[13] Thucydides, *History*, 145.
[14] Pseudo-Xenophon, quoted in *Kurt Raafluab* "Perceptions of Democracy in Fifth-Century Athens," in *Aspects of Athenian Democracy*, ed. W. Robert Connor (Copenhagen: Museum Tusculanum Press, 1990), 36.

Pseudo-Xenophon's remarks illustrate the development among the *thetic* class of an increasing awareness of their rightful "share in the polis." The imagery of the ship of state, here in Pseudo-Xenophon, later famously in *Republic,* captures the naval and ultimately democratic notion that all citizens and sailors shared the consequences of decisions made.[15]

This awareness found further expression in Greek tragedy. In *Antigone* Sophocles presents a protagonist making claims against tyrannical rule and for, to some extent, conscience.[16] Antigone makes a claim against arbitrary decree and in favor of the citizen's participation and immersion in a larger order. Over the fifth and fourth centuries BCE these ideas, born in theatres both military and literary, infiltrated Athenian culture. The transformation of the military from an aristocratic to a demotic institution, accompanied by cultural valorizations of participation as diverse as Thucydides and Sophocles, helped create a civic identity and public ethos with participation at its forefront.

Even with these developments, which were not entirely peculiar to Athens among the Greek city states, the unique institutions of democratic Athens demanded a level of popular participation unprecedented in the ancient world. Beyond the democratic character of Athenian offices, their sheer number demanded the involvement of every citizen. According to Phillip Brook Manville's calculations, the breathtaking number of offices rendered public service equal parts civic duty and institutional necessity. Indeed, the man excoriated by Pericles as "having no business at all" would have had to make it his business to avoid political life. As Manville notes

> The combined total of the quorum for the *ekklesia* (6000) annual *boulethai* (500) and the 700 different domestic *archai* mentioned by *Ath.*

---

[15] S. Sara Monoson, *Plato's Democratic Entanglements* (Princeton, Princeton University Press, 1977), 56.

[16] Hegel, in *Phenomenology of Spirit*, writes of Antigone's rebellion against Creon "The accomplished deed completely alters its point of view; the very performance of it declares what is ethical must be actual; for the *realization* of the purpose is the purpose of the action." G.W.F. Hegel, *Phenomenology of Spirit*, trans. A.V. Miller (Oxford: Oxford University Press, 1977), 285.

Pol. 24.3 gives one pause when measured against an adult male population of only about 40,000 in 431 and perhaps half that number in the fourth century.[17]

The extraordinary number of offices and the relatively small number of citizens made it virtually impossible for a citizen to spend less than a year in the service of Athens over the course of his lifetime. The reality of service to Athens as an inevitable consequence of citizenship combined with the experience of that service constituted a powerful source of the vigorous conception of Athenian civic identity.

Not only were citizens involved in the state to an unprecedented degree but the state, as it grew, increasingly involved itself in the lives of citizens. The Athenian state, in the structuring of its citizenship and in the innovations of government, both occluded from view family allegiances and increasingly supplanted the family in traditional roles. To return again to Pericles, we can see in Thucydides' account a shift from speaking of "forefathers" (*hoi pateres*) to the more general and necessarily diffuse "ancestors" (*hoi progonoi*).[18] The talk of ancestry as opposed to parentage suggests two complementary phenomena. The first and most readily apparent is the awareness, at least among the elite, of the fragility of any claim to Attic autochthony. As W. Robert Connor observes, "It was sufficient to know that *all* Athenians were autochthonous; no need, then, to trace one's ancestry back, either to a hero of the remote past or to a more recent immigrant."[19] On a second track, again in Pericles' Funeral Oration, by the middle of the fifth century, the Athenian state began to contemplate supplanting the family in the most critical of roles: the rearing of children and the burial of the dead. Pericles offers the city as a stand-in for the father's loss in war, and while the emergence of such a class of citizen's prompted the promised benefit it nonetheless entails imagining and implementing a new and novel state capacity.

---

[17] Manville, "Origins," 18–19.
[18] Barry S. Strauss, "Oikos and Polis," in *Aspects of Athenian Democracy*, ed. W. Robert Connor (Copenhagen: Museum Tusculanum Press, 1990), 120.
[19] W. Robert Connor, "The Problem of Civic Identity," in *Athenian Identity and Civic Ideology*, ed. Alan L. Boegehold and Adele C. Scafuro (Baltimore: The Johns Hopkins Press, 1994), 35.

> For the time being our offerings to the dead have been made, and for the future their children will be supported at the public expense of the city, until they come of age. This is the crown and prize she offers, both to the dead and to their children, for the ordeals which they have faced.[20]

Pericles' remarks indicate an openness, indeed in the language of "crown and prize" he offers even a valorization, of the occasions upon which the state replaces the family. Motivated by considerations of social solidarity, the Athenian state spoke of familial ties rarely and vaguely. This politically significant reticence in the fourth century accompanied a willingness, in some limited cases, to supplant the family altogether. The funeral oration served not merely to remember the dead but to promote the civic ideology for which they perished.[21]

I have attempted to briefly draw together three strands of fourth and fifth century Athenian life to illuminate the context in which education and later Plato's educational proposals took place. These strands, the emergence of a deep sense of civic identity, the necessity of a high degree of political involvement, and an increasing openness to an expanded role for the state made obvious by Socrates' lifetime the gravity and import of civic education in the life of the polis.

It is in this context that we find the presence of "freelance" teachers such as the Sophists and eventually Socrates endeavoring to teach the young men of Athens. This is the milieu first drawn and indeed caricatured in Aristophanes' *The Clouds*. The caustic depiction of Socrates in *The Clouds* illustrates not only Aristophanes' concerns but echoes popular concerns about the state of education in Athens. Athenian audiences, in appreciating Aristophanes' satire, recognized not only Socrates but the new type of student portrayed. The father and son students, Strepsiades and Phidepides, seek education for personal advantage, in particular the avoidance of debts. They seek an education suited for the Periclean man of "no business at all." What's worse, their eccentric teacher Socrates seems interested only in the natural world and even there is unable to distinguish the important from the trivial, the

---

[20] Thucydides, *History*, 151.
[21] Matthew R. Christ, *The Bad Citizen in Classical Athens* (Cambridge: Cambridge University Press, 2006), 28.

central distinction that grounds all politically prudent action. *The Clouds* portrays students who are unaware of the ends of education and a teacher who cannot discern what it is important to teach or how to teach it. At the play's conclusion, the enraged Strepsiades reasserts the traditional family roles and burns down Socrates' Thinkery. In this fiery end, Aristophanes illustrates the grave consequences of education gone wrong. In its popularity it captured an enduring concern for the future facing all democratic societies, individual freedom across generations generates enduring uncertainty. In its fatal prescience, Aristophanes' attack on Socrates is at least in part an indictment of a particular sort of education. *The Clouds* finds its comedy in the failure of Socrates' teaching to connect the citizen to the state, to prepare him for his share in the political, to ground him in the business for which he is destined. Plato's Socrates acknowledges as much in *The Apology*, considering the charges against him he admits

> I must read out their affidavit, so to speak, as though they were my legal accusers: Socrates is guilty of criminal meddling, in that he inquires into things below the earth and in the sky, and makes the weaker argument defeat the stronger, and teaches other to follow his example. It runs something like that. You have seen it for yourselves in the play by Aristophanes, where Socrates goes whirling round, proclaiming that he is walking on air, and uttering a great deal of nonsense about things of which I know nothing whatsoever. (*Apology* 19b–c)

Aristophanes' charge gains its peculiar gravity as a result of the importance Athenian society places on its young men; everything depends on them, on the education of their characters.[22] Those who would corrupt the young risk setting fire not merely to a school but to the city itself. The charge deepens in its poignancy when one contemplates how many among the Aristophanic audience later comprised the Athenian Jury.

---

[22] R.L. Nettleship, *The Theory of Education in Plato's Republic* (Oxford: Oxford University Press, 1935), 48.

Socrates and Plato as Teachers

Any work of philosophy, to the extent that it aims to reveal something amounting to wisdom, contains a teaching on education. Part of that teaching adheres in the truth claims and syllogisms offered by the philosopher, part adheres in the very structure of the work. Nowhere is this more the case than in a Platonic dialogue. Plato's decision to write dialogues (instead of treatises) bespeaks a deep recognition of the volatile nature of youth and the precarious place of the educator in a democracy, it is this recognition that is most conspicuously absent in the Aristophanic portrayal of Socrates. In contrast, a circumspect style of speech and an awareness of the political perils of education are primary qualities of Plato's Socrates. Farther into the dialogues the relationship between these two elements reveals a third wrinkle, the triumphant trompe l'oeil of Plato's prose inevitably points to the artist's presence[23] and raises the question: what is the relationship between the vivid Socrates and the murky figure behind known to us, in his own words, only through a handful of letters? Plato offers an impossibly intricate tapestry, he teaches with dialogues in which Socrates teaches others all the while reminding us that Socrates was, before all this work, his teacher. Plato and his Socrates tell us what to make of students, but lurking in the background a more sable-colored return to Aristophanes, what to make of teachers?

While political and philosophical writing may have a variety of purposes, exhortation, admonition, and lamentation for instance, at the bottom of all truly philosophical works *a case is being made,* something is being taught. Plato admits this while remaining acutely aware of the peculiar aspects of the written word that render philosophic and political prose problematic. The dialogues reveal in the person of Socrates the broadly philosophic recognition that not every lesson is for every person, not every argument is suited for every occasion. The character of the careful educator embodies the principles of the cautious writer.[24] Tellingly, Plato uses the idiosyncratic text of the *Cleitophon,* a "minor"

---

[23] This will be discussed at greater length below by exploring one of the few moments of explicit Platonic self-reference, see *Laws* 811c–d.
[24] Leo Strauss, *The City and Man* (Chicago: University of Chicago Press, 1964), 54.

dialogue that the dramatic action appears to place as a prelude to the *Republic*, to first establish the diaretic principle at the heart of his pedagogic practice. In the dialogue an ambitious would-be student named Cleitophon confronts Socrates demanding an explanation for Socrates' refusal to teach him about the nature of justice. In an atypical twist for Plato, Socrates speaks only once, at the beginning of the dialogue, to inquire as to whether Cleitophon has become the pupil of the Sophist Thrasymachus. Cleitophon responds angrily, admitting as much and suggesting that it is Socrates' fault, to the extent that he has refused to teach him. His intemperate peroration concludes

> *Cleitophon*: I have now given up persisting. I think you are better than anybody else at exhorting people to care about goodness, but one of two things must be true: either you can do only that and nothing that goes any further-which could also happen in the case of any other art; for example without being a steersman one might train oneself in making eulogies about how valuable the steersman's trade is for mankind and likewise for the other arts. The very same complaint might perhaps be lodged against you in the field of justice-people might say that you are none the more expert in justice because you make fine eulogies about it. Mind you that is not what I think, but one of two things must be true: either you know nothing about it, or you don't wish to share it with me. (*Cleitophon* 410b–d)[25]

As a prelude to the *Republic* this speech is fascinating; Plato portrays a student who accurately appraises Socrates' special genius and who is therefore understandably frustrated by the refusal of that genius to teach him. It elegantly sets the stage for Plato's expansive understanding of political and pedagogic speech and action in *Republic*. The *Cleitophon* provides the first suggestion that the success of civic education hinges as much on qualities that are inherent in the student as that of the teacher; it makes clear that the Platonic pedagogue practices prudence not only in how but in whom he educates.

---

[25] Plato, "Cleitophon," trans. Clifford Orwin, in *The Roots of Political Philosophy*, ed. Thomas Pangle (Ithaca: Cornell University Press, 1988).

The opening pages of the *Republic* sorely test this dual prudence in teaching. Returning from the Piraeus, Socrates finds himself pressed into dialogue with a series of young men at the home of a wealthy metic armorer named Cephalus. Young men surround and strong-arm Socrates into conversation, among their number the previously shunned Cleitophon. However other than a brief and allegedly inaccurate rehash of his new teacher Thrasymachus' views Cleitophon remains silent (*Republic* 340a–b). A dramatic change from the impassioned imprecations of their prior encounter. But does that mean he is not party to some education? Of course not, Cleitophon is in the room after all. He may not be spoken to directly, but he hears. Socrates' speech is delivered in full cognizance of the spurned students' presence. To the extent that the dialogue is a conversation overheard, a lesson to which we are a silent party, the reader plays a role akin to Cleitophon's. Plato crafts the dialogues in the same spirit, aware of the diversity of his readership. Like the guests of Cephalus, readers vary in character, ability, and intelligence, yet almost any may be "present." We may be party to the conversation but what we learn from it largely depends on us. In *The War Lover* Leon Craig captures nicely the heuristic principle at work.

> For in saying the same thing to one and all it implicitly acknowledges their common humanity, allowing everyone, without personal prejudice, an equal opportunity to make of the words what they will. And yet in intending different messages for different kinds of people, it treats them differently in due recognition of their unequal talents and efforts and character-in effect employing a sort of "labour theory" of intellectual entitlement.[26]

Craig here describes one of the cardinal virtues of the Platonic dialogue, one that represents a revolution in writing. Plato transforms the written word, enabling it to speak differently to its diverse readers. The Platonic dialogue replicates on the page the ideal relationship between student and teacher, a relationship where method and material are informed in structure and substance by the nature of the student.

---

[26] Leon Craig, *The War Lover* (Toronto: University of Toronto Press, 1994), xxxii.

Education and Diaresis

In all of the Platonic dialogues Socrates encounters few fellow philosophers. This may be because, as Stanley Rosen pointedly suggests, "Philosophers educate non-philosophers; they punish philosophers for their mistakes."[27] After all the overwhelming character of Socratic speech is pedagogic. Socrates shapes his speech to "fit" each person with whom he converses, indeed as Cleitophon's experience indicates, this sometimes means refusing to speak to someone altogether.[28] Especially in the case of an education in dialectics Socrates identifies the catastrophic consequence of ill-aimed lessons for both philosophy and the city. In *Republic* Socrates cautions

> "At any rate" I said, "the current mistake in philosophy-as a result of which, as we also said before, dishonor has befallen philosophy-is that men who aren't worthy take it up. Not bastards, but the genuine should have taken it up." (*Republic* 535c)

The genuine, Socrates makes clear, are those who are "capable of an overview" (*Republic* 537c). Such an education, when imparted to those incapable of an overview, does not merely fall upon deaf ears. Instead, the frequently aporetic character of Socratic dialectic, its studied openness, ceases to serve as a propaedutic tool, vanquishing unexamined prejudices and unchallenged assumptions. Among the ill-suited the ever-incomplete inquiry at the heart of philosophy instead mutates into an all too effective skepticism, a corrosive weapon, destructive of both the reputation of philosophy and the welfare of the city. Socrates cautions that when the character of the student is ignored and the rudimentary tools of dialectic are imparted without considerations of age and character, the recklessly schooled will

---

[27] Stanley Rosen, *Plato's Statesman* (New Haven: Yale University Press, 1995), 10.
[28] See also *Euthydemus* where Socrates discourages his friend Crito from sending his son to study philosophy. Socrates opines "But when I glance at any one of those who profess to educate people, I am horrified: each one I look at seems to me to be quite unsuitable, to tell you the truth, so I don't see how I am to direct the boy to philosophy" (*Euthydemus* 306e–307a). Plato, *Euthydemus*, trans. W.H.D Rouse in *Plato Collected Dialogues*, eds. Edith Hamilton and Huntington Cairns, 16ed. (Princeton: Princeton University Press, 1963).

...misuse them as though it were play, always using them to contradict: and imitating those men by whom they are refuted, they themselves refute others, like puppies enjoying pulling and tearing with argument at those who happen to be near. (*Republic* 539b)

While this consideration appears at first to be directed at those who learn dialectic too young, there is ample evidence in the preceding passages suggesting that such an education is at least as limited by innate faculties as it is by age and intellectual development (*Republic* 537d–e).

The opening action of the *Republic* first suggests a central Platonic theme, the careful tailoring of civic education to both the capabilities and the temperament of the student. Book I presents Socrates with three different accounts of the good and three profoundly different *dramatis personae*. The first exchange, with Cephalus the wealthy owner of the home in which the conversation is to take place, ends with Socrates' interlocutor declaring he must depart and attend to his religious obligations. Socrates allows him to depart their company in a piece of dramatic action structurally similar to the conclusion of the *Euthyphro*. In both cases Socrates converses with someone with a traditional conception of morality and a developed sense of piety and its concomitant duties. In both cases just as the beliefs of interlocutors begin to come into question, they are allowed to depart relatively unchallenged by Socrates (*Republic* 331d, *Euthyphro* 15e–16a). In each case, the message from the incomplete conversation seems to be that Socrates has measured his potential pupil and found, by dint of venerable piety or youthful religious zeal that the interlocutor is ill-suited to *any* substantive teaching. The continuation of the dialogue in the case of the *Republic* reveals the extra lesson: not only are some people ill-suited for some education but their very absence may make possible conversations their presence prevents. The dramatic action of the opening passages of the *Republic* suggests that the first task of the teacher is to sort and determine who is capable of what. More important for civic education specifically, the departure of Cephalus implies that some people must be literally sorted *out,* this is the first separation of natures necessary before any proper education can commence. It also constitutes a subtle application of the principle of justice first canvassed in Book I. Justice involves activity consistent with nature.

The departure of Cephalus allows for the gathered men to set aside the custom and propriety owed to a host and father to Socrates' subsequent interlocutor, Polemarchus. To illustrate consider Socrates' treatment of Polemarchus and Thrasymachus. While each, and Thrasymachus in particular, comes in for much rougher treatment than Cephalus, both remain long after Socrates has finished speaking directly to them. They may have gravely misguided conceptions of the nature of the just and their abilities to debate the great Socrates are clearly limited, but Plato has them stay. That they remain, unlike Cephalus, suggests something critical concerning the character of their exchanges with Socrates. Book I ends with Polemarchus and in particular Thrasymachus not so much silenced as subdued. The obvious result of their exchange is the "defeat" of the respective positions of Polemarchus and Thrasymachus, more subtly Socrates treats the two men with enough dialogical care that they will remain to hear what Socrates has to say. To invoke the imagery of the Cave the two men have had their chains broken, what remains now is for them to be turned. This rupture lies at the heart of Socrates' pedagogy, the surface action appears aporetic, but the deeper intent and consequence is propaedeutic. W.R. Newell in *Ruling Passion* captures the character of this experience nicely when he writes

> His [Socrates] relentless skepticism about his interlocutors' and his own conceptions of the good life provides the forceful rupture, the pain of parting with our cozy conception and lazy justifications, necessary for turning to face the light. Anyone who has had the good fortune to have a great teacher knows how exasperating their benevolence can be.[29]

The rupture that Socrates brings about in his students represents the starting point for any understanding of how he teaches. The rupture, breaking the grasp of false beliefs, constitutes the crucial step before the *periagoge,* the turning toward the light. Its significance to a discussion of Platonic civic education (as meaningfully and seriously distinct from

---

[29] W.R. Newell, *Ruling Passion* (Lanham, MD: Rowman and Littlefield, 2000), 85.

philosophic education) is that to some extent all of his major interlocutors experience some degree of this "rupture."[30] Moreover, by placing Cephalus, Polemarchus, and Thrasymachus side by side at the outset, each distinct from the others in belief, character, and intellect Plato highlights the philosophic, pedagogic, and civic essence of Socrates' craft. Book I depicts the unique demands of Socratic civic education, it must teach the different differently, sort the teachable from the unteachable and do so in front of other potential students without seeming vicious, duplicitous, or capricious. The Platonic project of civic education Plato initially presents in *Republic* three politically distinct pupils, the aging oligarch, idealistic democrat, and aspiring tyrant each embodying a different challenge.[31] From the outset the education of diverse students, pressed together by circumstances, social or civic, demands an education concerned with their diverse perspectives if not their politics. From the beginning of *Republic* all education begins in civic education.

The Civic Education of the Non-Philosophic in Plato's *Republic*

Plato's explicit discussion of civic education begins in the second book of the *Republic*. The conversation commences in response to Socrates' assertion that the contours of justice can be better discerned when considered in the context of a city (*Republic* 372e). The discussion moves through a detailed proposal for the education of citizens, an account which culminates infamously in the Noble Lie. (*Republic* 414b–415d). The explicit substance of that teaching, while obviously significant, pales in comparison to the subtler teaching concealed within the structure of Socrates' larger argument. Plato's presents the Noble Lie in Book III, but portions the full import of the argument out over the next four books. By slowly rolling out over the preceding four books the political commitments first

---

[30] For a possible exception to this rule see W.R. Newell, "The Problem of Callicles," in *Ruling Passion*.
[31] Henry Teloh, *Socratic Education in Plato's Early Dialogues* (South Bend, IN: University of Notre Dame Press, 1986), 85.

implied in his origin myth, Plato forestalls the natural snap judgments that the perhaps noble but fantastic myth would otherwise prompt. The full philosophical conception of education or more precisely of the process and nature of teaching and learning isn't realized until Book VII and appears disconnected from the Noble Lie by the scandal of Book V.

In particular, by dividing and delaying the propounding of his pedagogical assumptions Plato conceals from view the full implications for the non-philosophic citizen of the equally problematic Myth of the Cave. Plato alludes to the connection between Myth and Lie in the prelude to the Noble Lie. In *Republic* 414e Socrates explains to Glaucon how he will persuade the first rulers, the soldiers, and then the citizenry of the Callipolis of the veracity of the Noble Lie. The education they first receive, Socrates argues, will be made to seem like a dream. In its place they will learn to recollect a creation myth of their emergence into the light of day.

> I shall speak-and yet, I don't know what I'll use for daring or speeches in telling it-and I'll attempt to persuade first the rulers and the soldiers, then the rest of the city, that the rearing and education we gave them were like dreams; they only thought they were undergoing all that was happening to them, while, in truth, at that time they were *under the earth,* which is their mother within, being fashioned and reared themselves, and their arms and other tools being crafted. When the job had been completely finished, then the earth, which is their mother, *sent them up.* (*Republic* 414d–e, emphasis added)

This passage is traditionally read in part as a Platonic acknowledgment of the political problem of autochthony[32] but the subterranean imagery also constitutes a first pass at Plato's primary pedagogic metaphor. Plato understands education as the drawing upward of the previously concealed, an upward pull that entails, particularly in the *Laws,* the possibility of illumination if not necessarily enlightenment for all. In this first pass Plato presents a light refracted. The Noble Lie places the philosopher in the role of reflective satellite, illuminating partially and

---

[32] Connor, "Civic Identity," 35.

educating incompletely those who cannot bear the direct rays of the sun. In this initial allegory of education Plato has yet to even hint at the philosopher in the city. The Noble Lie and its prelude concern only the education of the non-philosophic.

Jumping forward to Book VII, but staying with both illumination and education Socrates' closing statements concerning the image of the Cave contain an explicit claim about the nature of the soul that goes conspicuously unqualified. Imagining potential pupils both bound and shuttered, Socrates embraces a periagogic account of education that, in all its necessarily differentiated forms, nonetheless includes an element of ascent and draws on a common capacity for sight that "indicates that the power is in the soul of each" (*Republic* 518c). Admittedly this is a long way from a claim that every soul must be able to make the full ascent to comprehension of Being. Nothing in the Myth of the Cave precludes the possibility of a partial ascent and an incomplete but edificatory paideia.[33]

Politically Plato reiterates the argument for a partial ascent in the account of the returned philosophers, the men of the best natures who are admonished to "go down, each in his turn, into the common dwellings of the others and get habituated along with them to seeing the dark things" (*Republic* 520c). For this return to have any significance it must be salutary for the subterranean society. Something of value must be imparted to them by the philosopher. Philosophic rule, Plato makes clear, must be an at least partially altruistic enterprise, informed by the interest of the whole community, opposed to faction and cognizant of the phantasmagoric character of the cave experience.

It isn't until after a discussion of the periagoge in general that, in the context of his conversation with Glaucon Glaucon, Socrates turns to the specifics of a philosophic education and its concomitant full periagoge. The structure of the argument first connects the periagogic "twirling of the shell" (*Republic* 521c), the imagery of ascent, and the question of education and politics with the non-philosophic *before the philosophic*. The logographic ordering draws out the connection between civic education and philosophic education, a connection that is critical both politically and pedagogically. Plato inextricably and symbiotically

---

[33] Eric Voegelin, *Plato* (Baton Rouge: Louisiana State University Press, 1966), 129.

binds *Republic's* central concerns, education and politics, returning again and again to the manifold ways each shapes and informs the other. For Plato this deep interconnectivity twice justifies civic education, first in the name of the polis and second in the name of philosophy.

Education and Socialization

This connection, between politics, pedagogy, and philosophy, constitutes the inevitable consequence of the Platonic understanding of the place of socialization in the education of young men. The polis is the first teacher, its culture the first classroom. Socrates describes the city and its opinions as the most influential sophist (*Republic* 492a–b), the source of much of the education and character formation of young people. Plato distinguishes his own teaching from that of the sophists by describing the socializing power of the city in explicitly sophistical terms. The city, like the sophists who ply their trade within it, unceasingly promotes a crudely utilitarian and prudential view of education. The valorization of being well adjusted and successful amid prevailing norms, independent of their actual merit, represents the hallmark of a sophistic or a decadent civic education.[34] The starting point of all of Socrates' proposals concerning education is the repudiation of this conception of teaching and an endorsement of education founded on human nature rightly understood.

From the education of newborns in rocking and steady motions to the ascent from the Cave by the philosopher, Plato's educational project is shaped by being in the face of becoming. Plato is not offering an Athenian education in civic virtue but an education that holds true, by dint of its appreciation of the true nature of the student, *sub specie aeternitas*. However, the assertion that the pupil has a true and permanent nature does not mean that this nature is the same for all. Plato draws a distinction which will echo down to Cicero and later even to Locke, Rousseau, and Smith. Plato's account of the course of education and the winnowing process it entails suggests a dual character to human nature.

---

[34] Voegelin, *Plato*, 81.

Each citizen is held to possess an intellect with common capacities what differs among human beings is the degree and potential of those capacities. The vast majority of Plato's potential students can only possess "true opinion," they may only inchoately grasp things in themselves and never apprehend their essence. Plato hints at this group of citizens with the rule to which the cave dwellers are subjected upon the return of the philosophers, a non-tyrannical rule blending compulsion and persuasion (*Republic* 519e–520a). The combination of compulsion and persuasion is crucial to understanding this passage and it is a pairing which reappears forcefully in the discussion of civic education in the *Laws*. The philosophers who return do not rule through compulsion alone, the fact that they persuade implies that a degree of persuasion is possible, that the citizens of the cave are capable of being, to an admittedly limited degree, *reasoned with*. They are citizens and not merely slaves. Indeed to whatever extent the new rulers of the Cave are able to persuade citizens to stop the "fight over shadows" (*Republic* 520b) they have been convinced of the epiphenomenal character of their subterranean existence. In the emergence of such a conviction the philosophical rulers of the cave implicitly transmit something of the reality being missed. This is a long way from revealing to them that they argue over becoming by showing them Being. Nonetheless, it suggests that they may at least be "turned" (ibid.) sufficiently to see becoming for what it is, that they may hold true opinion (*dike*) or belief without possessing true knowledge (*gnosis*).

Admittedly, this partial turning, the apprehension of true opinion as opposed to true knowledge, seems implausible when read in the context and the aftermath of the image of the Cave. In the pages of Book VII following the discussion of the Cave, Plato presents the perfect education and an able (though how able remains a question for Socrates later) student, this presentation might lead, were it not for repeated reminders, to a forgetting of the civic education which preceded it in Books II & III. The provisions of these preliminary books unmistakably lay out the groundwork for a partial periagoge, the therapeutic paideia of the ordinary citizens.[35] Plato presents a paideia capable of possessing not only

---

[35] Newell, *Ruling Passions*, 115.

nomoi that reflect natural justice but equally capable of creating citizens who understand the laws as such. It is this understanding which connects the citizens "partisan commitment to community *and* an openness to the universal truth that transcends partisanship" (my italics).[36]

Plato's *Republic* is not primarily a work on civic education. Indeed in important ways its teaching on education remains decidedly ambivalent regarding the civic education of its favored student, the young philosophic soul (*Republic* 596b). The lion's share of Plato's positive teaching in civic virtue is found in the *Laws*.[37] In *Republic* Plato explains and unpacks a specifically and singularly civic education primarily as the necessary condition for a philosophic education and life. The civic education of *Republic* serves the dual function of sorting the citizenry into intellectual types and protecting the interests and even the very possibility of a cohort of specifically philosophic students.

The most striking feature of the educational proposals of *Republic* is the universal character of the education. In contrast to the Cretan city of the *Laws* the *Republic's* Callipolis lacks any practice of slavery. One implication of slavery's absence is that a universal ability to be ruled by means beyond mere force and compulsion is possible. This further implies at least the rejection of private models of education contingent on status, which before the arrival of the Sophists and the concurrent expansion of Athens, had been the overwhelming Athenian practice.[38] Plato no longer sees parents as the source of education instead they are its opponents, exiled to prevent them passing on any of their "learning" to their offspring (*Republic* 541a). In the Callipolis the most striking aspect of early education is its inclusivity. This universality is initially justified by the nature of young pupils and eventually deemed politically necessary by the strictures of the Noble Lie. The contention that some children will be passed down or up based on ability as opposed to ancestry demands an initial universality, such a sorting is only possible in the context of an initial equality of pedagogic opportunity (*Republic* 415a–d).

---

[36] Ibid.
[37] Of course it has to be admitted that much of what Plato recommends regarding the withholding of the philosophic education from those who are ill-suited to it and of the consequences of a degraded philosophic education amount to a political and philosophic *caveat emptor*.
[38] Samuel Scolnicov, *Plato's Metaphysics of Education* (London: Routledge, 1988), 5.

Throughout the *Republic*, Plato's discussion of education is always deeply informed by his conception of the development of reason. From infancy through to middle age Plato prescribes a staggered education that opens up new subjects of study to students as they become "ready" for them. This staggered education develops concurrently with a winnowing out of students as they reveal themselves to have reached their respective limits of learning. This winnowing matters. As it occurs Plato's Socrates sets aside all but the philosophic student on the way to the final education in dialectic and philosophy. The readers of *Republic* rarely turn back to the early and intermediate levels of education, those afforded to the non-philosophic as a necessary condition of an informed act of diaresis. They overlook this process which nonetheless results in the generation of a politically virtuous non-philosophic class in the Callipolis. The literary linearity of *Republic* conceals the aggregating quality of the city described. Each step, each casting off in Plato's ideal education disappears from the text but continues to populate the city.

A degree of education for all of the citizens of the *Republic* is rendered essential by the character of an education in reason. Plato organizes his education through the complementary contentions of a pre-rational period in human development and a harsh "window of opportunity" conception of character education. Plato combines these claims with an explicit rejection of parentage as a legitimate indicator of intelligence or character that forces him to consider the merit of children, and more importantly their educational prospects, long before they can indicate by their own actions their worth as pupils. These realities explain Plato's reliance on a primarily musical early education. Music, Plato argues, is fundamentally pre-rational in character. Music teaches by imbuing fondness for the fine (*kaloi*) and the appreciation of rhythm and scale (*harmonia*). The pre-rational pupil embraces both of these without being able to render a rational account of why he appreciates either.

> He would blame and hate the ugly in the right way while he's still young, before he's able to *grasp reasonable speech*. And when *reasonable speech* comes, the man who's reared this way would take most delight in it, recognizing it on account of its being akin. (*Republic* 402a, my italics)

On this account reasonable speech emerges in an utterly unqualified manner. Plato does not say that reasonable speech comes to some and not others. But even if reasonable speech did not come to all citizens, during this early period of education it seems impossible to tell who it would and would not come to. The only prudent path, having rejected ancestry as an indicator, is to educate everyone. Admitting the most generous possibility, this education suggests that almost all might possess a degree of reason, at least in speech. Plato leaves open at least the possibility that a politically relevant portion of reason might be the educational inheritance of every citizen of the Callipolis.

The negative possibility of either mistakenly postponing learning or, on a set of wrong assumptions, incorrectly educating imposes further strictures on Plato's proposals. The need to identify and educate appropriately demands that pre-philosophic education encompass all potential citizens. Plato's motives for educational inclusivity emerge as much out of a desire to protect as to promote philosophy. While Book VII lists the dishonors that can and do befall philosophy as a result of its study by those ill-suited to its pursuit, Books II and III primarily address political consequences. Socrates warns that undue caution or an attempt to wait until the student "shows his stripes" comprise approaches precluded by the character of individual rational development. The unceasing growth and change in the pupil over time constitute the single most compelling stricture on selective education of children. Education, civic and philosophic, must at least partially resign itself to the realities of human growth and change over childhood and adolescence. Socrates admits that by the age of 10 if education has not been rightly begun it cannot be remedied.

> Don't you know that the beginning is the most important part of every work and that this is especially so with anything young and tender? For at that stage it's most plastic, and each thing assimilates itself to the model whose stamp anyone wishes to give it. (*Republic* 377a–b)

Plato initially justifies the education of all in *Republic* by acknowledging the impossibility of discerning the philosophic from the non-philosophic in infancy. Plato further explains his inclusive account on explicitly political grounds, admitting the necessity to protect the potentially philosophic among his young pupils from the hostile "stamp" of the sophist or popular prejudice. Confessing that the stamp placed on the souls of the young cannot be philosophic in nature, Plato insists that the unavoidable influences of early education remain open to philosophy and sympathetic to the virtues of the philosophers. For those ultimately unfit for philosophy the ideal "stamp" still renders them more suitably disposed to both civic virtue and to the externally originating dictates of reason than the education offered by the sophists. In *Republic* this second-tier education constitutes a *sine qua non* for the education of the philosopher, but it is also the *sine qua non* for a citizenry open to rule by a reason it cannot fully participate in.

True Opinion and Civic Education

The great problem with the discussion of civic education in *Republic* is that the actual practical pedagogy of the solely civic education goes largely undiscussed. In *Republic* Plato chooses not to explicitly describe the relationship of the things learned to the learner in the case of the non-philosophic citizen. We are told in great detail how the pupil educated in dialectic will be trained to evaluate beliefs, how dialectic will draw the soul out of the "barbaric bog, [and how] dialectic gently draws it forth and leads it up above" (*Republic* 533a). We know that in the end the successful philosophic student comes to a relationship of unmediated knowing of the truth. No such clear declarations are made concerning the education of the solely civic student. The evidence for how the non-philosophic citizen relates to the civic things taught remains both sparse and spread across the dialogue. Plato is either reluctant or, in *Republic* at least, evasive in explaining how the non-philosophic citizen *knows what he knows*. As a result, perhaps unintended, it appears at first glance that it is only by implication that this knowledge is epistemologically second tier. Yet this relationship is crucial to the Callipolis. After all, the vast majority of its citizens will relate to the truths of the city in this second (perhaps third?) tier manner. To not understand how they learn and know is to ultimately leave unexamined what the role of education and reason amounts to in the life of the polis as opposed to the academy.

The nature of purely civic knowledge[39] and how it is known by the citizen is implied at several different junctures in the *Republic*. That knowledge, Plato makes clear, takes the form of true opinion which unlike the knowledge of the philosopher is not so much known as possessed. Late in Book III Socrates alludes to the epistemological status of the civic beliefs of the Guardians.

> Now then, as I said a while ago, we must look for some men who are the best guardians of their conviction that they must do what on each occasion seems best for the city. So we must watch them straight from childhood by setting them at tasks in which a man would most likely forget and be deceived out of such a conviction. And the man who has a memory and is hard to deceive must be chosen and the one who's not must be rejected mustn't he? (*Republic* 413c–d)

The character of the guardian's memory plays the crucial intellectual role. The guardian possesses the ability to retain true opinion and simultaneously resist the charms of wrong (though often popular or self-serving) opinion. However, to discover *for themselves* what is and is not true remains noticeably absent from the intellectual capacities of the guardian. This absence explains the proprietary as opposed to revelatory language employed by Socrates in discussing knowledge. The guardians may come to possess the truth. The truth may arrive or depart, they cannot discover it but they can be deprived of it (*Republic* 413a). In a sense truth relates to the guardian as opposed to the guardian relating to the truth. Truth may be located within the guardian, but the guardian cannot, on his own, find the truth. In this account Plato begins the conversation about virtue and character completed in *Laws*. The guardian's relationship to truth relies at least partly on non-rational qualities of his soul.

In the interpretative essay accompanying his translation of the *Republic* Allan Bloom suggests that the exile provisions (541a) that mark

---

[39] I use the word knowledge here aware of its inaccuracy, a consequence of the limitations of the English language. We lack a specific word for the knowing that is not really knowing that I seek to describe in what follows.

the completion of the Callipolis are evidence of its impossibility, proof positive of the ironical character of the dialogue.[40] Accepting Bloom's contention, Plato surprises the reader, with the shift in his discussion away from education, illumination, and ascent to a discussion of decline. *Republic's* final three books outline the collapse of the city and in that collapse offer a concrete teaching not about rule by philosophers but rather the consequences of neglect of civic virtue. The final three books return to the explicitly political concerns of the first three. The account of the decline of the Callipolis concludes with Socrates reminding his readers of remarks made before the discussion took its *grand virage* into the education of women, communism of the family, and the end of private property. The mirror image of the critique offered at the end of Book VII, the second-best Socratic teaching, cautions against the neglect of the non-philosophic citizenry. The fall away from perfect rule is for the most part, save its point of origin, a non-philosophic fall. Excepting the rhetorical apex of *Republic,* the precious few moments at Book VII's conclusion, the decline from the rule of philosophy begins almost immediately. Socrates returns, in concern if not conversation, to the political realities represented by Cephalus, Polemarchus, and Thrasymachus.

Book IV first draws the distinction between the philosophic and non-philosophic among the citizen class. To that end, Socrates suggests that the philosophic class will constitute the smallest cohort, that "this class, which properly has a share in that knowledge which alone among the various kinds of knowledge ought to be called wisdom, has, as it seems, the fewest members by nature" (*Republic* 428e–429a). Socrates locates ordinary citizens directly below this class, a group defined by its relation to the quintessential civic virtue of courage. Of this group and its virtue Socrates asserts

> So a city is also courageous by a part of itself, thanks to that part's having in it a power that through everything will preserve the opinion about which things are terrible-that they are the same ones and of the same sort as those the lawgiver transmitted in the education. Or don't you call that courage? (*Republic* 429b–c)

---

[40] Allan Bloom, "Interpretative Essay," in *The Republic of Plato,* trans. Allan Bloom (United States: Basic Books, 1991), 409.

This class, as Plato describes in Book VII, will share in almost all the education of the philosophic, but their nature prevents them attaining the highest level of learning. Moreover, while they are party to the same early education as their philosophic compatriots their nature not only delimits their education differently but in its earlier conclusion it fundamentally transforms its effect. What on the surface appears to be an educational difference only of degree, in its completion for the philosophic becomes an educational difference in kind. The distinction between philosopher and citizen concerns that which they have a share in. Here the Platonic language is telling, if for Athenian democrats citizenship meant a share in politics for the philosophic it entails a share in wisdom; for the ordinary platonic citizen, a share in courage.

The soldiers of the Callipolis, educated in music and gymnastic, are educated to take upon themselves, even into themselves, the laws (*Republic* 430a). The language implies not comprehension so much as acquisition. In contrast to Book VII, the discussion of civic education and learning utilizes proprietary terminology. In Book IV, adding nuance to his account of what sharing in civic virtue entails, Socrates employs dying of cloth as an illustrative metaphor for how the citizen possesses true opinion. The metaphor is particularly suggestive, not least because the imagery of social and civic fabric will reappear in *Laws*. As Socrates expands upon it, the qualities of the metaphor suggest a second-best education, structurally if not substantively, similar to the education in dialectic reserved for the philosophic. In discussing the process of dying Socrates explains

> "Don't you know" I said, "that the dyers, when they want to dye wool purple, first choose from all the colors the single nature belonging to white things: then they prepare it beforehand and care for it with no little preparation so that it will most receive the color: and it is only then that they dye. And if a thing is dyed in this way, it becomes colorfast, and washing either without lyes or with lyes can't take away its color." (*Republic* 429d–e)

Education for the courageous involves stripping them of taints or imperfections in their "fabric," a necessary step before impressing upon them the true color that they will then go on to bear faithfully. Even for the non-philosophic education involves a rupture, it is not the turning into the light of the cave, but it does entail a break with traditional and parochial prejudices. Plato makes the "second-best" status of this education all the clearer by a comparison to Socrates' description of the foundations of philosophic knowing in dialectic.

> [Soc.] "When the beginning is what one doesn't know, and the end and what comes in between are woven out of what isn't known, what contrivance is there for ever turning such an agreement into knowledge?" "None" he said.
> "Then," I said, "only the dialectical way of inquiry proceeds in this direction, destroying the hypotheses, to the beginning itself in order to make it secure; and when the eye of the soul is really buried in a barbaric bog, dialectic gently draws it forth and leads it up above, using the arts we describes as assistants and helpers in the turning around." (*Republic* 533a)

The process of dialectal education appears to involve, albeit in a different type of knowing, a similar process of bleaching out the impurities and starting from white. Plato hints at the connection between the two forms of knowing with the image of weaving invoked in the description of non-dialectical knowledge, an image that will recur both throughout the *Statesman*[41] and significantly in the *Laws*.[42]

A crucial difference between the two kinds of knowing, one that is drawn out by the imagery employed to describe the knowledge of true opinion is the element of internal reflection. In dialectic the particular hypothesis being examined can be held out, separate from the examiner, and treated as distinct. The subject of inquiry is distinct and distinguishable from the inquirer. The image of dying entails that the cloth is dyed clear through, no part of the fabric is held distinct, it is all of a color. True opinion, unlike true knowledge, becomes not so much a thing that

---

[41] For an exhaustive treatment of the metaphor of weaving and cloth manufacture in *Statesman* see Stanley Rosen *Plato's Statesman The Web of Politics* (New Haven: Yale University Press, 1995).
[42] Plato, *Laws*, 734e.

is known but an aspect of the person. Civic education teaches not how to know but instead trains in how to be, true opinions function not as knowledge but as trait, true opinion acts as the governing principle in place of the fully realized logos the non-philosophic lack.

One of the strangest ironies of the *Republic* and the strongest evidence for its status as a philosophic propadeutic to the *Laws* is Plato's unwillingness to discuss civic life except in terms of its decline away from philosophic rule. While the virtues of the philosopher and the merits of that life are detailed at great length only half the promise is met as regards the civic. We are told that the primary civic virtue is courage, moreover it is made clear that a civic education will involve a second-best pedagogy that cleans and prepares the soul for the holding of true opinion, for the ability to be ruled from without by truth. This truth, Socrates suggests, will originate for the non-philosophic in the person of the lawgiver. However, while Plato presents the founding of the city, the grand context in which it operates (eugenics, communism, gender equity, etc.) at length, Plato leaves undiscussed the common life of the *Callipoloi*. Raising this concern, the pious Adeimantus naively remarks.

> It isn't worthwhile," he said "to dictate to gentlemen. Most of these things that need legislation they will, no doubt, easily find for themselves. (*Republic* 425e)

The ordinary business of the city doesn't interest Adeimantus. Adeimantus would rather discuss the content of the heavens than the conduct of the street. His ambitious brother Glaukon is equally uninterested in the civic life. How to rule and be ruled doesn't interest him. On the other hand, how to acquire rule utterly fascinates him. It may or may not be true that gentlemen will work out the daily business of city life with ease, what is certain is that Adeimantus and Glaukon have not yet become gentlemen. The *Republic* prepares them to find this legislation, it bleaches out their souls so that they make take the dye of Plato's *Laws*.

In the *Republic* the civic education of the non-philosophic seeks to inculcate a capacity to retain and live by and through true opinion. While Book VII concludes with the establishment of the rule by philosophers, in the concluding passages of Book IX we have the explanation of what ordinary citizenship in such a city would entail. The civic virtue of the non-philosophic, as Socrates makes clear, amounts to a willingness to be ruled by true opinion which emanates from above. It is in this openness to a truth possessed but not examined and understood, that civic virtue is expressed and that establishes comity between the rulers and the ruled.

> In order that such a man also be ruled by something similar to what rules the best man, don't we say that he must be the slave of that best man who has the divine rule in himself? It's not that we suppose that the slave must be ruled to his own detriment, as Thrasymachus supposed about the ruled; but that it's better for all to be ruled by what is divine and prudent, especially when one has it as his own within himself; but, if not, set over one from outside, so that insofar as possible all will be alike and friends, piloted by the same thing. (*Republic* 590c–d)

The reminder of the presence of Thrasymachus at this moment is crucial. It is not that Thrasymachus' conception of rule is finally destroyed, that happened long ago. The discussion between Adeimantus, Glaucon, and Socrates has not transformed Thrasymachus into a man capable of walking in the Platonic "light of truth," but it has rendered him willing and able to hear and perhaps even possess the true opinions being offered. Socrates rules Thrasymachus in a way that enables Socrates to practice philosophy and Thrasymachus to practice civility. Book IX ends with Socrates musing that all that they have laid out may make it possible for the truly wise to found the Callipolis within themselves, the invocation of Thrasymachus' name, the reminder of his continuing presence, opens the possibility that such a founding may move later to the colonization of other minds who practice virtues founded and imported from without.[43] Plato, when he mandated fifteen years of service to the Callipolis as a precondition but not a guarantee of the ascent to philosophy, institutionally established civic virtue as second to philosophy.

Plato's discussion concludes with a treatment of rule by true opinion formed without and received within by the strictly civic pupil. Plato implies that this reception develops qualities that mimic aspects of the

---

[43] Scolnicov, *Metaphysics*, 105.

philosophic student but that remain a secondary sort of knowing, lived as fully as their degree of removal permits. While the institutions of education described in the Callipolis provide for this education the provision is more meaningfully portrayed in the dramatic action of the dialogue. This is why Thrasymachus matters *more* not less in the books after his debate with Socrates in Book I. The aggressive young sophist who bursts onto the scene "like a wild beast" (*Republic* 336b) *at* the end of the dialogue sits in the manner of one *qui tacet consentire*. He has been rendered capable of rule from without by compulsion first but eventually his continued presence signals rule by persuasion. Thrasymachus, over the course of the evening, has ascended from slave to subject.

Read on its own the *Republic* stands as a stark caution against utopian thought. The educational program established within its pages culminates in the destruction of the family, the emptying of all blood and zest from dramatic poetry and music and most memorably the scandalous *mise en scene* of the gymnasium. At every stage of learning in the Callipolis fewer students are permitted to proceed, ultimately those who have been found worthy of the highest teaching reward the city that has made such learning possible with a universal exile of all those over the age of 10. Interestingly, Plato does not make clear what the rule of such enlightened men will do to education.[44] To the contrary, no sooner has the education of the philosopher kings culminated in their ascension to rule than the account switches to the sources of decay within the city.

Plato has fully countenanced the philosophic education and the general contour of the politically virtuous but non-philosophic citizen has been established as has his necessity. However, the immediate shift in the discussion of the city, from its climax in Book VII with the rule of the philosopher kings to the drawn-out denouement of its decline in Book VIII illustrates in the negative the necessity of a specifically civic education. The philosopher kings may be able to generate further philosophers,

---

[44] In fact to say that Plato doesn't make clear the innovations in education that the philosopher kings would either maintain or expand upon is an understatement. In the opening of Book VIII Socrates recounts what has been agreed upon and among the arrangements for women, communism of the family, and the quartering of the guardians among others the educational provisions are conspicuously absent (*Republic* 543a–c).

but such generation depends on a non-philosophic citizenry capable of being ruled. The *Republic* provides both for the education of rulers and the deep realization of the necessity of an education for the ruled. But within the pages of the *Republic* the necessity doesn't equal its full adumbration. As such, for the purposes of politics and education *Republic* serves as a prelude to *Laws*. The transformation of Thrasymachus, from an aspiring tyrant convinced of his own right to rule into a degree of gentleness (*proates*) prepares him not for a full education, a reprise of the *Republic* but for the reception of law. The *Republic*, by outlining the ultimate education both clears it out of the way and points to such a clearing as necessary to a discussion of the penultimate education. The striking educational character of the *Republic*, its pedagogical double irony, is that those who are taught are all ultimately found to be ill-suited for the education it alludes to. Furthermore, Plato never delivers the education for which they have been found fit, a full civic education. As such, the politico-pedagogic structure of the *Republic* suggests the undisclosed philosophic education with which Plato's *Laws* concludes. This mirroring renders each dialogue both a propaedeutic and an invitation to the other.

The Laws

It is easy to conclude, and it is often contended, that the *Laws* offers a prescription for what is affectionately known as Plato's "second best city."[45] This heuristic distinction between the Cretan city of the *Laws* and the *Republic's* Callipolis has served to both distort and diminish the importance of this, not insignificantly the longest, of Plato's dialogues. The distinction suggests that Plato somehow cropped off the idealism and the utopian elements of the *Republic* leaving only a more "realistic"

---

[45] The Athenian Stranger draws this distinction and employs this phrase in Book V, 739a. Its employment in Book V of *Laws* is far from co-incidental, the Athenian continues on to discuss why the city is second-best and refers immediately to commonality of property and the family in Book V of *Republic*. Considering the ironic political import of the *Republic's* provisions in Book V we must necessarilly take care not to treat the designation of second-best uncritically.

picture of a good constitution. Among other things, this crude but ubiquitous assertion misses the deep difference *in kind* between the projects of *Republic* and *Laws*. The latter constitutes Plato's most singularly political work; as a result, to the extent that politics is "second best" to philosophy the relationship holds. However, as I've attempted to show in the discussion of civic virtue in *Republic*, Plato doesn't conceive of philosophy and politics in reductively ordinal terms. The explicit concentration on the political import of legislation, education, crime, and punishment renders *Laws* not secondary but complementary, beginning where the *Republic* ends and ultimately, as I have argued earlier, ending where the *Republic* begins.

Plato's *Laws*, unlike the *Republic*, offers no description of a philosophic education. Indeed, the promise of such a description, made by the Athenian Stranger to his travelling companions Klenias and Megillos, jars in its absence from the dialogue's concluding passages. Of the philosophic education and in a cryptic fashion all too typical of his later writings Leo Strauss observes, "Naturally, the philosopher remains silent."[46] Naturally is key. The significance of the Athenian Stranger's silence, like his novel moniker and the extra-Athenian context of the dialogue, points to the differing terrain to be treated, an education in civic virtue cannot speak to philosophy, its pupils will never know the landscape outside of the Cave. Across the Sea of Crete, the conversations of *Republic* and *Laws* are worlds apart.

In the *Republic* Plato treats civic education as a *sine qua non*, necessary to the life of the philosopher, thrice justified as political necessity, propaedeutic and diaresis. In *Laws* the education of the non-philosophic citizen moves to the forefront, meanwhile the education of the philosophic, not a *sine qua non* by any means, exists primarily as an implication of Plato's argument and an undefined aspect of the mysterious Nocturnal Council. There are two aspects of Plato's discussion of civic education which are broadly drawn in *Republic* but receive their fullest expression in *Laws*. In *Republic* Plato began to draw out the elements of pre-rational education via habituation, in that dialogue this education

---

[46] Leo Strauss, *The Argument and the Action of Plato's Laws* (Chicago: University of Chicago Press, 1975), 185.

comprises a precursor to a philosophic education and is treated in those terms. In *Laws* we see the importance of habituation for the life of the citizen and by extension the city. Plato's *Laws* fills out the picture, only briefly outlined in *Republic*, of how true opinion dwells within the rightly educated citizen. Plato offers this dwelling within the breast of true opinion as the best possible education for the non-philosophic citizen, and one characterized by consonance (*sumphonia*) with the knowledge of the philosopher. The two components of a completed civic education, habituation directed at consonance and the possession of true opinion, are the core of the *Laws* vision of civic education. This concern completes the account begun in the *Republic* with the education of the philosopher. The *Laws* fills out the civic context of education, philosophy and politics first suggested in the *Republic* (*Republic* 519b–520a).

Education and Habituation

The educational connection between *Republic* and *Laws* first appears in the Athenian Stranger's discussion of physical, musical, and rhythmic education. The differences, in detail but also in substance, first suggest the consequence of Plato's shifting concern. For instance, in *Republic* gymnastic education serves the twofold purpose of indicating the crucial connection between the body and soul's virtues and pointing up the risks of utopian political thought in terms of radical gender equality (*Republic* 452a).[47] In the *Laws* with its very different concern the description of

---

[47] Leo Strauss, *The City and Man*, 116–118. Pangle makes a similar argument regarding ambidexterity and gender in *Laws*: "One might go so far as to say that the cultivation of ambidexterity is analogous to the best regime by nature, while the cultivation of right handedness is analogous to natural law (cf. 636b and *Ethics* 1134 b 30ff.) We see that reflection on our commonsense doubts about the simpler project of making all citizens ambidextrous is meant to illuminate the grounds for resistance to the idea of making men and women share the same military training." "Interpretive Essay," in *The Laws of Plato*, trans. T. Pangle (Chicago: University of Chicago Press, 1979), 481. The case for irony is not as strong in these passages as in the companion passages in *Republic*. While perfect ambidexterity is impossible a *degree* of ambidexterity is not only possible it seems reasonable. The stark and impossibly de-eroticized example of *Rep. V.* is absent in *Laws*, instead through accommodations for separate meals, lodging etc. the Stranger seems to suggest that gender difference is ultimately intractable but amenable to *some* amelioration.

education in music and gymnastic is more unified in purpose. The inculcation of the civic virtues in the citizenry is more singularly the focus of the *Laws'* treatment of civic education. The Athenian offers several different definitions of education in the *Laws* but they all share the common characteristic of promoting a harmony between the passions and virtue within the citizen soul. This harmony, the Athenian makes clear, must begin long before any reasonable expectation of education by rational persuasion or illustration. Indeed, as in the *Republic* (522a) not only must it begin before reason but it also forms the core of the non-philosophic education. The purpose of gymnastic and dance is not to promote a knowledge of the virtues *qua* virtues, but to promote an attachment to them.

Playing upon the dual meaning of *nomos*, as both rhythm and law, the stranger suggests that an educated man is one who has knowledge of the musical.

> Athenian Stranger: So the uneducated man will in our view be the one untrained in choral performances, and the educated ought to be set down as the one sufficiently trained in choral performances?
> Kleinias: But of course. (*Laws* 645a–b)

Plato is not suggesting that knowledge and ability in the choral is the substance and total of education in the Cretan city. Instead, the Stranger's account contends that the way that attachment to the substance and form of the choral comes to be in the citizen is structurally similar to the way in which the civic virtues are to be learnt. The learning occurs not as an explicit lesson but as a slow and steady enchantment by way of rhythm and tone.[48] It is not aimed at knowledge but at an attachment based on a pleasing familiarity.

The Stranger's vision of education rests on two key elements that operate at different times in the civic education of the child. From the very first moments of life a Cretan child should be rocked and caressed by its mother in order to introduce it, by way of rhythm, to the idea of order. As the Athenian argues

---

[48] Glenn R. Morrow, *Plato's Cretan City* (Princeton: Princeton University Press, 1966), 309.

> When someone brings a rocking motion from the outside to such passions, the motion brought from without overpowers the fear and the mad motion within, and, having overpowered it, makes a calm stillness appear in the soul that replaces the harsh fluttering of the heart in each case. (*Laws* 791a)

The steady rhythmic rocking of the child serves as a post-partum enchantment of the infant who would otherwise be struck by the chaos of being in the world. The rocking teaches even a newborn that calm and mastery of fear find their source in the experience of order.[49] This passage points to a deep difference, intimated earlier, between the *Laws* and the *Republic*. In *Republic* art, dance, gymnastic, and rhythm worked in the service of philosophy, that is in the early stages of the comprehension of order; in the *Laws* these selfsame work primarily in the service of order. The rocking of infants in the Cretan City aims not at their eventual comprehension of the nature of order but rather at the inculcation in the soul of *nomoi*. This initial neo-natal lesson aims at the settling of temperament not the elevation and illumination of soul, at knowledge of law not justice.

Plato further hints at his difference in the substance of education between the *Republic* and the *Laws* in his re-visitation of the naval motif in *Laws*. In *Republic* the nautical imagery concerns piloting (especially *Republic* 342d–e) and navigation by the stars (*Republic* 488e–489a). In *Laws* Plato employed a shipwright analogy, and the citizen far from being the shipwright occupies the place of ship itself. The Athenian Stranger suggests

> I'm trying to distinguish the outline of ways of life as they accord with characteristics of souls, and thus really "laying down their keels"- investigating, in the correct way, what device we should use and what characteristics we should at any time incorporate if we are going to be carried through this voyage of existence on the best way of life. (*Laws* 803a–b)

---

[49] Morrow, *Cretan City*, 328.

The words that follow "laying down their keels" hint at its deeper significance. As Thomas Pangle notes "The Athenian here plays on the Greek words 'keel' (*tropideion*) and 'characteristic' (*tropos*)."[50] The difference between the education offered by the *Republic* and the *Laws* is striking. The keel of a boat, the lowest and center timber in its construction, is key to its stability but does not participate in navigation. Pushing the analogy a little and bringing it into the context of the *Republic*, the keel has no knowledge of the stars, invisible from its submarine position. The characteristics that are inculcated through habituation share this aspect. The Athenian uses the verb "to carry" to describe what occurs, the cultivated characteristics bear the citizen through life, they do not navigate like the stargazer of the *Republic*. Plato carries the idea of being borne through existence by qualities that the citizens were habituated to as children a step further when the Athenian Stranger begins to talk of the educated citizen in terms of puppetry.

> This is the way our nurslings should consider things: they should believe that what's been said has been adequately spoken, but that the demon and god will suggest things to them regarding sacrifices and choral performances, thus indicating those whom they should offer games and propitiate, and when they should play each game for each, so as to live out their lives in accordance with the way of nature, being puppets, for the most part, but sharing in small portions of the truth. (*Laws* 804a–b)

This description of education and by extension of ordinary human life understandably angers the Athenian's Spartan interlocutor Megillos. Megillos is right to be angered by the playfulness with which the Athenian takes political life, it is the sum total of the Spartan's horizon, its diminishment is his diminishment. As Strauss remarks, "The dissension between Megillos and the Athenian is the dissension between the political man who necessarily takes the human things very seriously, and the philosopher."[51] But this is only part of the equation. Megillos takes umbrage with the imagery while missing the qualification "sharing in small portions of the truth." Like the keel of a ship, the characteristics of

---

[50] Pangle, *The Laws*, 531, n27.
[51] Strauss, *Argument*, 106.

the soul carry it and by dint of that, they participate in the journey even if the submarine timber senses little. The keel is steered by the stargazer and the stargazer in turn is borne upon the keel. So it is also in the virtuously ruled city. Like Megillos, the citizen's education and ability preclude him from speaking lightly of human affairs, from having the necessary philosophical freedom (*parrhessia*) to chart a course. However without the fundamental timber of men like Megillos no city, no voyage, is possible. The Stranger's remarks suggest that such "timber" not only shares in the truth, in however small a portion, it must be at least inchoately aware of its portion to continue to serve its purpose. It must recognize the truth even if this recognition is experienced as an epistemologically secondary opinion (*doxa*).

Reason and Calculation, Logos and Logismos

The invocation of puppetry in Book VII deliberately hearkens back to the discussion, at the dialogue's outset, of the different types of cord within the human soul. The first book of the *Laws* functions similarly to the first book of the *Republic*, it draws out all of the themes and implies all the tropes that will be explored in the remainder of the text. Education is first among these, as the discussions of both the divine cords and the "student symposium" make clear.[52] The puppetry image of Book VII hearkens back to the beginning of the dialogue and that hearkens back even further to the discussion of education in Book VII of *Republic*. In that discussion Plato describes education both as a turning (*periagoge*) and a form of coercion, more specifically a compelled "pulling" toward the light (*Republic* 515e–516a). In *Laws,* by setting the discussion of the two cords near the beginning of the dialogue the Athenian signals the civic nature of both pedagogy and pupil. This nature leaves room for an education both by persuasion and compulsion with a stronger element of the latter than is possible on the periagogic and optical analogy of the *Republic*.

---

[52] Strauss, *Argument*, 17.

Plato illuminates the status of the civic pupil, in stark contrast to the tripartite soul of *Republic*, when the Athenian depicts the soul as informed by a severe dualism. The Athenian contends that within a single person we find "two opposed and imprudent counselors, which we call pleasure and pain" (*Laws* 644c). These two imprudent counselors are further divided then de-anthropromorphized into divine cords of gold and iron.

> Now the argument asserts that each person should follow one of the cords, never letting go of it and pulling with it against the others; this cord is the golden and sacred pull of calculation, and is called the common law of the city; the other cords are hard and iron, while this one is soft, inasmuch as it is golden; the others resemble a multitude of different forms. (*Laws* 644e–645a)

This passage reveals a subtle shift of argument regarding the two "imprudent counselors." The two have now been divided into the one and the many with the two counselors sharing the latter category and introducing a new alternative. The gold is singular and expresses unity, like the substance of the civic education of the city's body politic. It implies in its singularity that all who cling to it, and are simultaneously pulled by it, will participate in the unity of its purpose and essence. Contrary to the golden cord is the diversity of purpose of the hard iron cord; its multiplicity reflects the diversity of selfish interests within the city.

The dichotomy of gold and iron, civic versus selfish, in the imagery of the cords complements a deeper hierarchy of reason and calculation. In describing the two cords the Athenian describes the image as a salutary civic myth, in this sense it is similar to the myth of the three metals in *Republic*. However, the Athenian draws out the difference between the two myths by referring to the two cords as an argument, one directed at encouraging a civically virtuous calculation.

> It is necessary always to assist this most noble pull of law because calculation, while noble, is gentle rather than violent, and its pull is in need of helpers if the race of gold is to be victorious for us over the other races. (*Laws* 645a–b)

The etymological connection between calculation (*logismos*) and argument (*logos*)[53] hints at the absence from this first outlining of the soul in the *Laws* as compared to the *Republic*. Plato attributes to logos within the tripartite vision of the soul described in the *Republic* the rational and ruling portion, in this discussion logos comes from the outside. *Logos* understood as argument aims at assisting the soul that clings to the second-best faculty of calculation, *logismos*. Plato further illustrates the difference between *logos* and *logismos* when, as in the *Republic*, its relation to the citizen's soul is expressed in proprietary language and not the language of ontology or native faculty. The citizen should acquire the argument and then live according to its precepts (*Laws* 645b). Calculation is something taught, a civic calculus that allows the citizen to derive consistent and valid answers to civic dilemmas.[54] Of particular civic import is the common nature of this calculus among the citizenry. The calculus is a "true reasoning" that by dint of its truth will generate consistent and valid answers over time and across the body politic. Unlike the varied and particular iron cords that represent the private and idiosyncratic desires of citizens and generate division and faction the true reasoning of calculation is common and creates correct answers. Of equal importance, it cultivates community.

Ultimately the myth of the cords serves a function similar to that of the three metals in *Republic*. Unlike the Noble lie it provides for a fuller existence for the non-philosophic than that offered by the Callipolis. Plato's Cretan citizens participate in a political arithmetic that possesses first principles to which they are deeply attached but not, as in the philosopher's principles, ones that have been independently and intellectually arrived at. The Cretan citizen's civic principles settle within his breast not in response to reason's determination but through the enchantment of sentiment.[55] These first civic principles, the Athenian makes clear will be the laws of the city, which the city should acquire "either from one of the gods or from this knower of these things, and then set

---

[53] Pangle, *Laws*, 517, n53.
[54] Amelie Oksenberg Rorty, "Plato's Counsel on Education," *Philosophy* 73 (1998): 165.
[55] Morrow, *Cretan City*, 309.

up the reasoning as the law for itself and for its relations with other cities" (*Laws* 645b–c). The Athenian is the "knower of these things" and he intends, in discussion with Kleinias and Megillos, to impart the principles of a civic calculus to which the citizens are to become deeply attached and through which they may calculate about politics.

Consonance

The education of the citizen in the Cretan city replaces the love and pursuit of wisdom (*sophia*) with a civic education built on consonance (*sumphonia*). In contrast to the *Republic*, the habituation in *Laws* does not strictly aim at diaresis and propaedeutic culminating in true knowledge (admittedly for an extremely select few) but rather at the epistemologically secondary true opinion. Here the two dialogues dramatically part ways. The Athenian's description of education stops abruptly right at the moment in the *Republic* where Plato introduces the education in dialectic (*Laws* 823b).[56] The three old men break off their speech at true opinion; this true opinion lives in the souls of citizens as a form of calculation, a secondary ability to reason, that operates in consonance/harmony with true knowledge. The necessity and priority of consonance define citizenship in the Cretan city. Returning again to the difference between the cities of the *Republic* and *Laws* Plato's inquiry in the latter concerns the nature of lawgiving and those for whom it is intended. In a sense, the Athenian stranger leaps over the central books of *Republic*, he is uninterested in the cave, instead he discusses the conditions that would prevent the civic decline that follows the philosopher's return. He is interested in the success of laws not the nature of forms.

The Cretan citizen's deeply held opinion is no mind-numbing orthodoxy. True opinion, as the Athenian Stranger makes clear, demands of the student/citizen far more than mere rote learning. Through his civic existence the citizen expresses, rather than merely recites his experience of true opinion. Not subservience, but a life lived in harmony with the city constitutes the aim of education. This explains the city's need not merely

---

[56] Strauss, *Argument*, 114.

for laws, which act as prohibitions or permissions, but also a series of admonishments and encouragements. These serve to delineate not only the bare minimums of civic expectation but to express the full panoply of virtues that comprise the ideal citizen. They aim at a totalizing vision of the citizen, one that demands of the founders of the Cretan city "that he write not only laws, but, in addition to laws, things interwoven with the laws, writings that reveal what seem noble and ignoble to him" (*Laws* 823a).

The correctly habituated student, schooled in the seeming of nobility and its opposite, feels pleasure and pain in a way that is consonant with civic virtue. These reactions and the consequent reactions they generate give first expression to consonance understood not merely as the holding of true opinions, but the practice of a life lived in harmony with those opinions. This deep inculcation of true opinion, an opinion that encourages a harmonic existence, demands the development of a civic and second-best reason. Consonance prepares the pupil for the second-best reason, calculation, which generates outcomes in harmony with the true good of the city[57] and this second-best reason entails a particular kind of active obedience. This second-best reason understood as an active virtue suggests that obedience to law entails preparing citizens to be ruled in a way that is distinct from simple use of force.[58] These are citizens not subjects. They may not participate in rule, but they meaningfully participate in being ruled. Being ruled, the Athenian Stranger makes clear, possesses an unmistakably transactional and reciprocal character. Rule in the *Laws* entails an admixture of compulsion and persuasion, compulsion in the process of habituation followed by persuasion that the pupil has been educated to accept. To illustrate the form that this persuasion will take Plato draws on a favorite paired analogy, sickness and health, doctor and patient. Turning to doctors first, *Laws* further bifurcates his analogy by describing two different types of doctors, one appropriate for slaves the other for free men. The Athenian argues that in a city populated by both slaves and free men the physicians that treat the two

---

[57] Seth Benardete, *Plato's Laws* (Chicago: University of Chicago Press, 2000), 55.
[58] For a similar interpretation of *Republic* see George Klosko "Demotike Arete in the Republic," *History of Political Thought* 3 (1982): 363–381.

populations practice medicine in fundamentally different ways. Slaves are for the most part treated by other slaves; they are attended by a slave-physician who offers his patients a roughshod bedside manner.

> None of these latter doctors gives or receives any account of each malady afflicting each domestic slave. Instead, he gives him orders on the basis of the opinions he has derived from experience. Claiming to know with precision, he gives his commands just like a headstrong tyrant and hurries off to some other sick domestic slave. (*Laws* 720c–d)

The Athenian explains the behavior of the physician in terms of both the education provided for the physician and the nature of the slaves themselves. The slave's physician acquires his art through a rote memorization of the commands of his master (*Laws* 720b), commands he then arbitrarily applies with some apparent brutality to the slaves in a manner seemingly independent of their actual ailment. The slave doctor does not so much practice medicine as re-enact or reiterate it. The Athenian further highlights the physician's lack of true medical knowledge by pointing out that while he has learnt "from experience" no sooner has he prescribed a cure than he "hurries off to some other slave." This moving along indubitably impairs his ability to learn from experience: any cure that doesn't result in immediate remedy (or morbidity) will have its effect go unobserved by the physician. The slave doctor's practice provides for no conversation, no exchange of information, no mechanism of action, response, and reply. Interestingly, it is the physician the Athenian describes and not the slave who resembles the "citizen" of the tyrannical regime. The "laws" of the Tyrant are obeyed uncomprehendingly and civic actions that are informed by them are as capricious as the orders themselves. The slave-patient is simply the object of those laws, acted upon but never really, consciously considered in their nature by those enacting the "law."

Of the enslaved patient himself little need be said. The slave doctor doesn't listen to his complaints because the slave, so uneducated, unhabituated, in his soul so utterly brutish, can neither explain meaningfully what ails him nor, if he could, would his words be deemed worthy of consideration by the physician. Ultimately, the uneducated doctor and his patient remain completely isolated from each other. Their relation resembles that of citizens in a poorly educated polis. No common education means no common language. The words and actions of each are mutually incomprehensible, they each speak and live a selfish and basely idiosyncratic existence pulled by their respective, particular, and narrow iron cord. They act upon each other as things, forces, objects in motion, not citizens in conversation and common endeavor.

The Athenian contrasts this with a different type of doctor and patient and a fundamentally different relationship between the two. The Athenian describes the free doctor in terms that place him in the long lineage of Platonic comparisons between physicians and philosophers.[59]

> The free doctor mostly cares for and looks after the maladies of free men. He investigates these from their beginning and according to nature, communing with the patient himself and his friends, and he both learns something himself from the invalids and, as much as he can, teaches the one who is sick. (*Laws* 720d)

The doctor in this passage constitutes an obvious stand-in for the philosophic lawgiver. In order to recommend a remedy, the doctor must first assess the nature of the citizen. This initial assessment and not the presenting malady comprises the starting point. The doctor who treats free men encounters an individual whose nature and malady are both comprehensible. The doctor communicates with and in turn understands the patient's response, his testimony, his "it hurts here." The distance between the knowledge of the doctor and the patient remains great but not unbridgeable. Indeed, the Athenian makes clear that the cure to the free man's malady lies in such conversation, connection, a common point of contact.

> He doesn't give orders until he has in some sense persuaded; when he has on each occasion tamed the sick person with persuasion, he attempts to succeed in leading him back to health. (*Laws* 720d–e)

---

[59] See especially *Gorgias*, 479–481.

The pedagogic import of this passage is obvious. That the doctor aims to persuade the patient suggests that the patient is amenable to more than mere compulsion, furthermore it implies that the patient can be a party to his own remedy, that he can learn to live in such a manner as to promote his health.[60]

What form does this persuasion take? The Athenian, by employing the term persuasion as opposed to argument, draws the important distinction between a conversation between two doctors and a doctor/patient conversation. The doctor speaks to the patient in a language comprehensible to the patient and provides him with the rationale for his prescription. Unpacking the analogy between patient and pupil reveals the relationship of civic education in the *Laws* to the education in philosophy and dialectics in *Republic*. In the medical analogy, if applied to the education of philosophers in *Republic*, Socrates would teach the patient to become a doctor. The philosophic patient would not be offered a detailed prescription, instead he would participate in the diagnosis, beginning with the first symptoms and an understanding of the idea of health itself. He would start at the very beginning and arrive by correct reasoning at true knowledge of his ailment (*Republic* 533d). The end product of this analogy grafted onto the pedagogical project of *Republic* would not be an educated patient and doctor but two doctors. This is not to suggest that the patient in *Laws* is not taught. He stands between the philosophic student of *Republic* and the slave/patient to which he is compared in *Laws*. The citizen/patient in *Laws* stands somewhere between subjection and illumination. Told the rationale for his course of treatment and possessing it as comprehended prescription the citizen/patient endeavors to live a life informed by it. The patient is lead back to health; walking with the doctor, as Megillos and Kleinias walk with the Athenian Stranger.

---

[60] C. Bobonovich, "Persuasion, Compulsion and Freedom in Plato's *Laws*," *Classical Quarterly* 41 (1991): 373.

Plato's Civic Prescription

What is the political prescription in the Cretan City? In discussing the merits of literary education for the young the Athenian Stranger provides a startling answer. He begins by outlining a variety of techniques for teaching the young in the written tradition of the poets. The Athenian Stranger then suggests that the morally ambiguous nature of much of this poetry renders it dangerous to the civic welfare of students. However, in contrast to the careful censorship of *Republic*, the Athenian does not offer a philosophically reduced and revised canon but rather an altogether new one. In a moment of striking Platonic literary innovation the Athenian remarks:

> Inasmuch as I'm not altogether at a loss for a model. As I looked now to the speeches we've been going through since dawn until the present-and it appears to me that we have not been speaking without some inspiration from the gods-they seemed to me to have been spoken in a way that resembles in every respect a kind of poetry. It's probably not surprising for me to have had such a feeling, to have been very pleased at the sight of my own speeches, brought together, as it were; for in poems, or poured out in prose like what's been said, these appeared to me to be both well-measured, at any rate, of all, and especially appropriate for the young to hear. (*Laws* 811c–d)

With these words Plato writes himself into the dialogue. Plato's place within the *Laws* resembles in prose the self-portrait of Raphael in *The School of Athens*. Plato implicates himself here as surely as Raphael. At no previous point in the dialogue has mention been made of the conversation being recorded, nor has a fourth participant, a silent stenographer been implied. And yet the Stranger talks as if he has their speeches, the substance of their conversation, in front of him. The Stranger goes further in suggesting that a record has been kept by declaring that he is pleased at the *sight* of his speeches, speeches which have been "brought together." But who has done this work? The recorder must be Plato, slipped ever so briefly into the forefront to remind the reader of the task at hand.[61] It is hard to overstate the significance of this move for the education of the citizen. In a single moment Plato transforms and elevates *Laws* from diagnosis to prescription and remedy. In an important sense the dialogue becomes suddenly and, in both senses, dramatically self-aware. It remains an investigation, but it is now also an artifact subject to that investigation. A critical aspect of the sudden inclusion of the author in the action is the sudden honing into view of the author as artist/craftsman and therefore the conversation as the product of that art. With the appearance of the author, we are explicitly invited to wonder what Plato aims to produce in the dialogue and further what it is that law is meant to produce.[62] The reader sees the three soujourners, but most especially the Athenian Stranger, as distinct from Plato, as creations combining in the service of a larger project. The most striking consequence of this act of authorial revelation appears with the Athenian Stranger's plans for the record of their conversation. By the Athenian Stranger's order, the record of their conversation will be handed over to the Cretan City's Supervisor of Education who may supplement it also with poetry and prose deemed to be in spirit and substance "brother" (*Laws* 811e) to the dialogue.

The *Laws* reconceived of as not only concerning the Cretan city but also *of* the city becomes the prescription of the philosophic doctor for the civic patient. Here what seems most striking for citizenship in the Cretan city is the transparency of the founding. The arguments which culminate in the laws of the new city are to be available to the entirety of the political class. The availability of the principles of the founding stands on the surface at least, in stark contrast to the hidden nature of the

---

[61] Of incidental importance this passage seems to me to be the strongest argument against the Athenian being considered a stand-in for Plato as opposed to Socrates. In this passage Plato's presence *over and beyond* the three interlocutors prevents such a conclusion. He is recorder and craftsman he cannot therefore be character.

[62] Production has in fact been on the table since at least Book IV where the governing art is equated with a series of other arts, as Curtis Johnson observes "It is noteworthy that where Plato does explicitly refer to rules as 'craftsmen' (*technitai*) as in the *Laws* (709a–d) he is also clear that these rulers (unlike the philosopher-rulers of the *Republic*) are "lawmakers-that is, exercise a function that issues in an unmistakable product; separate from the makers themselves" Curtis Johnson "The "Craft' of Plato's Philosopher-Rulers," in *Politikos* ed. Leslie G. Rubin (Pittsburgh: Duquesne University Press, 1992), 216n17.

founding principles of the Callipolis.[63] However this stark contrast holds only if the purposes of the two dialogues are simplistically understood of in terms of best and second best. The *Laws* does not aim to teach the philosopher but the citizen, this teaching is not simply second best it is profoundly different.

The citizen's study of both the terms of the dialogue and its dramatic action provides the substance of the civic teaching to follow. Plato's civic teaching emerges explicitly in the discussion of specific civic provisions, commonality of meals, the division of neighborhoods, admission of new citizens for example. More subtly but perhaps more substantially that civic teaching emerges in the citizen's encounter with Platonic dialogue. In providing for the transcription of the day's conversation Plato hints at the political potential of his revolutionary literary form.[64] Offering a dialogue as the founding *nomos,* in contrast to Homer or Hesiod, let alone Solon, speaks volumes about the nature of the civic. Contrasting the literary legacy of the poet with that of the lawgiver, and thus by implication himself, Kleinias and Megillos, the Athenian Stranger argues.

> How do we conceive writing about laws in the cities should be: should the writings appear in the shapes of a father and mother, caring dearly and possessing intelligence, or like a tyrant and despot, should they command and threaten, post writings on the walls and go away? (*Laws* 859a)

In speaking of a tyrant who departs, Plato recalls the practice of the slave doctor. The tyrannical lawgiver declares and then departs. Subsequently, the citizen of such a city passively receives the law, a law given without rationale and obeyed without reason. The citizen submits to the law's command out of a singular obedience lacking any portion of comprehension. The laws weigh upon him. They do not dwell within.

In contrast, the Athenian Stranger's constituting dialogue, subtly opposed to the Athenian practice of writing the laws on the walls of the city, founded an enduring and continually reconstituting conversation. It encourages within the citizen not merely a sort of behavior but a sort

---

[63] Bobonovich, *Compulsion*, 377.
[64] I will return to this them in the discussion of Cicero's *De Re Publica* and *De Legibus*.

of character, namely that of a person fit to comprehend and utilize the laws, able to learn their calculus and employ it in civic life.

Plato offers a three-fold explanation for the status of *Laws* as the basis of the Cretan City's education in laws: the nature of law, the nature of the philosopher, and the nature of the citizen. These justifications speak respectively to the fundamental nature of even the best of laws: incompleteness, scarcity, and spirited tension. The arch-tectonic character of *Laws* provides the first rationale assigning it the role of founding civic education and law. Unsettled, Kleinias cautions the Athenian Stranger that this assigning can only be appraised once their daylong discussion has reached its destination and conclusion (*Laws* 812a).[65] In his alarm Kleinias' desire for conclusions indicates an important twofold misunderstanding of the nature of both dialogue and of law. By writing a dialogue Plato admits that all law is incomplete, all constitution writing partial. The breadth of the political prohibits its encompassment by the written word, no matter how well crafted. By virtue of this endless variation Kleinias concerns can never be fully answered, at least in the form he expresses them. The purpose of the education is to provide an argument out of which the citizens and their educators may generate, in conversation with the dialogue, innovations that address situations unforeseen and unforeseeable within the context of law. The dialogue both reveals and addresses the necessary limits of a legal order that exists in a politics characterized by inevitable change.

Plato further binds the laws and educational program of the city to the dialogue through another subtly self-conscious discussion of his own role in the enterprise depicted. Plato slowly reveals the inevitable awareness, on the part of the philosopher, of the uncommon nature not only of his lesson but also of his type. The Athenian is an extraordinary person, a type that appears rarely in human affairs. Employing the dialogue as both textbook and law allows the philosopher to provide a framework of action and counsel that continues on after his death or departure.[66] Plato draws out the necessity of providing for a future without the philosopher most obviously with the age of the interlocutors and the dramatic action

---

[65] Benardete, *Laws*, 216.
[66] Strauss, *Argument*, 92.

in which they participate. Old men all, they journey through the day into night. In marked contrast to Socrates' often youthful interlocutors, the Athenian Stranger's aging fellow travelers are poignantly aware that a founding document must inevitably stand in for the deceased founders. Their conversation, their education, their positions, will be reexamined, reaffirmed and newly applied by subsequent generations who learn by engaging with the record of this founding conversation.[67] In this way the Athenian Stranger in *Laws* and perhaps Plato in all the dialogues found a partial remedy for the exceptional nature of the true philosopher and the wise lawgiver.[68]

In Book VII of *Laws* Plato turns to an explicit discussion of the ends of education and the limits of its possibility in the Cretan city. Having established the necessity of the *Laws* itself to the future well-being of the citizens and city the conversation, seemingly inexplicably, turns to hunting. Closer examination reveals a twofold rationale for this sudden switch: It addresses both the limits of the education dictated by the nature of the *Laws*, and the limits of education dictated by the nature of men. The *Laws* considers political education, more specifically political education as opposed to philosophic education. As in so many of Plato's dialogues, this dyad seems axiomatic, the two invariably imply one another. In the *Republic* an education in the political was a step on the ladder of learning which ultimately, for a select few, culminated in a philosophic education and the prerogatives of rule. From its outset the *Laws* focuses on a lower rung of the ladder. Its concern is not to adumbrate philosophic education but rather to fill out the political education existent primarily as *sine qua non* in *Republic*.[69]

---

[67] The late correspondence between John Adams and Thomas Jefferson seemed designed to serve just this purpose for subsequent generations seeking to navigate what Benjamin Rush famously described as the North and South poles of the American Revolution. As Adams famously wrote, in opening their reconciliation in old age, "You and I ought not to die before we have explained ourselves to each other" (July 13, 1813).

[68] For an interesting further discussion of the written word and its relationship to wisdom see Benardete's remarks on the *Laws* and the *Phaedrus* in Benardete, *Plato's Laws*, 353.

[69] This is not to suggest that the education of the philosopher-ruler in the Callipolis doesn't receive an education in politics, but rather to suggest that inasmuch as that education is presented it is a lesson for the philosopher and *not* for the citizen.

The sudden switch to hunting in the *Laws* Book VII sets in stark contrast the divergence in pedagogic paths from the discussion of education in Book VII of *Republic*. In the *Laws*, at the moment in the argument where the student should stand, pedagogically, at the mouth of the cave his instructor takes him into the fields and streams in search of prey.[70] The dramatic action with which the dialogue concludes offers the same message. At the end of the day's walk the old men approach the shrine of Zeus and the Athenian Stranger's promise, to speak of philosophic education draws near. Instead, the dialogue ends with the silence of the philosopher. To no avail Kleinias and Megillos implore the Athenian to remain and assist in the Cretan City's founding. In his silence the Athenian Stranger reveals the tension between philosopher and city, between politics and wisdom. Ultimately, in his silence the Athenian Stranger embodies the unwillingness of the philosopher to rule.[71] In his silence he acknowledges the decisive pull of the golden cord first spoke of early in the day. The Athenian Stranger, at the cave, turned suddenly taciturn, expresses the enduring estrangement of politics from philosophy.

The explicitly pedagogical import of the dramatic action complements this hypothesis, buttressed by the parameters of the discussion laid out in the opening of the dialogue.

> I expect it would not be unpleasant for you to pass the present time discussing the political regime and laws, talking and listening as we go on our way. The road from Knossos to the cave and temple of Zeus is altogether long enough. (*Laws* 625a–b)

The conversation *must end* where it does, to continue further would be to explore beyond the political regime and laws, more explicitly to venture into the cave and into a discussion of matters treated elsewhere. As I argued at the outset, the dramatic action of *Laws* points to the *Republic*, the philosopher remains silent not only because of the tension between philosopher and politics but because the philosopher has already

---

[70] Strauss, *Argument*, 114.
[71] Pangle, "Interpretive Essay," 509. See also Strauss, *Argument*, 114.

spoken of these things. Kleinias and Megillos wish to found a city, for them the conversation has ended, for the reader who wishes to continue the conversation beyond lawgiving, to journey onto the fundamental grounds of justice and the good the dialogue ends not with silence but with a pregnant pause.

The discussion of education in Book VII of the *Laws* ends with a discussion of hunting for a second reason, oddly juxtaposed with the first. The discussion of hunting points first to the end of education and then as the discussion continues it points increasingly to the unending nature of education. It points to the presence of spirit in politics and the impossibility of completely "training" spirit. The incompleteness that is an aspect of both thumos and eros and their ceaseless longing to be expressed demands an equally unceasing education. By turning the conversation to hunting the Athenian draws out the limits of an education of the sentiments in terms of the training of the passions. Hunting points to the extension of the passions outside the walls of the city, outside of the civic. It points to conquest. The hunting of animals is rooted in the same passion that compels men to hunt one another both in warfare[72] and friendship (*Laws* 823b). The Athenian Stranger intends, in the teaching of types of hunting and fishing, first of game and then inevitably of men, to imbue in the passions of citizens a law of war, a pleasure in the just and a pain in the unjust as it pertains to affairs between cities. Hunting, like warfare, is by definition extramural. Outside of the city walls the true mettle of an education in the noble and ignoble becomes fully, terribly manifest. In the absence of effective sanction, it is the clearest case of a law that cannot simply be written on the wall. The teaching of hunting is the training of the martial soul, the Athenian Stranger remarks

> Having said these things as preliminary, what would come next is a measured praise and blame as regards hunting; there should be praise for the sort that makes the souls of the young better and blame for the opposite sorts. (*Laws* 823d)

---

[72] Plato, *Sophist*, trans. F.M. Cornford, in *Plato Collected Dialogues*, eds. Edith Hamilton and Huntington Cairns, 16ed. (Princeton: Princeton University Press, 1996), 219c.

The kinds of sport that will be encouraged are those that encourage the martial virtues of stamina, courage, and resourcefulness.[73] Those condemned, like hunting at night and fishing with traps, encourage the politically corrosive passionate capacity for guile, deception, and sloth. The distinctions drawn for instance between hunting on water and bird-hunting versus hunting on land and with dogs seems at first and even second glance to be vague and ambiguous, the further nuance that sacred hunters are to be permitted a degree of these behaviors adds to the mystery and points perhaps toward the capricious. Including these details, even confusions, Plato indicates the ambiguities that exist and define the law as it exists outside the city walls. Piracy, prohibited by the Athenian Stranger (*Laws* 823e), bears a striking resemblance to naval battle. It is not always clear which is which. The consequences of this ambiguity for the characters of the soldiers are equally ambiguous.[74] This partially explains the hunting of men for friendship. Friendship pulls the passions away from the beastly aspect of war and sustains the civic spirit through the passion for association and against the wildness of war. The city must encourage friendship in war, it must teach a virtuous camaraderie that anchors the rightly educated passions and true opinions learned within the city walls. This is an education that cannot end without the impossible end of conflict. As long as there is war this sort of salutary and restorative education must always be available to the citizen-soldier lest following war he returns to the city he defended unfit to live within its walls. At this point in the *Laws* the formal discussion of education comes to an end (*Laws* 824c), the discussion of hunting amounts to the admonishment that in the life of the citizen the discussion and experience that *is* education ends only in death.

---

[73] Morrow, *Cretan City*, 335.
[74] Benardete, *Plato's Laws*, 230.

An End and an Invitation

In discussing civic education in both the *Republic* and the *Laws* I have not primarily spoken of what specific virtues each dialogue aims to inculcate. Instead, I have emphasized the grounding of those virtues, the soul that is crafted to bear them, the framework on which they hang. Both dialogues in describing civic and non-philosophic education seek to establish a habit of soul that prepares and makes gentle the pupil so that he may bear the civic virtues. This chapter has not sought to describe and countenance the specific civic virtues but rather how they are to be taught, not what a good citizen is, but how they are crafted. The one task inevitably entails the other to some extent, but the tasks are not the same.

The explicitly civic virtues of the *Laws*, moderation, courage, and piety are the foundational elements of a civic algorithm. The dialogue as a read and experienced artifact aims not at a complete understanding of these foundational elements but at their adoption. To understand Platonic civic education is to get behind these foundational elements and examine how the algorithm itself is taught. Eventually such an enterprise points at the enduring openness of the equation, it points to the bounds, the calculative and inquisitive limitations of the political. It points back to the *Republic*. However, the *Laws* even in its conclusion recalls its peculiar status as inquiry into law and law itself, inquiry into education and education in itself. Plato knows that *Laws* lives beyond him, that the dialogue and not merely the Athenian Stranger must remain silent to some. In its length, it's difficult and dry prose, the speechifying of the later books and the relative absence of dramatic action, it enacts the diaresis first outlined in *Republic*. In its structure and substance *Laws* sorts the non-philosophic from the philosophic. Reading the dialogue most of the future Cretan citizens will greet the Athenian's final silence with relief and turn back to the affairs of the city. A few readers, arriving at the Cave of Zeus will see in the darkness and silence an invitation.

3

Cicero's Civic Education at the Dawn of Empire

It has never been natural, it has seldom been possible, in this country for learning to seek a place apart and hold aloof from affairs. It is only when society is old, long settled to its ways, confident in habit, and without self-questioning upon any vital point of conduct, that study can affect seclusion and despise the passing interests of the day. America has never yet had a season of leisured quiet in which students could seek a life apart without sharp rigors of conscience, or college instructors easily forget that they were training citizens as well as drilling pupils;

Woodrow Wilson, "Princeton in the Nation's Service" October 21, 1896[1]

---

[1] Woodrow Wilson, "Princeton in the Nation's Service" Speech of October 21, 1896 from *Collected Papers*, Volume 10. http://www.princeton.edu/~mudd/exhibits/wilsonline/indn8nsvc.html.

© The Author(s), under exclusive license to Springer Nature Switzerland AG 2022
G. C. Kellow, *The Wisdom of the Commons*, Palgrave Studies in Classical Liberalism, https://doi.org/10.1007/978-3-030-95872-5_3

Introduction

Athens, in its rise, decline, and capture fascinated Rome. Cicero, in life and thought, embodied this fascination. Two pillars of his oeuvre, the *Letters to Atticus* and *On Duties*, are epistolary exercises that literally spanned the Ionian Sea. He owed most to Plato and Aristotle and in the strangest homage of all gave Plato's *Politeia* its enduring Western title, *Republic*.[2] As a philosopher and prose stylist Cicero followed Plato and Aristotle in writing both dialogues and letters on questions philosophical, ethical, and political. More closely, and tragically in common with Plato's mentor Socrates, Cicero found himself an outspoken philosopher at the mercy of and eventually murdered by forces politic. Despite sympathies political, philosophical, and biographical Cicero's discussion of the role of the philosopher in public life and in citizen education reveals a deep tension between the Athens of the early Academy and his own Rome. Profoundly indebted to Athens, Cicero's thought is ultimately turned to and was perhaps overwhelmed by the Rome of the late Republic. In a very real sense, the urgency surrounding the collapse of the Roman Republic drove Cicero to employ Greek means for Roman ends.

The fragmentary nature of Cicero's two most explicitly Platonic dialogues, his eponymous *Laws* and *Republic* provide the greatest hurdle to any attempt to understand Cicero's conception of civic education and its debt to Plato. More regrettable still is the almost complete loss of the fourth book of *De Re Publica*, the section that apparently contained Cicero's clearest and most succinct account of civic education. However, this loss, lamentable though it is, does not present the same challenges as say the loss of Book Seven of Plato's *Republic* would to a similar enquiry into Plato's views on education. Beyond the fact that more of Cicero's writing[3] has survived from antiquity than that of any other ancient philosopher, the unique structure and the literary character of Cicero's surviving writing reveals a great deal about his views on civic education.

---

[2] This influence is direct but it also read through the Neo-Platonic tradition and in particular Polybius and Panaetius (The latter's thought is known to us primarily through Cicero's writing).

[3] This fact alone should (but consistently does not) silence those who argue for the relative philosophic insignificance of Cicero, if he has so little original to say why is his literary and philosophic corpus so assiduously guarded over the millennia?

3 Cicero's Civic Education at the Dawn of Empire

It is a relatively banal truism that any philosopher's prose, the structures, and style he employs to convey his ideas, reveals an aspect of how he believes the reader (always an implied student) should be taught.[4] A dialogue, a book, even a learned letter is implicitly pedagogic, in how it teaches it reveals a theory of teaching. This is more desperately true for Cicero than most. Living through and struggling against the decline of the Roman republic, Cicero's political philosophy, civic pedagogy, choices of *dramatis personae*, place and theme, style and structure, spoke volumes. It could not be otherwise. Much of Cicero's extant philosophy was written during periods of exile and political and mortal danger. Cicero intended these works to be read into a failing political culture and politics to serve as a Republican tonic restorative of the fortunes of the Senate, Roman society and, quite frankly, himself. Both Cicero's dialogues and his epistolary prose are explicitly intended to serve as a timely and restorative civic paideia.

The Athenian Capture of Rome

The most conspicuous element of Cicero's project is his use of Greek political philosophy and philosophical form to restore Roman intellectual life. Cicero clearly attempted to translate (sometimes literally) Greek political philosophy into the Roman political milieu. At the same time Cicero was no antiquarian or sentimental philo-hellenist. Indeed, as I shall argue below, Cicero's employment of Athenian means concealed both the degree of his break with Plato and Platonic precursors and the profundity of his own innovations.

To the careful reader Cicero reveals a subtle set of innovations and novel ideas, especially as concerns the capacity to reason and therefore the status of the student. These innovations and novelties mark a concerted and conscious break with Plato. Cicero heightens the significance of these pedagogical and ontological breaks with an even more revolutionary

---

[4] Like many supposed banalities this observation contains depths, these are beyond the scope of my purposes here, for the classic modern exploration see Leo Strauss, *Persecution and the Art of Writing*, Chapter 2 (Chicago: University of Chicago Press, 1992).

reassessment of the relation of politics to philosophy. In what follows I plan to chart the fraught course of Cicero's thought on philosophy and civic education from introduction and adaptation to innovation and reconstitution, the path of enquiry laid out by the philosopher himself.

The Roman poet Horace perfectly captured the complex and often ambivalent character of the encounter and dialogue between Rome and the Peloponnese: "Captive Greece made her savage victor captive and brought the arts to rustic Latium."[5] Writing little more than a generation after the murder of Cicero, Horace found Rome still wrestling with the multiple tensions, philosophic, political, and cultural that inevitably accompanied its ever-expanding empire. These concerns increasingly preoccupied Cicero in the last years of his own life and those of his beloved Republic. The encounter with Greece not only informed Cicero's ideas it offered him comfort in exile and personal loss. In *Tusculan Disputations* he concludes of philosophy "at any rate in my cruel sorrows and the various troubles which beset me from all sides no other consolation could have been found" (*Tusculan Disputations* V.xli.121).[6]

Understanding the significance of Cicero's philosophical writing and in particular his vision of Roman civic education begins with understanding his place in the encounter between Greece and Rome. Too often characterized as an unoriginal thinker, a mere popularizer (and by logical extension *bastardizer*) of Greek political thought[7] Cicero engaged in much more than simply an act of cultural enrichment, an infusion of hellenic flavors into the Latin *metier*. Cicero's late philosophical writing constitutes an attempt at synthesis, nothing less than the hybridization of two distinct political and philosophical traditions, those of oratory and philosophy, into a single civic culture and intellectual practice. Cicero laid this out plainly in the opening paragraph of his single most important and influential work: *De Officiis*. Addressing his son Marcus, at

---

[5] Horace, *Epistolae* II, 156. quoted in H.I. Marrou, *A History of Education in Antiquity*, trans. George Lamb (London: Sheed and Ward, 1956), 242.

[6] Cicero, *Tusculan Disputations*, trans. J.E. King (Cambridge: Harvard University Press, 1943).

[7] Perhaps the single most troubling proponent of this view is Elizabeth Rawson, who in an otherwise brilliant biography of Cicero begins by suggesting "Cicero's greatness resides, indeed, less in his creative originality than in the form and life that he could give to the Latin tradition, enriched by a wide knowledge of Greek civilization." Elizabeth Rawson, *Cicero A Portrait* (London: Penguin Books, 1975), 3.

the time studying philosophy in Athens, Cicero encouraged him to remember and *apply* what he has learned in Rome to his studies in Greece. Of his own education and encounter with things Greek he recalled

> I myself have always found it beneficial to combine things Latin with things Greek (something I have done not only in philosophy but also in the practice of rhetoric), I think you should do the same that you may be equally capable in either language. (*De Officiis* I.1)[8]

A careful reading of this crucial exhortation reveals no clear cultural hierarchy concerning Rome and Greece. Cicero inverts the initial precedence of Latin over Greek in the description of the things studied, which is first and which second, Roman or Greek? Philosophy or Rhetoric? The closing sentence leaves them equally recommended; they are to be combined in a manner that leaves both practices informed by the other. The nature of that relationship, its apparent ambiguity and equivalency, constitutes the first step in Cicero's political project of civic education.

The presence of equally significant poles, both in terms of culture and intellectual enterprise, is central to understanding the Ciceronian project. Indeed, the significance of intellectual tradition, culture, and history sets Ciceronian political philosophy off in a decidedly non-Platonic direction from the very outset. As a young man Cicero had studied and traveled throughout the Hellenic world and had seen its ruination at its own hands and those of its new Roman masters. He lamented the reduction of Sparta and Spartan ritual to a mere tourist attraction, the enslavement of the Greeks and the utter destruction of Corinth.[9] At the same time recognizing the decline of the Greeks combined with a political awareness of the deep cultural significance of the idea of the 'rise' of Rome, pushed his thinking towards a nascent theory of historical development. Early in the *De Re Publica* Cicero acknowledged that this movement constituted

---

[8] Cicero, *De Officiis*, translated and edited by M. Griffin and E.M. Atkins (New York: Cambridge University Press, 1991).
[9] Manfred Fuhrmann, *Cicero and the Roman Republic*, trans. W.E. Yuill (Oxford: Blackwell Publishers, 1990), 30.

a clear break with Greek tradition and in particular with Plato and the dialogue upon which his work is at least exoterically modeled.

> I will have an easier time in completing my task if I show you our commonwealth as it is born, grows up, and comes of age, and as strong and well-established state, than if I make up some state as Socrates does in Plato. (*De Re Publica* II.3)[10]

The difference in task did not lead Cicero to abandon Plato altogether. Rather, following his advice to the younger Marcus, Cicero pursues in Plato what his Latinate wisdom recognized to be of importance in his own time, ever approaching Greece from the vantage point of Rome. In particular, Cicero focused on the development of philosophy in time, of the pursuit of wisdom as an accretive historical process. In an additional wrinkle, Cicero contended that the encounter with cumulative wisdom itself possessed imperatives dictated by historical circumstance. Cicero insisted that the Roman philosopher could adopt Plato's ideas while rejecting his priorities. Consequently, when Cicero turns to Plato's *Republic*, he pursues not the significance of the Callipolis but the lessons of its decline, not the best city but the nature of regime change (*De Re Publica* II.21).[11] It is in this context, against a background both of Hellenic philosophy and Roman moral and political collapse, that Cicero considers civic education with the former put in the service of the growing demands of the latter.

Cicero's transformation of Greek philosophy amounts in part to an act of filtering the content and inverting the order of emphasis and significance. Cicero's "mining" of Greek philosophy is accompanied by constant reminders that the extraction is an act equally prompted by Roman wisdom and Roman necessity (ibid.). Turning again to what appears at first to be the most Platonic of Cicero's dialogues, *De Re Publica*, we see that the encounter between Cicero and Plato is informed

---

[10] Cicero, *On the Commonwealth and On the Laws*, trans. James Zetzel (New York: Cambridge University Press, 1999).

[11] Dorothea Frede, "Constitution and Citizenship: Peripatetic Influences on Cicero's Political Conception in the *De Re Publica*," in *Cicero's Knowledge of the Peripatos*, eds. William W. Fortenbaugh and Peter Steinmetz (New York: Brunswick Transaction Books, 1989), 79.

from its very outset by the earthy wisdom of "rustic Latium" and achieved by the frequent allusion to and even quotation from the Roman political pantheon. Drawing on the authority of Cato, Cicero writes

> He [Cato] said that there never was a genius so great that he could miss nothing, nor could all the geniuses in the world brought together in one place at one time foresee all contingencies without the practical experience afforded by the passage of time. (*De Re Publica* 2.1)

This passage restates the intent spoken of with equal primacy at the commencement of *De Officiis*. Roman wisdom, acquired through its long and glorious history, stands combined with Greek wisdom not displaced by it. Indeed, Cicero implies more: Greek philosophical wisdom and learning are secondary in perspicacity to Roman historical experience. A repeated theme in Cicero, the introduction of Greek wisdom must be informed by Roman experience. "Experience afforded by the passage of time" has led Rome to a more prudent employment of wisdom than the political hubris of constitution making.[12]

The Roman understanding of historical development is not *historicist*. Change and progress are forever tied to continuity and connection with the past. The concept of continuity, of permanence, within change, and across history, was central to the Roman sense of virtue and the sense of civic life in the late Republic. Cicero returns again and again to this quintessential republican tension: the wish to retain the Republic unchanged and the recognition that change and development defines republican politics. Politically and institutionally this tension was best expressed in the tension between Oratory and Jurisprudence, between the ever-changing Roman law and the Roman "constitution" the Twelve Tables primarily honored in the breach.[13]

---

[12] Jean-Louis Ferrary, "The Stateman and the Law in the Political Philosophy of Cicero," in *Justice and Generosity*, ed. Andre Laks (New York: Cambridge University Press, 1995), 55.
[13] Rawson, *Cicero*, 323–324. In his life as a lawyer Cicero often boasted of his childhood memorization of the Twelve Tables and yet as an adult he acknowledged both the tenuous connection between the practice of Roman law and the Tables and the practical superiority of Oratory over Jurisprudence.

In politics, Romans had traditional resolved the tension between an ahistorical conception of republican virtue and a profoundly historical experience of civic life around the idea of virtue's embodiment. In the popular tradition of Rome's great families, over generations, the first families continuously embodied specific virtues. So, the Claudii embodied pride, the Quinctii austerity, the Cassii democratic sensibilities. In each case generations inherited and expressed a virtue that transcends them.[14] Cicero embraced this idea of virtue's embodiment and recognized in it the resolution of the tension between development and permanence. This resolution understood history as teaching not only, or even primarily, what it was to be Roman but what it *is* to be a Roman as a set of qualities comprising character which individual generations express.[15] In Cicero's famous epistle to Brutus, *Orator*, he describes this as the central lesson of Rome's history.

> To be ignorant of what occurred before you were born is to remain always a child. For what is the worth of human life, unless it is woven into the life of our ancestors by the records of history? (*Orator* 120)[16]

The Roman past manifests itself in the present in the lived virtues of Rome's citizens as such while Rome's borders and fortunes may change the Roman *vir* remains constant.

Cicero suggests another element with the imagery of weaving, imagery also present in Plato's *Laws* and *Statesman*. New generations like new additions to a tapestry or carpet are indeed additions, they are new, but they must also be made to fit, they must connect and they must match. Rome extends itself over time and increasingly by Cicero's age, over space expanding the fabric must not only be connected but rendered similar in tone and texture to the original. Roman history not only endures as virtue into the present, but it extends demands into the present, it is

---

[14] H.I. Marrou, *Education in Antiquity*, 236.

[15] This can be seen most clearly in the personification of virtue qua virtue as *Virtus* portrayed both as male and female but always bearing the sword and shield of victory. *Virtus* appears in Roman statuary but is most ubiquitous on the back of imperial coinage.

[16] Cicero, *Orator*, trans. H.M. Hubbell (Cambridge: Harvard University Press, 1962).

present both as lived ideals and as an openness that impresses itself upon the future.

The Dream of Scipio, with which Cicero concludes *De Re Publica*, perfectly captures this relationship between history and virtue.[17] In the dream three generations of the Scipii converse about the nature of history, the endurance of memory, and the role of honor. Speaking to his son, P. Cornelius Scipio, Scipio *pater* recalls his victorious son to his place in the Scipionic and ultimately Roman fabric of virtue.

> Scipio, you should be like your grandfather here and like me your father in cultivating justice and piety: it is important in relation to your parents and family but most important in relation to your fatherland. (*De Re Publica* VI.16)

The three men are woven together in a fabric of virtue, knotted strands of family and country. Both Grandfather and grandson were awarded with the honorific cognomen "Africanus" for separate victories over Carthage. Bringing them into conversation Cicero establishes that the original connection, drawn to Scipionic Rome through the use of Laelius and P. Cornelius Scipio, goes back even farther, that seemingly singular men of the likes of Scipio act as embodiments of virtues that exist over generations of Romans. In the Republic's decline Cicero recognized the desperate need to emphasize the permanence of virtues against the constant change of politics, especially the change represented by Caesarism. Revolution, to the extent that it constitutes a break with the past shatters the careful balance between historical development and virtue's continuity, between Rome's political development and its moral foundation. The end of the Republic, more importantly its replacement not only by empire but by an emperor broke this connection. An emperor, or rather a new emperor involves an utterly novel set of virtues. In this context Caesar cannot embody that which went before; the first Emperor has no ancestors.

Cicero, perhaps more than any other Roman thinker, understood the deep significance of the rustic past of Rome and the importance of

---

[17] This is but one aspect of the Dream's significance, an equally important element will be discussed below.

historical context to an ever-expanding and increasingly insatiable Rome whose only check was the cultural claim continuity made against its civic character. Recognition of the cultural and political significance of embodiment and its claim of continuity informs the structure of Cicero's writing at least as much as his careful study of the place of dramatic action and argument in Greek thought. Cicero's characters often speak Greek philosophy, but the words are placed in the mouths, language, and virtues of the Romans.[18] By employing embodiment and vernacular Cicero sought an effect neither of mimicry nor novelty but of incremental and established change. He provides Greek philosophy with Roman ancestors. In embodying Greek thought in figures of Rome's illustrious past, the Scipii, Crassus and others, Cicero wove it into the context of Roman history, like the victory over Carthage, Greek thought becomes not novel innovation but honorific cognomen. Cicero's careful prose equates the legitimacy of Scipio *Africanus* with a new Roman Greek.

Roman History and Greek Philosophy

It is an odd and ironic consequence of the deftness of Cicero's intellect and prose that his most significant political and cultural accomplishment is held against him by modern scholars. Cicero, deeply cognizant and for that matter supportive of traditionalist Republican sensibilities, introduced both Greek philosophy and his own original thought into the Roman context without ever appearing to innovate or transform. He was a profound and innovative thinker who appeared to his contemporaries and to later readers as a conservative voice and above all a defender of the Roman tradition.[19]

The Romans, like the Athenians before them, wrestled with the problem of autochthony and its place in their political life and public history. In introducing his own ideas and those of the Greeks to the

---

[18] In contrast in Cicero's letters to his friends and in his political speeches he often employed Greek.

[19] There are exceptions to this interpretive tradition, most notably the revolutionary and proto-revolutionary writers of the Enlightenment in France and America.

Roman tradition Cicero began by 'back-writing' Roman prehistory in order to graft onto Roman public history a legitimate tradition of adapting to and incorporating Greek ideas and individuals. In the second book of *De Re Publica* the "marriage" of the Sabine women to the first generation of Roman men provides Cicero with his first example of Roman cultural plurality and incorporation of difference. Cicero's Scipio highlights the specifically political character and consequence of the "marriage": a treaty with the Sabine king, sanctioned by Romulus, that "admitted the Sabines to citizenship and joint religious rituals" (*De Re Publica* II.13). Later Scipio recounts the first major encounter of the Romans with the Greeks, an encounter which was "no mere trickle from Greece that flowed into the city, but a full river of education and learning" (*De Re Publica* II.34). The significance of Scipio's description is twofold. First, it establishes a tradition not only of Roman cultural incorporation. Second and more importantly, the presence of Scipio as historical narrator suggests that such incorporation has not hindered the generation of Roman virtues in their highest human embodiment.

Scipio continues his history of Early Rome by recounting how one of the Greeks who had flowed in on this river, Lucius Tarquinius, a longtime friend of King Ancus, upon the monarch's death, was elected king.

> And so at the death of Marcius [Ancus] the people unanimously elected him king under the name of Lucius Tarquinius: that was how he had changed his name from what it had been in Greek, so as to be seen to follow the customs of this people in all respects. (ibid.)

In recounting this story and the story of the Sabine women Cicero establishes a dual legitimacy both for the idea of a broad even pluralistic conception of Latin autochthony and for a well-established pattern of popularly vindicated contact and co-penetration of Greek and Roman society. The Scipionic version of these episodes in Roman history, the introduction of new foreign things, and in particular Greek things, becomes not an innovation but part of a consistent pattern, a Roman tradition. Returning to the historical dictum of Cicero's *Orator*, by Scipio's lights, if a Roman wishes not to remain ever a child he must embrace the Greek.

Cicero's revisions of the Roman tradition also express themselves in the character and dramatic action of the dialogues. In several of the most important dialogues the voices of Cicero's most novel ideas and in particular those gleaned from the Greeks, are espoused by illustrious figures from the Roman past. The Scipios in *De Re Publica* serve this end but equally important, especially for understanding Cicero's educational project, is the use of the famous Consul and Censor Crassus in *De Oratore*. By employing these characters Cicero achieves two goals, he makes the foreign familiar and he invests the new with the imprimatur of the illustrious dead who speak it.[20]

In the centuries immediately following Cicero's murder his eloquence and mastery of Latin grammar rendered his letters, speeches, and dialogues sources of authority concerning correct speech rivaled only, and not coincidentally, by Virgil.[21] Quintilian went so far as to suggest Cicero to students as "an incomparable model of oratory and oratorical theory."[22] That later Roman readers saw Cicero's prose as standard in its usage is, perhaps above all else, a testament to his gift for innovations that were amenable to deeply traditionalist Roman sensibilities.

Alongside his discourse transforming Latin style, Cicero possessed a profound familiarity and grasp of the Greek language and spoke and wrote in it often. However, in his works of political philosophy he refrained almost completely from employing Greek terminology. While eschewing Hellenic terminology Cicero nonetheless subtly imported Greek ideas into Roman political thought. Buried deep in his introduction of Greek thought to the Roman context, his linguistic and terminological introduction of Greek thought into Roman civic education was as significant and essential to his political project as the literary, historic, and dramatic devices he employed. Cicero repeatedly massaged the meaning of the Greek words he translated into Latin by quietly, even covertly, changing the meaning of both. On the surface Cicero's treatment of Greek terminology appeared trans-literal in character but a closer

---

[20] R.F. Hathaway, "Cicero's Socratic View of History," *Journal of the History of Ideas* 29 (1968): 6.
[21] Aubrey Gwynn, *Roman Education from Cicero to Quintillian*, 2nd ed. (New York: Russell & Russell, 1964), 155.
[22] Quintilian, *Institutio Oratorio* III.i.20, quoted in Gwynn, *Roman Education*, 187.

examination reveals a dramatic catachresis. The rough packing together of the transliterated *philosophy* and *philosopher* into the Latin *prudentia* and *prudens* or *sapientes* marks perhaps the most brazen of Cicero's attempts at terminological hybridization, the most critical and deliberate act of philosophic catachresis.[23] Once again, in equating the philosophers of Athens with the wise men of Rome's early history Cicero attempts to conceal the novelty and distinctness of the practice he seeks to introduce and legitimate. Cicero sets the very first philosophers, indeed all those up to Pythagoras apart from philosophy and deliberately described them with the more general and therefore less alien *Sapientes*, wise men. Cicero writes

> And those we see that philosophy is a fact of great antiquity, yet its name is, we admit, of recent origin. For who can deny that wisdom itself at any rate is not only ancient in fact but in name as well. (*Tusculan Disputations* V.iii.7)

By catechrestically forcing philosophy and its practitioners into *prudentia* and *sapientes* Cicero deracinates political philosophy. He places it in the context of general human history as opposed to a particular and foreign practice a novelty brought into Rome by virtue of its expansion. He sets out to deny the cultural trope later expressed in Horace's "Captive Latium."

In a very real sense Cicero seeks to locate philosophy inside the boundaries of Rome, the very opposite of the extramural setting and multicultural motif with which Plato begins *Republic*.[24] Cicero presents philosophy as only nominally native to Greece and in particular to Socrates and after.[25] By introducing the philosophic terminology in Latin and subtly transforming wisdom into a stand-in for philosophy Cicero essentially transforms the Greek legacy into a broadly human inheritance.

---

[23] Seth Benardete, *Plato's Laws* (Chicago: University of Chicago Press, 2000), n358.
[24] *Republic*, 327a.
[25] The distinction between 'original philosophy' and Socrates and after is of particular importance to Cicero and will be discussed further below.

Of course, by broadly human Cicero means Roman. Cicero created and popularized through the process of catachresis a Latin language[26] for a Greek practice while denying all the time that such a creation was necessary, claiming that to the contrary Latin was always up to the task. Early in his life, in a work he would look back on as juvenilia, but which set the tone for his later project. Cicero went even farther arguing "the Latin language, so far from having a poor vocabulary, as is commonly supposed, is actually richer than the Greeks" (*De Finibus* I.iii.10).[27]

Cicero, in an act of uncharacteristic (and disingenuous) humility, claims that to the extent that he does cite Aristotle and Plato it is little different than when Ennius "borrows from Homer, and Afranius and Menander" (*Fin* I.iii.7). On the one hand, Cicero describes his enterprise as merely the bringing in of exotic elements for their aesthetic appeal, a question of style and flourish at best. On the other Cicero invests his work, by associating it with Ennius (and also Terence and Caecilius), with the status of an established Roman practice. Finally, by creating a philosophical terminology in Latin he enables his own philosophical work immeasurably. To an extent bested only by Plato, Cicero milled and manufactured the linguistic material and apparatus necessary to construct his own political philosophy.[28]

A full understanding of Cicero's political philosophy must acknowledge the centrality of education. At the same time such acknowledgment requires of the reader a sensitivity, approximating Cicero's own to the declining Roman context into which he was writing. Such sensitivity, combined with a simultaneous sly exhorting of wisdom and civic virtue in a language and with imagery familiar to his readership was a lesson Cicero learned at Plato's knee. In *De Legibus* Cicero explicitly invokes this lesson from its eponymous predecessor declaring

---

[26] Marrou, *Education in Antiquity*, 253.
[27] Cicero, *De Finibus*, trans. H. Rackham, (Cambridge: Harvard Unversity Press, 1967).
[28] Furhmann, *Cicero and the Roman Republic*, 160.

> But I think I must do as Plato did, the most learned of men and also the most serious of philosophers, who first wrote about the commonwealth and also wrote a separate work about its laws, namely speak in praise of the law before I recite it. (*De Legibus* II.14)[29]

The process of rendering in Latin the Greek tradition undertaken by Cicero is the necessary first step. The first praise of philosophy is to declare that it is of us, it is our own. Each of his main works of philosophy, by placing the Greek tradition within the Latin and changing its timber and rhythm to suit Latin ears, forms a prelude: a prelude not so much to the laws as to a new and novel type of learning and teaching of civic virtue. Cicero further marries the prelude, a Greek innovation, to a specific Roman pedagogic practice; the treatment of Greek political thought becomes the Roman practice of the *praelectio*. In the Roman schoolroom the introduction of a new text traditional began with the *grammaticus* reading through of the text aloud with explanatory but purely exegetical comments on its content.[30] The *praelectio* was the students first encounter with the new text. It served to familiarize the ear with the surface of the material, to ameliorate its novelty, to prepare the student for his own deeper engagement with the text. Cicero's transformation of Greek thought into latin phrasing, cadence, and cultural context constituted the necessary first social and political *praelectio* to any deeper Roman engagement with political philosophy and with civic education. After Cicero the sound of political philosophy and particularly the teaching on civic education no longer jars the Roman ear. Virtue, civic virtue as conceived by Cicero and Plato, is rendered familiar, it is rendered Roman in a context in which this is the essential first praise of the law recited.

---

[29] That Cicero's description of the relationship between *Laws* and *Republic* is inaccurate is not significant to my purposes here but will be returned to below.
[30] Marrou, *Education in Antiquity*, 279.

Innovation and Transformation

The first step in Cicero's program to reclaim and reconstitute Roman civic education was the attempt to tune the Roman ear to the philosophical and political timbre and rhythm of Greek material. The second task was the transformation of that thought to better suit the demands of the Roman world. While Cicero recognized enduring similarities between political life in the Greek polis and the challenge of the late Republic, he also acknowledged the profound differences between the Socratic introduction of political philosophy into Athens and the same enterprise undertaken in the imperial milieu of Rome. Cicero writes poetically of the tenuous place of philosophy and philosopher in Rome when he has his old mentor L. Licinius Crassus lament

> However, the streams of learning flowing from the common watershed of wisdom, as rivers do from the Appenines, divided in two, the philosophers flowing down into the entirely Greek waters of the Eastern Mediterranean with its plentiful supply of harbors, while the orators glided into the rocky and inhospitable Western seas of our outlandish Tuscany where even Ulysses lost himself. (De Oratore I.xix.69)[31]

Aside from the careful *praelectio* that is characteristic of all of Cicero's dialogues in their treatment of Greek thought, Cicero also engaged in a careful and culturally informed selection from Attic sources more informed by Cicero's sense of *officia* than his undeniable *sapientia*. To the extent that Cicero mined Greek thought for ideas and anecdotes that seem apt in the Roman context he fit within the established manuscript culture of late Republican Rome.[32] However the profound philosophical and political elements of Cicero's method shaped and transformed Greek material far beyond the crude efforts of Terence's *Medea* or much later Seneca's *Phaedra* and *Oedipus*.

Cicero never lost the connection with Greece. This explains why his innovation and transformation of Greek thought into the Roman milieu

---

[31] Cicero, *De Oratore*, 2 vols., trans. E.W. Sutton (Cambridge: Harvard University Press, 1942).
[32] David Burchell, "MacIntyre, Cicero and Moral Personality," *History of Political Thought* 19 (1998): 105.

is often mistakenly equated with the leaden efforts of Seneca and Terence. Indeed Cicero, at least partially, intends such a misconstrual. However, a close reading of Cicero's dialogues in particular shows a profound awareness of the meaning and import of action and setting in Plato, a significance Cicero as the preeminent Latin stylist does not hesitate to employ in his own writing. Indeed, it is in using things Greek within a Roman setting and dramatic action that Cicero both follows Plato and sets off his own thought from Plato's. A close look at the setting of *De Oratore* illustrates Cicero's technique nicely.

> Then Cotta went on to say how on the morrow, when those older men had rested sufficiently and everyone had come into the garden-walk, Scaevola, after taking two or three turns, observed, "Crassus, why do we not imitate Socrates as he appears in the *Phaedrus* of Plato? For your plane-tree has suggested to my mind, casting as it does, with its spreading branches, as deep a shade over this spot as that one cast whose shelter Socrates sought-which to me seems to owe its eminence less to 'the little rivulet' described by Plato than to the language of his dialogue-and what Socrates did, whose feet were thoroughly hardened, when he threw himself down on the grass and so began the talk which philosophers say was divine, -such ease surely may more reasonably be conceded to my own feet" "Nay," answered Crassus, "but we will make things more comfortable still," whereupon, according to Cotta, he called for cushions, and they all sat down together on the benches that were under the plane-tree. (*De Oratore* I.vii.28–29)

On the surface the invocation of the *Phaedrus* here makes obvious sense. In Plato's dialogue the subject, ostensibly at least, is writing and by extension speechmaking and as such the comparison seems apt. A closer look reveals within the context much deeper differences, differences that highlight the profound philosophical distance between Rome and Athens. The *dramatis personae* are the first and most powerful hint. Cicero begins the third and final book of *De Oratore* by recounting how Crassus' interlocutors M. Antonius, Q. Lutatius Catulus, and C. Julius Caesar Stabo Vopiscus all fall victim to Marius. On the other side of the conflict between Mariusand Sulla, P. Sulpicius Rufus, a Marian, is proscribed and then murdered by Sulla's forces. To any Roman reader acquainted with the Platonic corpus the list of victims of the collapsing politics of the late Republic draws attention not to *Phaedrus* but *Republic*, not to the styles of rhetoric but the state of politics. Each dialogue is peopled with the victims of leaders who seize the opportunities for tyranny peculiar to declining republics. With this collection of *dramatis personae* Cicero's indicates that his ideal orator[33] is someone acquainted not only with rhythm and eloquence but with wisdom, politics, and a sense of consequence.

This sense of consequence is also implicit in the contrast between the settings of *Phaedrus* and *De Oratore*. In the *Phaedrus* the interlocutors seek shade outside the city walls, in *De Oratore* we find them outside the walls of Rome but hardly in bucolic repose. As Cicero's party approaches the plane tree we discover that it already has benches underneath it. People have been to this spot before. They have come often, they have made it comfortable, they have civilized it. The significance of the benches, accentuated by the ease with which Crassus orders cushions to be provided, suggests the impossibility of ever truly being outside the walls of Rome. Rome's boundaries have encompassed the whole world. Crassus' order that cushions be brought for the group to sit upon reminds the reader that not only has the empire engulfed the known world but furthermore that the empire is characterized by luxury. From its opening *De Oratore* reminds us of the Ciceronian teaching on civic education that appears throughout his political writing, the wisdom of the Greeks must always be read, discussed, and understood in the new Roman context.

Attached to this insight about how the Greeks should be read Cicero includes a critique of Greek philosophy and in particular of Platonic political philosophy and its various descendants. Some of these descendants, Cicero argues, have neglected the critical connection between philosophy and politics, between the philosopher and the orator. In Cicero's assessment this neglect of politics is not only politically deleterious it constitutes a fundamental breaking of faith with philosophy's

---

[33] I use the term orator here interchangeably with politician and in its ideal case statesman. For Cicero the distinction between the three is of less significance than the distinction between orator and rhetorician.

origins in questions of the good life within the city.[34] Cicero returns again and again to the decline in political philosophy, beginning with the Academy, which he believes allowed it to slip into empty dogmatism and the ivory tower study of subjects utterly without value to the functioning of the city.

The charge that philosophy abandoned political engagement equals in its gravity the consequent charge that philosophy can no longer defend itself against the unphilosophic city. It is no small irony that in so accusing philosophy Cicero clearly echoes the accusation of Callicles in the *Gorgias*.[35] However a critical difference between the two claims again illustrates the unique character of Cicero's attempts to transform Greek philosophy into a complement to Roman teaching. According to Cicero, the failure of the true philosopher to defend himself constitutes not a personal or philosophical but a profound political failure. In a very real sense Cicero's indictment is much graver than Callicles' ad hominem impugning of a Socrates "unable to help himself or save himself from the gravest dangers."[36] To Cicero the failure to render unto Rome the wisdom it requires amounts to a form of passive injustice: the failure to provide the city with protection from the gravest dangers.[37] A philosopher unable to prevent his execution or exile because of willful neglect of political virtues and most especially oratory neglects his civic duty and denies the services of philosophy to his city.

Cicero's limited indictment of Socrates and of Greek philosophy can be expressed roughly but adequately in the simple assertion that things that belonged together, wisdom and eloquence, the two essentials for wise rule, had been unwisely separated by Socrates and his intellectual descendents (*De Oratore* III.xvi.60). Raymond DiLorenzo captures Cicero's charge nicely writing

---

[34] Barlow, "The Education of Statemen in *De Republica*," *Polity* (1987): 358.
[35] *Gorgias* 484c–e, trans. W.C. Helmbold (Indianapolis: Library of the Liberal Arts, 1952).
[36] *Gorgias* 486b.
[37] Martha Nussbaum, "Duties of Justice, Duties of Material Aid: Cicero's Problematical Legacy," *Journal of Political Philosophy* 8 (2000): 194–196.

> Unlike many Greeks before him, he [Socrates] thereby severed the heart (*cor*) from the tongue (*lingua*), the life of political service from the pursuit of knowledge, the teachers of speech from those of thought.[38]

Fundamentally, Cicero's civic education project entails the reconnection of philosophy to oratory, of tongue to heart, of the pursuit of knowledge to civic duty.

Cicero's project of reconnection involves more than a reappraisal of the Platonic separation of eloquence from wisdom, a separation that he was interested in from his earliest writing and acknowledged even then was more complex than a simple repudiation of eloquence.[39] It also entails a fundamental reordering of the relationship between the political and the philosophic. Such a reordering comprises the second theme informing all of Cicero's most important writing in political philosophy. Indeed, in both *De Officiis* and *De Re Publica* the idea that philosophy must serve the city appears not only as explicit principle but in the very modes of expression and form that Cicero's inquiries take. Writing in his own voice at the beginning of *De Re Publica* Cicero argues

> Furthermore, virtue is not some kind of knowledge to be possessed without using it: even if the intellectual possession of knowledge can be maintained without use, virtue consists entirely in its employment, moreover, its most important employment is the governance of states and the accomplishment in deeds rather than words or the things that philosophers talk about in their corners. (*De Re Publica* I.2)[40]

The reference to philosophers "in their corners" makes two things clear. Cicero is fully aware of the public/private division in Greek philosophy and he is fully cognizant of the ambivalence between the good of the philosopher and the good of the city in Greek political philosophy. In

---

[38] Raymond DiLorenzo "The Critique of Socrates in Cicero's *De Oratore: Ornatus* and the Nature of Wisdom," *Philosophy and Rhetoric* 11 (1978): 248.

[39] See Book 1 of *De Inventione*, undeniably part of Cicero's juvenalia and a work about which Cicero's feelings in later life were highly mixed, it clearly indicates an interest from his youth onward in the relation of oratory to philosophy.

[40] The second element of this passage that bears noting is the synthesis it represents not merely between Rome and Athens but between Platonic and Aristotelian accounts of virtue.

the Roman milieu Cicero condemns this ambiguity not as innately false but as luxurious, something the declining Republic can ill-afford.

> Consequently let us dismiss the master in questions, without any derogatory comment, as they are excellent fellows and happy in their belief in their own happiness, and only let us warn them to keep to themselves as a holy secret, though it may be extremely true, their doctrine that it is not the business of a wise man to take part in politics-for if they convince us and all our best men of the truth of this they themselves will not be able to live the life of leisure which is their ideal. (*De Oratore* I.xvii.64)[41]

Cicero rejects the philosophical ambiguity concerning the relationship between philosophic wisdom and politics. In referring to philosophy's "holy secret" he suggests that the esoteric moment has passed or at least that its return may yet still be prevented. This explains his otherwise curious insistence on dismissal without derogation. The tensions within and the challenges without simply preclude the kind of philosophic practice Cicero sees embodied in Platonic and Neo-Platonic philosophy. Such philosophers must either serve the city or at least stay out of the way.

While pragmatic political concerns, often of an immediate and pressing nature, are indubitably a substantial component of Cicero's political writing it would be a mistake to suggest that his rejection of the supremacy of philosophy over politics is purely pragmatic and/or contingent on the peculiar demands of Roman society. At the very heart of the critique is a deeply held conviction that in fact it is right and proper that politics and philosophy be reordered to give politics the place of primacy and render philosophy its handmaiden. For Cicero duty supersedes inquiry.[42] This principle emerges not only in terms of the modes of speech (public/private) in which philosophers speak but also

---

[41] Of course, this phrase contains a typically Platonic ambiguity inasmuch as it seems to say that the philosophical wise men may stay "in their corners" as long as they do not recruit anymore "wise men" to their cause, that if they remain silent while their way of life is passively unjust (see *De Officiis* I.71) it may be acceptable. Cicero hints at the same ambiguity in the concluding pages of his epistle to Brutus *Orator*, when he refers to a kind of wise speechlessness (*plerumque prudentes*). *Orator* 236.

[42] Walter Nicgorski, "Cicero's Focus: From the Best Regime to the Model Statesman," *Political Theory* 19 (1991): 233.

the subjects to which they turn their attention. Duty not only supersedes inquiry it delineates the boundaries of that inquired into. Duty demands that inquiry concern itself with questions of human nature and political life, consequently Cicero finds real and significant fault in "some men [who] bestow excessive devotion and effort upon matters that are both abstruse and difficult, and unnecessary" (*De Officiis* I.19). Here Cicero reconsiders the relationship of the political to the philosophic, first adumbrated in Plato's *Laws* and *Republic* in complementary if not truly reciprocal terms. Cicero assigns the political not only sole power to bound the philosophic but furthermore to rule over it within those bounds.

In reversing the order of the political and the philosophical Cicero makes a claim similar to the characterization of philosophy he first offered in introducing Greek thought into the Roman context. The supersession of philosophical inquiry by civic duty, Cicero contends, comprises the true and original intention of the pre-Socratic Attic thinkers. In a somewhat convoluted argument, Cicero connects the confusion of order between philosophy and politics to both Rome and Athens.

> But just as the old pontiffs owing to the vast number of sacrifices decided to have a Banquet Committee of three members, though they had themselves been appointed by Numa for the purpose among others of holding the great Sacrificial Banquet of the Games, so the followers of Socrates cut connexion with the practicing lawyers and detached these from the common title of philosophy, although the old masters had intended there to be a marvelous and close alliance between oratory and philosophy. (*De Oratore* III.xix.73)

Close attention to Cicero's curious institutional history here reveals two important elements. First, in a revolutionary elision and argument made famous in both 1688 and 1776, Cicero declares himself engaged in a restorative act. He seeks a return to the original intent of both philosophers and statesmen, the founding order of things. Cicero presents himself, to speak anachronistically, as a Roman whig.

The subtlety and rich substance of Cicero's position is further suggested by the equation of pontiff with philosopher, political office with the practice of law. Pontiff and philosopher share a parallel path away from origins and founding intentions. By appointing a committee to oversee official Roman banquets Numa's "old pontiffs" lost their original purpose, retaining an office but no longer an authority. In retreating to philosophical corners (*De Re 1.2*) philosophers had done the same. Philosophers and Pontiffs both surrendered responsibility while retaining title. The old pontiffs by delegating their authority to the Banquet Committee of three took an authority which once resided in their person, and placed it outside, lessening themselves and becoming dependent. In the same way, the separation of lawyers from philosophy left them without the source of their original authority and made them dependent on others. This is a recurring theme of Cicero's critique, the philosopher, unarmed with political savvy is unable to defend himself, the orator without philosophical learning is unable to ground his positions, to speak not only eloquently but also prudently.[43] The citizen educated in the law, its source in human nature and philosophic investigation thereof (*De Legibus* I.17), is the only truly politically competent and independent citizen.

The strong contention that virtue is inextricably connected with action represents the final important element of the Ciceronian equation of the origins and early history of philosophy with the ancient Roman pontificate. The pontificate in turning over their responsibilities had reduced their capacity to act virtuously. In similar fashion, the disconnect between philosophy and oratory Cicero attributes to Socrates removed a way of being virtuous from possibility for the philosopher. According to Cicero virtues, and especially virtues of the mind such as prudence, temperance, courage, and justice, are fundamentally characterized by volition (*De Finibus* V.xiii.36). Dependent on volition these virtues succumb to an intellectually voluntarist principle. To the extent that the philosopher is unschooled in the political he cannot exercise

---

[43] G.M.A. Grube, *The Greek and Roman Critics* (Toronto: University of Toronto Press, 1965), 170.

these virtues or even will their exercise in their most important incarnations. As such, the philosopher disconnected from the political stands morally diminished in much the same way the old pontiffs, no longer able to perform their duties, stand politically diminished. The orator, in the political realm, unschooled in the virtues of the philosopher stands equally diminished. Both the unphilosophic orator and the apolitical philosopher reject their full potential and, in their ignorance of the connection and order of things political and philosophic, reduce their ability to contribute to the virtue of the city.

In the opening dramatic action of *De Re Publica* we see on the philosophical side how Cicero conceives of such a reconnection between philosophy and politics and of the necessity to turn those engaged in non-civic studies in philosophy away from their holy secrets and into profane public life. The dialogue commences with Tubero, a young Roman citizen asking Scipio if he has witnessed the solar phenomena of the "two suns"[44] (*De Re Publica* I.15). That the great general would be questioned not about military affairs, his African campaign or Roman politics is curious to say the least. Indeed, more than curious young Tubero's chosen path of inquiry reveals that his education, while clearly significant in the area of natural philosophy remains profoundly wanting in the appropriate intellectual and civic virtues. His schooling left him either in ignorance or in apathy towards the affairs of the city. His inquiry and therefore in all likelihood his conduct remains uninformed by duty. Tubero's question reminds us, this time with more gravity than levity, of the Aristophanic representation of Socrates and his students in *The Clouds*. He is unable to discern the appropriate place and priority of intellectual and astronomical inquiry.

Tubero asks his question "before the others arrive" (ibid.) eventually Philus and then later Laelius arrive. Laelius is the oldest among the interlocutors, Scipio's friend and counsel, and the representative of the city.[45] Upon hearing the question Laelius demands "Are we so well informed about the things that concern our homes and the commonwealth that

---

[44] A sun dog or parhelion.
[45] Barlow, "The Education of Statesmen," 363.

we are asking questions about what is going on in the sky?" (*De Re Publica* I.19) Laelius' phrasing makes the admonishing tone of his question unmistakable. Laelius' rebuke marks the beginning of the serious discussion of *De Re Publica* and from the perspective of civic education it captures the tone and temper of Cicero's project concerning philosophy's place.

The Decline of Roman Education

The introduction and transformation of Greek political thought comprises the necessary starting point for understanding the Ciceronian vision of civic education is. The second and equally important component of Cicero's project consists in the application of the substance of his new teaching to the structure of Roman education. In the application Cicero's argument is ever informed by the undeniable decline in the quality of Roman education and the obvious and dire consequences for the Republic such a decline heralded. It is very much amidst these consequences, both personal and political, that Cicero writes. Perhaps the most obvious of these, the ostensible purpose of his writing *De Officiis*, is the education of his son Marcus. Marcus, along with his nephew Quintus, had been the special students and even the educational project of Cicero since they were young boys.[46] Cicero had initially taken on the education of the boys as a result of his dissatisfaction with the quality of Roman schooling. However, as the boys grew older their education inevitably involved professional teachers. Away from Cicero's tutelage first Quintus and then (albeit to a lesser extent) young Marcus turned against Cicero and towards Caesar. In the case of Quintus the turn was so complete as to lead him to side with Caeser against Pompey and possibly even to conspire against his uncle.[47] For Cicero the corruption of his son and nephew painfully illustrated the moral and civic decline in both the Roman *iuvenes*' character and in the quality of their education. In both his thought and his parenting of young Marcus Cicero identified the

---

[46] Gwynn, *Roman Education*, 80.
[47] Fuhrmann, *Cicero and the Roman Republic*, 156.

latter as the source of the former. For a son to ponder turning against his father was outrage enough to the *mos maiorum*[48] but to turn against Cicero in particular, who had done so much to protect and preserve the Republic added immeasurably to the father's fears concerning the decline of Roman schooling.

According to Cicero the decline in the appreciation of the *iuvenes* for the *mos maiorum*, as a result of their education, was of such grave political consequence because the old customs were the foundation on which Rome had been built. Cicero begins Book V of *De Re Publica* by quoting Ennius "The Roman state stands upon the morals and men of old" (*De Re Publica* V.1). To the extent that the teachers of Quintus and Marcus, of the Roman *iuvenes* in general, failed to pass on the lessons and narratives of the past Cicero believed they were undermining the very foundation of republican government. Cicero concluded that this has already come to pass, the institutional structures remained but the morals and the history which filled and supported them had bled away leaving only the empty husk of the old Republic.

> What remains of the morals of antiquity, upon which Ennius said that the Roman state stood? We see that they are so outworn in oblivion that they are not only not cherished but are now unknown. What am I to say about the men? The morals themselves have passed away through a shortage of men; and we must defend ourselves like people being tried for a capital crime. It is because of our own vices, not because of some bad luck, that we preserve the commonwealth in name alone but have long ago lost its substance. (*De Re Publica* V.2)

Cicero laments the passing of the morals of antiquity at the same time as he hints at the means of their recovery. The connection drawn between men and morals in this passage closely resembles the relationship between virtue and action that first appeared in Cicero's criticism of philosophy. The decline of Roman morals derives from the failure of those morals to be lived by men, they passed away not because they were fatally flawed themselves but because they were inadequately lived. They perished of a "shortage of men." As a result, what was most needed was

---

[48] Rawson, *Cicero*, 251.

a new civic education. Roman restoration depended on the education of men back into the ways of life that nourished and sustained Republican government.

In light of Cicero's comments about the sources of Rome's decline his proposal is all the more audacious. Cicero simultaneously advocated a return to the *mos maiorum* and introduced Greek innovation. He was a conservative innovator, an utterly novel traditionalist. Writing into new life representations of Cato the Elder, Crassus and Scipio alongside his first person and epistolary prose, Cicero aimed at refilling the frame of the Republic. He meant for his writing to be read and experienced by students not as a new teaching but rather as a new memorial or history. Cicero aimed at repopulating the cultural horizon and reinventing the political landscape with new memorials, new triumphs, new testaments to the *mos maiorum*.

> I myself, whatever assistance I have given the republic, if I have indeed given any, came to public life trained and equipped by my teachers and their teachings. Not only when they are alive and present do such men educate and instruct their assiduous students; they continue the same task after death by means of their writings, which they leave as memorials. (*De Officiis* I.155–156)

Cicero's writings, at their most public level, by portraying in conversation Scipio, Crassus, Scaevola, and even Cicero himself seek to rectify the shortage of great men needed to teach the young. Through Cicero's efforts his readers hear again the voice of Scipio in the Forum. In his dialogues Cicero revives a community of men for the *iuvenes* to look to and from whom to draw the knowledge of duty and virtue.

The apparent novelty and peculiarity of Cicero's endeavor makes more sense once it is placed within the context of Roman education in the late Republic. In the early and middle periods of Roman antiquity most education, if not quite all, was acquired in the home, for sons it meant that their education was primarily a duty, a deeply respected and serious duty, of the *paterfamilias*.[49] However, by the time of Cicero's

---

[49] Marrou, *Education in Antquity*, 232.

own education teaching had moved almost entirely out of the home. The early stages of education, performed at the primary level by the *ludi magister* and at the secondary in reading and writing by the *grammaticus* were considered basic and relatively noncontroversial elements in a boy's upbringing. Indeed, the primary and secondary school teachers were held to perform a task so rudimentary that they earned little and were held in general contempt, regretfully a circumstance little changed by the ensuing millenia. The civic education of a young Roman man began simultaneously with his initiation into adulthood, the removal of his juvenile *toga praetexta* and its replacement with the *toga virilis* of manhood. This was followed by his formal presentation into the forum where he was to receive his formal training in law and public life, the *tirocinium fori*.[50] It was at this stage of learning that Cicero believed the rot had truly set in.

Education in the Forum constituted the crucible that cast all the great political leaders of the past. Reflecting on his own schooling in the Roman Forum Cicero recalled that

> In fact public life was my education, and practical experience of the laws and institutions of the state and the custom of the country was my schoolmaster. (*De Oratore* III.xx.74–75)[51]

Cicero looked upon the Forum of his adulthood and saw a much narrower and socially destructive form of education that had displaced the rounded education he had received from Crassus and Scaevola. In place of their broad learning the *tirocinium fori* increasingly consisted of showmanship and displays of clever language and flourish.[52] The teachers of the past who had been educators but also lawyers and orators in their own right had been replaced by teachers trained solely in elegant and persuasive speech. Such teachers, utterly unschooled in the moral and

---

[50] Marrou, *Education in Antiquity*, 236.
[51] Of course Cicero typically overstates the case, compare his remarks in *Orator* 12 "I confess that whatever ability I possess as an orator comes, not from the workshops of the rhetoricians, but from the spacious grounds of the Academy."
[52] Stanley F. Bonner, *Education in Ancient Rome* (London: Metheun & Co, 1977), 332.

political traditions of Rome, offered only the simulacra of a true education in oratory and therefore also only an imitation of an education in civic virtue. Of them Cicero lamented

> My reason for dwelling on these points is because the whole of this department has been abandoned by the orators, who are the players that act real life, and has been taken over by the actors who only mimic reality. (*De Oratore* III.lvi.241)

Cicero easily identified the immediate and deleterious consequences of a theatrical education increasingly at odds with the imperatives of the political. A narrow rhetorical training transformed the already deeply agonistic character of politics and law. What becomes explicitly valued is no longer the search for the best answer to a given problem or the correct verdict in a given proceeding but simple victory or even more narrowly domination, even if that success runs against the interest of the Republic. The fault attributed to the departure of true orators is the mirror image of the critique of philosophy represented in Tubero's odd inquiry of Scipio in *De Re Publica*. Tubero pursued philosophy for philosophy's sake; the actors who "mimic reality" pursue political success equally for its own sake. Each error expresses a break with the civic imperative that ideally undergirds both intellectual enterprises.

Recalling that Cicero, employing the criteria of duty, placed politics above philosophy we can see in his distress at the decline of the teaching of rhetoric echoes of both Socrates' critique of Gorgias' reckless rhetorical teaching (*Gorgias* 459b–461b) and the more serious charge against the irresponsible teaching of dialectic in the *Republic* (*Republic* 539a–b). Cicero cautions that like Plato's imprudent young dialecticians, ambitious young men armed with rhetoric absent proper schooling will likewise tear "with argument at those who happen to be near" (ibid.). In a manifestly Platonic tenor Cicero cautions

> If we bestow fluency of speech on persons devoid of those virtues, we shall not have made orators of them but shall have put weapons into the hands of madmen. (*De Oratore* III.xiv.55)

Cicero further warns that the mimetic and performative structure of Roman education endows these weapons with a particularly dangerous capacity for self-replication. The education in public life in the Forum involved learning and practicing oratory in front of crowds of other young men. Here in institutionalized form, Cicero finds a situation catastrophically close to that warned of by Plato (*Republic 491e–492b*) except now rather than being excoriated it has become praised and assessed as a crucial element of Roman civic education. Cicero himself admits in *Brutus* "the orator who inflames the court accomplishes far more than the one who merely instructs it" (*Brutus* 89).[53] This volatile mix could only deteriorate, and deteriorate dangerously, with the increased specialization and showmanship, at the expense of a broader civic education, of the teachers and practitioners of rhetoric.

Cicero condemns the teachers of rhetoric not only for the reckless and mercenary way in which they teach but also for the nontechnical "social curriculum" they offer. In place of an education in civic virtue, the *mos maiorum*, and the *artes liberales* Cicero accuses the Roman rhetoricians of teaching a politically and morally corrosive love of luxury and valorization of greed. In Cicero's estimation, as Rome moved from the austere rigors of war to a pacific imperial luxury, Roman virtue succumbed to its own success.[54] Granting this Cicero disagrees with those who believed that Rome's virtues were predicated on constant military readiness.[55] Instead, Cicero contends that it is the conjunction of luxury with the legitimation of greed that corrodes civil society in times of war *or* peace. Describing the situation Cicero quotes Themistocles.

> 'I myself', he replied, 'prefer a man that lacks money to money that lacks a man.' And yet, conduct has been corrupted and depraved by admiration for riches. What does someone else's great wealth concern any one of us? It may perhaps help him who has it. It does not always even do that; but grant that it does. He may, it is true, be better provided; but how will he be more honorable? (*De Officiis* II.71)

---

[53] Cicero, *Brutus*, 89 quoted in Bonner, *Education in Ancient Rome*, 85.
[54] T.N. Mitchell, "Cicero on the Moral Crisis of the late Republic," *Hermathena* 136 (1984): 27.
[55] Mitchell, "Cicero on the Moral Crisis," 26.

Cicero captures the key consequence of the new imperial prosperity in the opening statement of preference, manhood is always preferable to money. More precisely Cicero wonders, in the increasingly commercial context of Imperial Rome how long manhood can coexist with money. Again, the cause for Cicero's alarm lies in the structure of Roman schooling. That educational structure's essential mimetic component inevitably magnified the consequences of the decline Cicero countenances. Much of a student's learning consisted of the public and performative emulation of his mentor and of admirable others within the Forum. As a result, not simply the lives but the lifestyles of the preeminent within the Forum comprised a critical component of the social curriculum. As a result, the teachers of rhetoric ran behind the ever-emerging patterns of social stratification, they taught how to praise and imitate that which had already become praiseworthy in the eyes of the Roman citizenry. Cicero both fears and acknowledges that students increasingly seek to emulate not the virtue and honor of the wise and the just but the ostentation and opulence of the wealthy. Again, Cicero offers in *De Officiis* a critique of Roman civic education that matches the critique of philosophic education young Tubero represents. Tubero fails to honor the city and perform his duty because his gaze has been turned inappropriately skyward by philosophy, students of the decadent *tirocinium fori* suffered the opposite vice: they could no longer lift their gaze from the base and earthly pleasures. The emulation of wealth and luxury, like the pursuit of abstruse philosophy, precludes the emulation of true Roman custom and duty.

The Status of the Student

The single most significant difference between Cicero and Plato concerns the status of the student. In stark contrast to Plato Cicero posits what, on the surface at least, appears to be a fundamentally and even radically egalitarian account of the person.

> If distorted habits and false opinions did not twist weak minds and bend them in any direction no one would be so like himself as all people would be like all others. Thus, whatever definition of a human being one adopts is equally valid for all human beings. (*De Legibus* I.30)[56]

The equality Cicero is positing in this passage is peculiar for several reasons. First and most obvious to the modern reader is the language and imagery of what Christianity would describe as "fallenness." This partially explains the importance of Cicero to the early Latin Church and in particular St. Augustine. However, reading Cicero's education proposals it is important to recognize that he offers only a definitional and original equality. According to Cicero individuals are originally equal in some respects but important aspects of that equality do not endure as we grow and mature. Equally significant, Cicero repeatedly describes the qualities and faculties that human beings possess but he does not commit to these qualities and faculties being identical in proportion and expression across humanity. For Cicero man has most in common with man but that does not entail that the relevant common characteristics are shared equally among all men.[57]

Cicero offers an account of the human being that encompasses both commonality and difference while eschewing simple natural equality. Human beings share a common core of innate abilities and even innate beliefs, but these characteristics and beliefs are possessed and realized to differing degrees across the species. First and foremost, among these characteristics is a capacity for reason, a capacity that all human beings participate in. More importantly humans participate in them to an extent that is both morally and politically relevant. Again, returning to *De Legibus* Cicero writes

> All the same things are grasped by the senses; and the things that are impressed upon the mind, the rudiments of understanding which I mentioned before, are impressed similarly on all humans, and language,

---

[56] We will see this assertion echoed again in strikingly similar terms in both Rousseau and Smith whose debt to Cicero's educational thought is substantial and conspicuous in their own.
[57] Leo Strauss, *Natural Right and History* (Chicago: University of Chicago Press, 1953), 135.

the interpreter of the mind, may differ in words but is identical in ideas. There is no person of any nation who cannot reach virtue with the aid of a guide. (*De Legibus* I.30)

A careful reading of this passage reveals a couple of key tenets of Cicero's theory of education and his conception of the person/pupil. Critically, every person contains the rudiments of understanding. This is a recurring theme in Cicero concerning not merely intellection but also virtue. Describing Nature's gift of virtue to human's he writes "But of virtue itself she merely gave the germ and no more" (*De Finibus* V.xxi.60). The metaphor of rudiment and seed fundamentally informs and transforms the task of the civic educator. By Cicero's account all humans possess a basic substance or essence, out of which virtue and intellect are "grown" by the educator.[58] Civic education continues to possess the element of discernment and discrimination present in Plato, but it now gains a new role as much creative as revelatory. To bruise the allegory somewhat if Socrates was a midwife Cicero is a gardener. Cicero's civic education entails recognizing the seeds of ability and then growing them into a virtuous citizen and perhaps statesman. Cicero offers an account of education that moves beyond the practice of *diaresis* and *periagoge* of Plato and into more explicitly constructive territory. The seminal and horticultural motifs point to the delicate balance between the Platonic discovering, uncovering, and orienting what is innately present and the Ciceronian account of civic pedagogy that draws out and into full being through education.

At the same time discernment and even discrimination remains central to Cicero's civic education. While he posits broad commonalities across the species, he also argues explicitly that within the species differences of ability especially as they concern politics are politically relevant.

> For just as there are enormous bodily differences (for some, as we see, their strength is the speed that they can run, for others the might with

---

[58] Maryanne C. Horowitz, "The Stoic Synthesis of Natural Law in Man: Four Themes," *Journal of the History of Ideas* 35 (1974): 14.

which they wrestle: again, some have figures that are dignified, others that are graceful) similarly there are still greater differences in men's spirits. (*De Officiis* I.107)

According to Cicero each human being possesses a dual *persona*, on one hand they are deeply similar to all other human beings; their species *persona* is the degree to which they share qualities makes them more like each other than like any other animal. Conversely, within the species there are tremendous differences, morally and politically relevant differences, these differences create the second mask the unique individual *persona* (ibid.). The educator must discern among his potential pupils the various degrees and distribution of characteristics of this second *persona*. Unlike the noble lie concerning the three metals in Plato's *Republic*[59] Cicero presents two ontological dyads: commonality and difference, equality and hierarchy. Instead of different metals that connote profound differences across the citizenry Cicero descries a citizenry possessing the same metals distinguished only by the ratio of their individual admixture. In so conceiving of the nature of human being Cicero in many ways places himself closer to the modern account of the pupil than that of his preceding Platonic account. In positing a universal capacity for justice, Cicero sounds more like Locke or even Thomas Jefferson than Plato's Socrates or the Athenian Stranger.

Statesmen and Teachers

As Rome expanded the task of the Roman educator became ever more distant from that described by Plato in either *Republic* or *Laws*. The civic educator increasingly diverted his focus from those great in spirit, the statesman, and more and more toward the continually swelling ranks of those who were destined to be ruled. This concern, more than the degree of human difference or the nature of equality, defined the difference between Cicero and Plato. Cicero's educational goal in the face of

---

[59] *Republic* 415a–d. What this comparison admittedly overlooks is the different context and propositional status of Cicero's ontological claims compared to the place and status of the Noble Lie in *Republic*.

the collapsing Republic was to manage and transform a populace that is hostile not only to philosophy but to politics. As such Cicero sought to educate for citizenship not subjection, he aimed at a populace fit to be ruled as opposed to tyrannized.[60]

Cicero acknowledges as much when his Scipio stands in favor of a mixed polity in the *De Re Publica*. The contrast between the republicanism of Africanus and the ambitions of Caesar could not be more starkly drawn. Scipio does not advocate a simple or crude equality, rather he suggests that republican virtue resides in the citizen's choosing to entrust themselves to the best men.

> But if a free people chooses the men to whom to entrust itself (and it will choose the best people if it wants to be safe), then surely the safety of the citizens is found in the deliberations of the best men. That is particularly true because nature has made sure not only that men outstanding for virtue and courage rule over weaker people, but that the weaker people willingly obey the best. (*De Re Publica* I.51)

Scipio further contends that republics succeed or fail not on the judgments of the best men, for surely the judgments of best men must almost invariably be correct, but on the judgment of the populations who choose to entrust themselves to the great. Scipio implies that Republican government is inextricably predicated on the civic education of the ordinary citizen. If the popular character of the citizenry renders it incapable of discerning the best, then the best will be unable to rule on their behalf. This fundamental Republican dilemma brings to mind the plight of the true doctor in the *Gorgias* and the stargazer in the *Republic*. However important differences, rooted in the status of the student/citizen, permit Cicero a degree of optimism absent in Plato. This optimism finds its source in Cicero's contention that all citizens possess the rudiments of reason, an *inchoata intelligentia*.[61] Cicero seems genuinely convinced

---

[60] As a result to some extent Cicero's specifically political education is closer to Aristotle than to Plato, see *Politics 1259*.
[61] Horowitz, "The Stoic Synthesis," 7.

that the citizenry can be taught a basic civic virtue which permits discernment of the best men and the entrusting of same with rule (*De Re Publica* V.8).

Cicero claims that he has learned all he knows from great men. Ciceronian civic paideia essentially offers the same advice. When the Republic thrived, when the frame was filled with a robust sense of Rome's history and a profound attachment to the *mos maiorum* emulation meant living and honoring the Roman virtues and in the case of the patriciate the particular virtues embodied in previous illustrious generations. Roman education, predicated on embodiment and emulation, sees in the absence of a Scipio or Crassus a lack of not only a leader but the politically salutary example crucial to education.

In Cicero's civic paideia the statesman is the captivating and illuminating example that draws the people upwards towards virtue. This process is realized through the statesman's multivariate employment of the Ciceronian dual *personae* in the realm of the public and political. In political oratory "the very cardinal sin is to depart from the language of everyday life, and the usage approved by the sense of the community" (*De Oratore* I.iii.8). Speaking in ordinary language allows a statesman to communicate what he shares with the citizenry and convey their shares in virtues that he more perfectly embodies.[62] By acting and speaking in a manner that conveys both commonality and superiority the statesman embodies the Ciceronian dual *personae* and in so embodying encourages emulation among the citizens similar to that first practiced when they don the *toga virilis* in the Forum. Hearkening back to the account of the two physicians in Plato's *Laws* (*Laws* 720d–e) Cicero further allows not merely for emulation but participation. In the common space of both words and nature between statesman and citizen the civic diagnosis discerned by the statesman's superior insight is transmitted to and comprehended by the citizen as true opinion.

Cicero places justice at the center of the nascent virtues that citizens are born with. In his own *Laws* Cicero unequivocally declares that all humans are by nature "made to receive the knowledge of justice" (*De Legibus* I.33). For the ordinary citizen that reception of justice emerges

---

[62] Gary Remer, "Political Oratory and Conversation," *Political Theory* 27(1999): 54.

3 Cicero's Civic Education at the Dawn of Empire

out of reflection on the character and conduct of the statesman that populate his polity's past and present.

> If you view the course of past history, you can see that the state has been of the same character as its greatest men; and whatever moral alteration takes place in the leaders soon follows among the people. That is quite a lot closer to the truth than Plato's opinion. He says that when musicians change their tunes the condition of states also changes; but I think that the character of states changes when there are changes in the life and habits of the nobles. (*De Legibus* III.31–32)

The significance of the leader to the character of the state and citizenry in Cicero cannot be overstated. Cicero presents much more than the prosaic assertion that wicked behavior invariably harms the state and just behavior usually benefits it. According to Cicero there is a politically salutary and even divine character to the life and actions of the just ruler. The character of these actions, resulting from both greatness of spirit and a full education attains to nothing less than "the development of an incredible, divine, virtue" (*De Re Publica* III.5). For the ordinary citizen, the development and public expression of this divine virtue in the statesman nourishes and illuminates their own (admittedly lesser) participation in that virtue. According to Cicero virtue spreads into the rich seed bed of a healthy republic. It moves downward from its original stately source, nourishing within all citizens an innate and "divine spark of genius and of mental capacity" (*De Re Publica* III.1) which duty demands they exercise in the interest of the city.[63]

On the highest level this illuminative characteristic is the crucial pedagogic element in the encounter between the two Scipios. Throughout his nocturnal encounter with his illustrious grandfather the younger Africanus continually turns his face to the earth, to the quotidian concerns of his daily existence, and repeatedly Scipio who stands above it all chides him "I wonder how long will your mind will be fixed on the ground?"(*De Re Publica* VI.17) The older Scipio, in his personage as

---

[63] Ferrary, "The Statesman and the Law," 65.

much as his sublunar location, draws the younger Africanus to the divine in himself, draws him upward.

> Therefore look on high if you wish; contemplate this dwelling and eternal home; and do not give yourself to the words of the mob, and do not place your hope in human rewards: virtue itself by its own allurements should draw you towards true honor. (*De Re Publica* VI.25)

Contemplating the divine in his ancestor draws the younger Scipio upward and away from the base. At first the apparition dazzles and confounds the younger Sciopio. He is dumbfounded and even frightened. Eventually his gaze steadies upwards in contemplation of his divine ancestor. As he steadies the conversation turns to virtue, embodied in Scipio virtue itself draws the younger Africanus upwards. In Scipio this upwards is not towards the heavens, not yet at least (*De Re Publica* VI.26), but towards recognition of his divine spark. In the city the just ruler stands in the same position as the elder Scipio. Virtue, shining brightly in the statesman, is dimly shared however by the general citizenry like a common moral cognomen, it draws them towards duty and civic virtue.

A Shortage of Men

On the surface Cicero's understanding of the education of the ordinary citizen appears relatively undemanding.[64] For the individual and ordinary citizens this may be a fair account of Cicero's position. However, returning attention to Cicero's initial diagnosis of the cause of the decline of civic virtue in Rome, "the shortage of men," reveals necessary conditions for civic education that are actually quite demanding. Cicero's contention that the civic virtue of the wider citizenry is dependent on men of stature whose conduct, comportment, and character they seek

---

[64] For an interpretation that sees citizen education as almost *completely* undemanding see Cary J. Nederman, "War, Peace and Republican Virtue: Patriotism and the Neglected Legacy of Cicero," in *Instilling Ethics*, ed. Norma Thompson (Lanham, MA: Rowman and Littlefield, 2000).

to emulate necessarily implies that the state that lacks them will lack civic virtue. The generation of such men explains the peculiar exhortative character of Cicero's epistolary prose, a character most apparent in his letters to the younger M. Cicero but also present in his letters to Brutus. *De Officiis* in particular reads like an instruction manual for *both* civic virtue and political success. Indeed, more than fifteen centuries after his murder Cicero's *De Officiis* was one of the most influential political text of Renaissance humanism, regarded as essential reading for leaders and more important perhaps, the ambitious who aspired to leadership. Its influence and import were further evidenced in 1465 when it became the first philosophic text of classical antiquity to be introduced to the printing press.[65] More philosophically significant Machiavelli's *The Prince*,[66] while corrupting its message of duty and honor almost absolutely, unmistakably parodies the structure and style of *De Officiis*.[67]

De Officiis like *The Prince* takes for granted the presence of young and ambitious men,[68] it begins with the assumption that the young Marcus and Quintus and their confreres are drawn to politics and assumes as the most urgent task drawing them to Republican politics and virtue and away from the thrall of Caesar and later Antony. Cicero's writing aims at more than the simple vitiation of the reckless appeal of Caesarism, it aims at bringing up men who stand equal to Caesar in political stature and tower above him in virtue.

Cicero introduces the *artes liberales*,[69] history, literature, rhetoric, law, and philosophy to young Marcus and others as being essential not to the character of their soul but rather to their political ambitions. Cicero contends that the orator schooled in all these will stand above all others in the forum. The genuine and therefore successful orator must have knowledge of the "whole of the contents of the life of mankind"

---

[65] A.A. Long, "Cicero's Politics," 214.

[66] The breadth of influence *De Officiis* exercised on the late medieval and early modern development of political philosophy is demonstrated by its influence over both Machiavelli's *The Prince* and its near perfect antithesis Erasmus' *The Education of a Christian Prince*.

[67] J. Jackson Barlow, "The Fox and the Lion: Machiavelli Replies to Cicero," *History of Political Thought* 20 (1999): 629.

[68] Ibid.

[69] Gwynn, *Roman Education*, 118.

(*De Oratore* III.xvi.54–55). Most notably in the early pages of *De Oratore* Cicero maintains that learned discourse, speech accompanied by education constitutes the very source of political community.

> To come, however, at length to the highest achievements of eloquence, what other power could have been strong enough either to gather scattered humanity into one place, or to lead it out of its brutish existence in the wilderness up to our present condition of civilization as men and as citizens, or after the establishment of social communities, to give shape to laws, tribunals and civic rights? (*De Oratore* I.viii.33–34)

To argue this position alone would not leave Cicero in a position significantly different from that of the rhetoricians he castigates as putting weapons into the hands of madmen. Oratory's initial appeal to the young is rooted in ambition but the experience of an ideal oratorical education begins in the political and indeed brutish passions but concludes with the transformation of the entire person.[70] The ideal education draws civic virtue and the citizen into being in the same way that the ideal lawgiver in his eloquence creates the city itself.

Cicero employs a unique brand of political and moral cognitivism here contending that the study of the *artes liberales* and philosophy in particular is an inherently salutary and civilizing[71] enterprise. To illustrate it is useful to quote in full a passage cited briefly above. In *De Re Publica* Scipio exhorts the young and intellectually apolitical and irresponsible Tubero to study politics.

> Therefore we should consider those who have discussed the proper conduct of human life to be great men (as indeed they are); let them be considered learned men, masters of truth and virtue. But this too should be something deserving of considerable respect (as in fact it is): the study of civil society and the organization of peoples-whether it was discovered by men who had experience in the range and forms of commonwealth or

---

[70] The transformational character of the education of the Oratory is perhaps the single most striking difference between *De Officiis* and *Il Principe*. If anything, Lorenzo unreconstructed passions are given opportunity for increase.

[71] By "civilizing" is intended not banalities of comportment but the rendering of the pupil fit to live in the city, the *cives*.

was the object of study in the leisure time of philosophers-a study which brings about in good minds now, as often in the past, the development of an incredible, divine virtue. (*De Re Publica* III.4)

Cicero maintains that the study of whole societies and forms of rule involves the intellect in a revelatory experience of a virtue already present. Political philosophy is the sun towards which the nascent state of their virtue, the *elementia virtutis*,[72] grows. An education in political philosophy draws the ambitious pupil up to the vantage point shown to the younger Scipio in his dream encounter with the elder Africanus (*De Re Publica* VI.12). To behold whole societies and contemplate their rise and fall draws the student into the same philosophic orbit as the younger, dreaming Scipio. Cicero's civic education renders the student cognizant of immediate affairs but equally aware of eternity and the place of virtue and duty within the realm of permanence. In political life the student so elevated, standing in divine virtue halfway between the street and the transcendent becomes in his person an education in civic virtue for the ordinary citizen.

Cicero never intended his introduction of Greek thought into the Roman context to restore the *mos maiorum* to their original state. Cicero knew that much of Rome's rustic founding ideals had either disappeared or ceased to appeal to ambitious young men. The introduction of Greek thought, carefully transformed and rendered into Latin, was meant to appeal to young men after the type of Tubero or Cicer's own son Marcus. Cicero appealed initially to their shared enthusiasm both for novelty and things Greek hoping and believing that ultimately it would turn them towards civic virtue and duty and raise some select few to the stature of the Scipii.

Cicero's hope and his teaching for the few sought to generate a similarly salutary civic paidiea "once removed" for the ordinary Roman citizen. Cicero's educational writing served a twofold purpose that traced his dual *personae* conception of the person. For individuals distinct in their greatness of spirit Cicero's political dialogues, his new horizon of great men, sought to draw them upwards. It sought in politics to recreate

---

[72] *De Finibus* V.xxi.59 quoted Horowitz, "The Stoic Synthesis," 14.

what he depicted in the Dream of Scipio and to create in them a new class of great men, equal in stature to those who formerly peopled the Republic living and thereby sustaining its virtues. To those who shared only the common *personae*, distinguished not from one another, a whole containing spirit but not in great quantity, possessing lesser amounts of both *inchoata intelligentia* and *elementia virtutis*, the new class of Republican men of stature that Cicero's "textbooks" sought to generate would provide the sun towards which the ordinary citizen turned in imperfect emulation. In the Dream of Scipio this is the secondary civic import of the younger Africanus' location. As Scipio stands above the expanse of the Roman world (*De Re Publica* VI.21) he not only looks down, but others implicitly look up. In the Roman street men of Scipio's stature draw up the citizenry as surely as Scipio is drawn up by his distinguished grandfather. Scipio aspires to his share in the honorific *Africanus*, Cicero hopes the young Marcus and others, in following his teaching and rescuing the Republic, will encourage the citizenry to equally aspire to their share in the Republican honorific *Romanus*.

4

Locke's Education for Ordinary Life and Liberal Citizenship

Certainly the prolonged education indispensable to the progress of Society is not natural to mankind. It cuts against the grain. A boy would like to follow his father in pursuit of food or prey. He would like to be doing serviceable things so far as his utmost strength allowed. He would like to be earning wages however small to help to keep up the home. He would like to have some leisure of his own to use or misuse as he pleased. He would ask little more than the right to work or starve. And then perhaps in the evenings a real love of learning would come to those who are worthy – and why try to stuff in those who are not? – and knowledge and thought would open the 'magic casements' of the mind.

Winston Churchill, *My Early Life*[1]

---

[1] Winston Churchill, *My Early Life* (Montreal: Reprint Society of Canada, 1948), 47.

Introduction

In tracing the course of a specific incarnation of civic education from the ancients through to modernity as much must inevitably be overlooked as emphasized. In moving from the dying days of the Roman Republic to the birth of the Enlightenment much must be passed over. Most conspicuously perhaps we pass over the Renaissance restatements of ancient civic republicanism, civic virtue, and its inculcation. Admitting this, there are compelling reasons to mark John Locke's philosophy and especially his *Some Thoughts Concerning Education* as the beginnings of a truly modern theory of civic education, as nothing less than a "Lockean Revolution in Education."[2]

This revolution involved, in a number of essential respects, a fundamental break not only with the classical understanding of civic education but also that of some of Locke's near contemporaries. Among these contemporaries John Milton's brief pamphlet *Of Education* is both a prominent and a typical example of pre-Lockean conceptions of civic education. Written only fifty years before the publication of Locke's *Some Thoughts Concerning Education*[3] Milton's pamphlet embraced key elements of the classical and renaissance vision of education.[4] In particular, the requirement for formal institution and a scrupulous attention to the specifics of curriculum comprise the twin pillars of Miton's *Education*.[5] The public nature of the university constitutes most obvious influence of the classical tradition on Milton. In *Of Education*, he makes clear that civic education represents a pressing public responsibility, one possessing such essential urgency that Milton commends the construction of universities to "every city throughout the land."[6] By placing

---

[2] Lorraine Pangle and Thomas Pangle, *The Learning of Liberty* (Lawrence: University of Kansas Press, 1993), 54.

[3] John Locke, "Some Thoughts Concerning Education," in *The Educational Writings of John Locke*, ed. James Axtell (Cambridge: Cambridge University Press, 1968).

[4] Of course, Milton also breaks with the ancients and in particular Cicero and Plato in important respects which will be countenanced below and that place him closer to Erasmus' *Education of a Christian Prince* than to either ancient source herein treated.

[5] John Milton, "Of Education," in *Areopagitica and Of Education*, ed. George H. Sabine (Arlington Heights: Harlan Davidson, 1951).

[6] Milton, "Of Education," 63.

the concern for and location of civic education in the public sphere, Milton conspicuously connected himself to the ancient tradition of colocating institution and subject. Locke on the other hand, whose *Some Thoughts* shares Milton's epistolary structure, commences his discussion by explicitly *removing* civic education from the city. Locke breaks with the tradition I've been tracing back at least as far as Pericles' *Funeral Oration*. Locke's revolution in education begins by declaring that education, including education crucially connected to the good of the community, is primarily a private concern. Education may concern the public, but in its essence, it is *res privata* and not *res publica*.

> The well education of their children is so much the duty and concern of parents, and the welfare and prosperity of the nation so much depends on it, that I would have everyone lay it seriously to heart and, after having well examined and distinguished what fancy, custom, or reason advises in the case, set his helping hand to promote everywhere that way of training up youth with regard to their several conditions which is the easiest, shortest, and likeliest to produce virtuous, useful, and able men in their distinct callings[7]:

What precipitates this change? In part at least, the reorientation of education reflects the modern reorientation of the state facilitated in significant part by Hobbes and Machiavelli.[8] This reorientation of the state moved it away from a common seeking after communal forms of the good in political life and transformed it into an institution for the management of conflict and the protection of private interest or "commodious living."[9] Gone are the shared meals of Plato's Cretan City, gone too is the Roman life spent in the Forum, in its place a society of private households joined together not for a common good but out of a set of common interests. Locke recognized that this shift from ancient to modern in political life, from the common good to shared interest, entailed a profound lowering of civic and ethical horizons of political

---

[7] Locke, *Some Thoughts*, 9.
[8] Leo Strauss, *Natural Right and History*, 189.
[9] Ibid.

community.[10] Of course Locke was both describing and advocating for just this change. To this end Locke famously declares in *Two Treatises of Government*.

> The great and *chief end* therefore, of Mens [sic] uniting into Commonwealths, and putting themselves under Government, *is the preservation of their Property.*[11]

Surely no ancient or even a near contemporary would've seen in Locke's chief end much of civic or political greatness. As Locke well knew, his conception of the fundamental sources of political community twice prohibits a system of public education in civic virtue. Essentially, the constraints on limited government that Locke's definition entails permit few of the resources, moral and material, for a common education. More importantly a state with so diminished a *raison d'etre* seems not merely ill-suited to provide for public institutions, its constitution and intention render it incapable of generating a genuinely salutary teaching on civic virtue.

Locke's *A Letter Concerning Toleration* displays, starkly, how far his thinking has traveled from the classical tradition of Plato and Cicero. Education, especially the education provided by the laws, stands transformed from a vital source of the *res publica* to a mere arbitrator between competing conceptions of the *res privata.*

> Laws provide, as much as is possible, that the Goods and Health of Subjects be not injured by the Fraud or Violence of others; they do not guard them from the Negligence or Ill husbandry of the Possessors themselves. No man can be forced to be Rich or Healthful, whether he will or no. Nay God himself will not save men against their wills.[12]

---

[10] The divide between ancient and modern in educational theory, as this chapter will assert, is much more ambiguous.
[11] John Locke, *Two Treatises of Government*, ed. Peter Laslett (Cambridge: Cambridge University Press, 1994), II.124.
[12] John Locke, *A Letter Concerning Toleration* (Indianapolis: Hackett Publishing, 1983), 35.

4 Locke's Education for Ordinary Life and Liberal Citizenship 111

Locke's assertion speaks both to his assessment of the nature of the student and the efficacy of the law. Breaking with the ancient tradition in terms equally of the sole power and legitimacy of the latter and the seeming weakness of the former Locke can easily be misread in his explicitly political works as being unconcerned with education aimed at civic virtue.[13] There is no doubt that the breadth of the divide between Locke and the classical tradition in the political works does conceal some deep (albeit partial) sympathies in his educational writings. The profound distinctions between ancient and modern politics and communities undeniably transform, for Locke, the conduct of education. However, this transformation is not total. This revolution is not complete. Some continuities endure. Lockean civic pedagogy, with its subtly adumbrated and intertextually dispersed account of the nature of the student, sits closer to the means if not the ends of Cicero and Plato than the more crudely and obviously sympathetic Milton.[14]

Locke, Cicero, and Plato agree that the polis is inevitably concerned with the character of the citizen. However, for Locke that concern does not generate a political prerogative. Indeed, the common concern with civic character that ties Locke to the ancients also divides him from them. Locke relocates civic education because he recognizes that it is inevitably also moral education and therefore the legitimate concern primarily of parents.[15] This prohibition does not mean that education and especially moral education does not directly affect or concern the political. The concerns Locke raised in *A Letter Concerning Toleration* regarding the citizenship status of atheists points powerfully towards the necessity if not the efficacy of the public sphere's engagement with virtue.[16] For Locke the transfer of legitimate authority from the public to private in education differs materially from the transformation of politics that liberalism demands. The shift in location in education, unlike liberalism's

---

[13] Thomas Pangle observes the ease with which Locke facilitates this misreading in *Two Treatises of Government* wherein the terms morality, morals, moral virtue, and ethics never appear. Thomas Pangle, *The Spirit of Modern Republicanism* (Chicago: University of Chicago Press, 1988), 204.

[14] Contrast Milton's casual description of the pupil's nature and lesson in *Of Education*, 62 with the prudent discrimination of Plato, *Republic* 535c and Cicero, *De Oratore*, III.xiv.55.

[15] Pangle and Pangle, *Learning of Liberty*, 55.

[16] Locke, *Letter*, 51.

constriction of the legitimate purview of politics, implies no necessary diminution of the social significance of education. The pedagogic remains an object of profound public interest and concern. Locke justifies the relocation of its practice almost exclusively in terms of efficacy as opposed to the more substantial ethical, ontological, and prudential justifications for the transformation of the political.

The stark declarative character of so much of Locke's prose tends to highlight its revolutionary aspects while concealing deeper continuities. In *Some Thoughts Concerning Education* the transfer of pedagogic power to parents appears at first to be the most revolutionary aspect of Locke's educational theory. This remarkable break challenges any reader's efforts at uncovering the deep sympathies and deeper divisions between Locke and the classical tradition. At its most basic, Locke's crisp declarations on education conceal the presence of other ideas, more subtly packaged, more carefully constructed, and perhaps more revolutionary still. Locke deliberately disperses his educational and by implication political teaching across several key works. This move between explicit and implicit, the pervasive presence of pedagogy in almost all his works, the subtle ways in which his arguments both introduce and undermine liberal assumptions, all point to deep sympathies in the practice of teaching with his ancient precursors.

Recognizing the expansive and intertextual character of Locke's enquiry constitutes the first task of any reader attempting to come to terms with Locke's conception of education. Locke's philosophy of education, like his political thought, discourages by its breadth.[17] Rejecting the very compartmentalization that would later virtually define liberalism and its study, Locke's educational theory comprehends epistemology, ontology, pedagogy, political philosophy, and more. As the first post-Reformation philosopher to write a book-length treatment whose sole subject is education, Locke tempts us to forget that all of his major works allude to education, that in concord with the classical tradition he sees education and politics as equiprimordial. Acknowledging Locke's method and breadth this modest treatment of Locke's conception of civic

---

[17] John Dunn, *The Political Thought of John Locke* (Cambridge: Cambridge University Press, 1969), 203.

education begins with ontology and epistemology, with the *tabula rasa*. It moves from the character of human being and knowing to the scope of reason and rationality and ends with the education of the citizen.

The Teaching of the Tabula Rasa

Locke is as concerned with education in virtue and in civic virtue as the ancients.[18] Locke most visibly departs from the classical tradition in the assignation of responsibility for this education to the private sphere and in particular to parents. On the surface this difference, explained all too handily by his liberal commitments, pales in comparison to the profound differences between ancient and modern concerning the nature of the student and consequently the potential of education. The common concern for virtue hints at a basic (albeit somewhat limited) agreement about the nature of education, the divergence concerns the means of education. Concerning the nature of the pupil the opposite condition inheres. Locke quietly accepts the cornerstone of ancient civic pedagogy: education must be suited to the nature of the student. At the same time Locke almost completely rejects the ancient account of that nature.

Locke begins *Some Thoughts Concerning Education* with what appears to be a propitious declaration.

> I may say that of all the men we meet with, nine parts of ten are what they are, good or evil, useful or not, by their education. 'Tis that which makes the great difference in mankind.[19]

This passage, despite its clear recollection of Cicero,[20] was taken to mean that education held out the possibility of overcoming what had

---

[18] This is not to suggest that the specific teaching regarding virtue is the same, merely that both teachings are concerned with the question of virtue.

[19] Locke, *Some Thoughts*, sec. 1.

[20] Cicero's declaration differs not in the account of the pupil but in the pessimistic tone only. "If distorted habits and false opinions did not twist weak minds and bend them in any direction no would be so like himself as all people would be like all others. Thus, whatever definition of a human being one adopts is equally valid for all human beings" (*De Legibus* I.30).

previously been perceived to be the pupil's intractable if not wholly irremediable nature. Locke's assertion takes on this character only when placed in clumsy conjunction with his description of the person as initially a *tabula rasa*. This depiction, famously offered in *An Essay Concerning Human Understanding*,[21] appears to imply that to the extent that humans are uniformly "blank" at the outset our ability to acquire and develop characteristics through education must be similarly uniform. The simple equation, offered by many English writers in the eighteenth century,[22] posited both fundamental equality and perfectibility to be the consequence of Locke's *tabula rasa*. Enthusiasm for this view expressed itself most hysterically in Lord Chesterfield's declaration that

> A drayman is probably born with as good organs as Milton, Locke, or Newton; but by culture, they are much more above him than he is above his horse.[23]

Of course, exponents of this view faced the daunting question of authorial intent. Locke never explicitly connects his declaration, or for that matter any other proposition or portion of *Some Thoughts Concerning Education* with *An Essay Concerning Human Understanding*.[24] This is not to suggest that no connection exists, indeed a profound connection undeniably exists, it is not however the connection that a simplistic combination of Locke's recognition of the import of education to character and the *tabula rasa* might imply. This is most apparent in Locke's *Some Thoughts*. Locke is clearly not directing his pedagogical counsel at the population as a whole, and most certainly not to draymen. Instead,

---

[21] John Locke, *An Essay Concerning Human Understanding*, ed. Peter H. Nidditch (Oxford: Oxford University Press, 1975), II.i.2.

[22] This simplistic reading of the *tabula rasa* is not limited to the past, see David M. Post, "Jeffersonian Revisions of Locke," *Journal of the History of Ideas* 47 (1986): 149.

[23] *Letters Written by Lord Chesterfield to his Son*, quoted in W.M. Spellman, *John Locke and the Problem of Depravity* (Oxford: Clarendon Press, 1988), 3. This motif, connecting a lowly profession to a higher one appears as early as Demosthenes and is restated, perhaps most famously, by Adam Smith in *The Wealth of Nations*. There the comparison is between a street porter and a philosopher in the context of the division of labor. Chapter 6 will deal with return again to this motif, these specific passages, and their larger significance.

[24] J.J. Chambliss, "Reason, Conduct, and Revelation in the Educational Theory of Locke, Watts, and Burgh," *Educational Theory* 26 (Fall 1976): 376.

4 Locke's Education for Ordinary Life and Liberal Citizenship

as the opening declarations make clear, Locke aims to teach gentlemen, or rather the sons of gentlemen.[25] If the enthusiasms of the Eighteenth century represented an accurate appraisal of the *Essay* and its relation to *Some Thoughts* then at the very least Locke could be accused of failing to follow through his thought to its logical, and apparently obvious, conclusion. However, a closer reading of both the relevant passages in the *Essay* and their true correlates in *Some Thoughts* reveals Locke's more modest estimation of the potential of education and his equally restrained belief in the malleability of the person.

The *tabula rasa* constitutes the centerpiece of Locke's critique of innate ideas. Locke rejects the claim that any of our beliefs about justice or the good indeed that any ideas at all are present prior to education or experience. In so contending Locke breaks immediately and definitively with Cicero. This break is all the more remarkable considering the singular prevalence of Cicero in Locke's considerations of education. Cicero seems to suggest at the very least a notion of incipient innate qualities, most obviously when he contends that man is that unique being possessed of reason, and "born for Justice."[26] Ciceronian civic education aims to draw out of the pupil the full potential for justice lying nascent within. Locke offers no such account of his pupil's progress.

Locke's *tabula rasa* further rejects, with equal zeal, the Christian and soteriological understanding of education. Unlike prior early modern and Christian thinkers, perhaps most notably Erasmus, Locke simply does not countenance a role for education in either salvation or in mitigating the tendency to sin. Again, returning to Locke's near contemporary Milton, the author of *Paradise Lost* offers a poignantly phrased account of the relation of an innate nature to education in his own *Of Education*.

> The end then of learning is to repair the ruins of our first parents by regaining to know God aright and out of that knowledge to love Him,

---

[25] Locke, *Some Thoughts*, sec. 6.
[26] Cicero, *De Legibus*, I.x.28.

to imitate Him to be like Him, as we may the nearest by possessing our souls of true virtue, which being united to the heavenly grace of faith makes up the highest perfection.[27]

Of course, Locke's hostility to any legacy of Adam, positive or negative, political or educational is well documented.[28] Locke's central concern, in education if not in politics, remains the nature of the subject and not the nature of rule. Investigating the nature of the subject Locke descries no innate tendency towards good or evil. In the absence of either a nature directed towards justice, after the fashion of Cicero or conversely a Miltonian fallen nature, Locke takes his rejection of innate notions a step further. Locke conspicuously fails to discern within the person any genuinely innate ideas concerning even fundamental questions of good and evil. In place of innate nature and notion Locke finds only experience. Experience, including education, impresses itself upon the blank page of the person.

Rejecting the mistaken belief in innate ideas represents the first of Locke's many nods in the *Essay* to the import of education for character. Close examination, Locke contends, reveals innate ideas as in fact our first lessons, lessons learned so early their teaching predates the age of first recollection. Locke concludes that these forgotten first lessons and not any innate nature is the true source of our first beliefs "come by these means, to have the reputation of unquestionable, self-evident and innate Truths."[29]

Locke's *tabula rasa* blurs the clean borders of education. It opens up and unframes education presenting a previously unrealized range of possibility. Locke's contention simply obliterates the prior notion of education as the means to either counter or cultivate the fundamental character of the pupil and by extension the citizen.[30] The argument

---

[27] Milton, *Of Education*, 59.
[28] Indeed this repudiation and the elucidation of its liberal political consequence constitute the lionshare of Locke's neglected *First Treatise on Government*.
[29] Locke, *Essay*, I.iii.22.
[30] James Tully, "Governing Conduct," in *Conscience and Casuistry in Early Modern Europe*, ed. Edmund Leites (Cambridge: Cambridge University Press, 1988), 21.

against innate ideas in the *Essay* subtly replicates for the citizen's conception of place and relation to authority the argument against divine right offered in the first of the *Two Treatises*. The ruler is no more naturally endowed with a patriarchal nature and entitlement than the subject is endowed with a nature innately inclined to accept and succumb to that rule. Locke replaces an innate citizen identity with an identity founded on custom and education.[31] Locke broadens his experiential understanding of the sources of personal identity and expands it to countenance its civic component. Citizen identity, now founded on education and custom, serves Locke as both public foil and private foundation for his civic pedagogy.

The Reintroduction of Nature and the Philosophic Student

Locke's contention, and surely his revolutionary intention, meant that human beings now understood to possess a common original status as *tabulae rasa*, would open up the possibilities both for education and for understanding the differences between individuals within society. At first glance, Locke appears to suggest that the obvious differences between people are to be attributed primarily to education and custom as opposed to reflecting innate differences in nature or capacity. This reading injects a near fatal dose of contingency into structures of social difference and rank and their reification in the structure and substance of education. Primordial blankness, the universal experience of the world as completely and perfectly new to each new life,[32] seems to entail fundamental and original equality among humans. However, this position remains tenable only on the crude equation of innate ideas with innate ability, an equation absent from Locke's account. Indeed, within Locke's *Essay, Some Thoughts Concerning Education, On the Conduct of the Understanding* and the *Two Treatises* there are repeated references not merely to the

---

[31] Locke, *Two Treatises*, II.101.
[32] Peter Laslett, introduction to *Two Treatises of Government*, by John Locke, ed. Peter Laslett (Cambridge: Cambridge University Press, 1994), 84.

differences emerging out of education and custom but also to differences attributed to nature and regarded as independent of, indeed to some extent even unaffected by, education. At the high end of ability Locke subtly alludes in the final pages of *Some Thoughts* to the existence of a class of students apart from the ordinary gentlemen, the student born with a nature and inclination open to philosophy. At the bottom end Locke coarsely acknowledges in the *Two Treatises* the existence of those whose nature defeats even the most basic and salutary effects of education, the "*lunaticks and ideots.*"[33]

While Locke's opposition to innatism does not necessarily entail a fundamental equality among human beings, it does entail more than the simple eliding of equality into sociality, the *simile simili gaudet* attributed to Cicero.[34] Between these two positions Locke concludes that the character of human equality is understood best in comparison with other species. Human beings resemble each other to a degree far beyond any cross-species comparison. Nonetheless Locke contends that a general conspecificity need not entail uniformity of ability. On the contrary, in discussing the extent of our similarity Locke admits of a diversity of ability within the species great enough to bring into question its very boundaries.

> And yet, I think, I may say, that the certain Boundaries of that *Species*, are so far from being determined, and the precise number of simple *Ideas*, which make the nominal Essence, so far from being setled, and perfectly known, that very material doubts may still arise about it: And I imagine none of the Definitions of the word *Man*, which we yet have, nor Descriptions of that sort of Animal, are so perfect and exact, as to satisfie a considerate inquisitive Person[35];

According to Locke the breadth of difference between individuals is so great at birth, the moment of most perfect "blankness," that controversies about whom to baptize are not uncommon.[36] Locke's inclusion of such

---

[33] Locke, *Two Treatises*, II.60.
[34] Strauss, *Natural Right*, 135.
[35] Locke, *Essay*, III.vi.27.
[36] Ibid.

4 Locke's Education for Ordinary Life and Liberal Citizenship 119

controversies undergirds his assertion that the simple commonality of qualities across the species is accompanied by a vast diversity in degree and extent to which individuals possess these qualities. Indeed, the degree of difference is so great that religious and therefore moral and potentially political decisions are affected.

Locke's description of the differences across the human species and the inadequacy of any single and simple definition to comprehend humanity strikes an immediate and jarring note when compared with his declaration of just such a definition in the *Two Treatises*. Far from interrogating the relatively fine points surrounding the boundaries of the species Locke writes of the political characteristics of the species with the bluntness, surety, and resolute simplicity he clearly eschewed in the *Essay*.

> The *state of nature* has a law of nature to govern it, which obliges every one: and reason, which is that law, teaches all mankind, who will but consult it, that being all *equal and independent*, no one ought to harm another in his life, health, liberty or possessions.[37]

This passage poses two problems for Locke's theory of education. First and foremost, the passage indicates that any person "who will but consult it" appears to have reason adequate enough to discern the law of nature. The radical egalitarianism of Locke's phrasing *could be* disqualified by the practical limitations in the distribution of education and the enduring power of both custom and prejudice save that the law of nature is knowable in the state of nature and therefore comprehensible independent of education. Given Locke's assessment of natural reason and the implied self-awareness thereof it is hard to imagine how the species boundaries of creatures endowed with such a degree of reason could ever be contentious. Set in one text alone it presents real barriers, perhaps insuperable, to offering a coherent account of Lockean pedagogy. The resolution to this difficulty emerges by placing it in the larger context of Locke's writing on both the law of nature and education. In reading the problem this way the apparent simplicity and intertextual contradiction of the declarations in the *Two Treatises* and the *Essay* points away from

---

[37] John Locke, *Two Treatises*, ed. Peter Laslett (Cambridge: Cambridge University Press, 1994), II.6.

contradiction and toward the stratified complexity of Locke's conception of the character of reason, the range of human knowing, and the discriminating character of education.[38]

Locke resolves the apparent conflict between the two texts by considering the *Essay* and the *Two Treatises* not in isolation but as parts of a larger whole. The difficulty of bringing into agreement the various positions within the Lockean corpus, when each is considered in isolation, reveals the deeper sympathies in pedagogy and heuristic strategy between Locke and the ancients that his break with them over the *tabula rasa* conceals. Reading Locke's work in close combination the specific and surface intentions of each particular text drop into the background and a more complex and broader vision emerges, it is the very presence of this emergent perspective that first reveals Locke's deeper sympathies with the classical tradition in education. The distribution of ideas across Locke's writing, the necessity of encountering all of them in order to get a clearer picture of each, amounts to a Lockean intellectual "labour theory of value"[39] consonant with the same literary and pedagogic practices in the dialogues of Plato and Cicero.

Even a peremptory intertextual examination of the law of nature, knowledge of which was considered readily available to almost all according to the *Two Treatises*, provides a conspicuous path mark illustrating the consonance between ancient and modern approaches. Turning to the *Essay*, Locke's explicitly epistemological and profoundly skeptical declarations concerning the knowledge of natural law and his further rejection of any but the weakest conception of moral cognitivism seem to leave little room for the claims of the *Two Treatises*.[40] In even greater contrast Locke fails even to mention the question of a law of nature anywhere in *Some Thoughts Concerning Education*.[41] However, while a law of nature is conspicuously absent the *Thoughts* does suggest to the potential Lockean pedagogue, that is the ideally careful and intended

---

[38] Leo Strauss, "Locke's Doctrine of Natural Law," in *What Is Political Philosophy?* (Chicago: University of Chicago Press, 1988), 206.

[39] Leon Craig, *The War Lover*, xxxii.

[40] Locke, *Essay*, I.iii.6, I.iii.13, and II.xxvii.6.

[41] Nathan Tarcov, *Locke's Education for Liberty* (Chicago: University of Chicago Press, 1984), 93.

reader, an alternative understanding of his declaration in *Two Treatises*. Instead of a claim for innate and self-conscious rationality when read through *Some Thoughts* Locke's famous declaration is transformed from an isolated and independent political and philosophic assertion into a practical pedagogic artifact. Read this way Locke is not making a claim about human nature but rather providing an example of how to teach it.

> I grant that good and evil, *reward and punishment*, are the only motives to a rational creature; these are the spur and reins whereby all mankind are set on work and guided, and therefore they are to be made use of to children too. For I advise their parents and governors always to carry this in their minds, that children are to be treated as rational creatures.[42]

Locke introduces a truly remarkable turn of phrase, rational creatures. Moreover, in the emphasis on reward and punishment Locke has also rendered rationality in exclusively creaturely terms. With this reduced and uniquely modern rationality, one first emerging with Machiavelli and Hobbes and attaining an apogee of philosophic nuance in Hume, Locke reconciles the tension between his politics and his ontology. When placed alongside the *Essay* and the *Two Treatises* this passage offers a subtle reconciliation of the surface incompatibility. As the above passage makes clear, Locke intends his declaration in the *Second Treatise* as a political lesson shaped by the need to treat the pupil *as rational*. The opening remarks concerning reward and punishment, and the remarkable equine imagery suggest to Locke's ideal teacher the true substance of that teaching and the best approach to his inevitably less than ideal student.[43] The very structure of Locke's writing constitutes a tacit rejection of a universal and identical education for all. Instead, in its intricate intertextual structure the dispersed and layered nature of Locke's

---

[42] Locke, *Thoughts*, sec. 54.
[43] There is an awkward and poignant contrariety in seeing the equine imagery unwittingly echoed in the words of Thomas Jefferson arguably Locke's greatest political pupil. Writing on the impending 50th anniversary of the Declaration of Independence, "The general spread of the light of science has already laid open to every view the palpable truth, that the mass of mankind has not been born with saddles on their backs, nor a favoured few booted and spurred, ready to ride them legitimately, by the Grace of God." Thomas Jefferson, "Letter to Peter Weightman" quoted in Michael Zuckert, *The Natural Rights Republic* (Notre Dame: University of Notre Dame Press, 1996), 41.

educational thought allows his writings to speak to different people differently.

Beyond the perhaps "too esoteric by half" intertextual justification for an approach to education that recognized gradations of intellect, Locke's own explicit declarations in both *Two Treatises* and *Some Thoughts* acknowledge the existence of remarkable individuals who by the force of their intellect escape the pedagogical *reductio* of asking after the teacher of the first teacher. These individuals not only escape this dilemma but provide a further justification for considering Locke's pedagogy as prudently discriminating between students concerning both the structure and substance of their education. Of them Locke writes

> And therefore, though perhaps at first, (as shall be shewed more at large hereafter in the following part of this discourse) some one good and excellent man having got a preheminency amongst the rest, had this deference paid to his goodness and virtue, as to a kind of natural authority, that the chief rule, with arbitration of their differences devolved into his hands, without any other caution but the assurance they had of his uprightness and wisdom[44];

Locke clearly rejects the idea, first stated at the outset of the second of the *Two Treatises*, that almost all people can know and be governed by the law of nature. Indeed, he suggests that to the contrary the very possibility of civil society rests as much on the initial emergence of the gifted few able to discern, develop, and implement institutions and laws on behalf of those who simply cannot possess this superior wisdom[45] as it does on an original contract among the population as a whole.

The distinction that Locke adumbrates politically concerning the founding of civil society in the *Two Treatises* could potentially be ignored if the recognition of such profound differences in intellect were restricted to great men and the rarified and mostly historic world of foundational politics. However, in *Some Thoughts Concerning Education* Locke explicitly provides room for the education of the philosophic nature,

---

[44] Locke, *Two Treatises*, II.94.
[45] Hans Aarslef, "The State of Nature and the Nature of Man in Locke," in *John Locke: Problems and Perspectives*, ed. John Yolton (Cambridge: Cambridge University Press, 1969), 136.

for the teaching of the student capable of superior wisdom. Late in *Some Thoughts*, hinting at both the appropriate timing of the education and the necessary care needed to discern the philosophic student, Locke begins to account for this teaching of a nature set apart. Neither custom nor education, rather the nature of the student alone determines whether or not he is suited to a philosophic education. Dividing students by dividing subjects, Locke distinguishes philosophy from history, and in so doing separates philosophic from civic education.

> In history the order of time should govern, in philosophical inquiries that of nature, which in all progression is to go from the place one is then in to that which joins and lies next to it; and so it is in the mind, from the knowledge it stands possessed of already, to that which lies next and is coherent to it, and so on to what it aims at, by the simplest and most uncompounded parts it can divide matter into.[46]

The passage is telling beyond the clear indication that the very possibility of philosophical study is explicitly dependent on nature. Locke characterizes education as a linear process. The pupil progresses through stages of interconnected learning, a progress halted at the moment when each pupil, respectively, reaches their intellectual limits. Such a limit is reached when the matter inquired into ceases to be "coherent" to them. Locke phrases it in *Concerning Reading and Study* as a hard law of intellection "The extent of our knowledge cannot exceed the extent of our ideas."[47] Earlier in the same section of *Some Thoughts* Locke presents this conception of learning, and in particular of philosophical learning, in a discussion of the education of young gentlemen in Greek. The Greek language, Locke opines, is the language of the scholar and not therefore his concern in a work ostensibly about the education of young gentlemen. Nonetheless Locke continues on to describe the unique qualities of both the subject and its student, in more than passing he admits

---

[46] Locke, *Thoughts*, sec. 195.
[47] John Locke, "Concerning Reading and Study," in *Educational Writings of John Locke*, ed. James Axtell (Cambridge: Cambridge University Press, 1968), 399.

> When he comes to be a man, if he has a mind to carry his studies farther and look into the *Greek* learning, he will then easily get that tongue himself; and if he has not that inclination, his learning of it under a tutor will be but lost labour, and much of his time and pains spent in that which will be neglected and thrown away as soon as he is at liberty.[48]

Locke began the section with a discussion dedicated simply to the learning of the Greek language but slips almost unnoticeably into a discussion of the "Greek learning." Locke further hints at the true nature of the intended pupil of *Some Thoughts* and the difference between pupils when he remarks that Greek learning is best begun in manhood. Greek learning, philosophy, is thus set chronologically outside the bounds of the text, which famously ends when the young student, gets "within the view of matrimony."[49]

The discussion of philosophic education in *Some Thoughts* is peculiar in its lack of substance and rigor. Locke dedicates multiple paragraphs to the salutary quality of break of day bowel movements, but the highest education is spoken of only in passing or by inference. Philosophic education is education *after* the education Locke is primarily concerned with in *Some Thoughts*. Philosophic education, for whomever it is suited, is not to be found in *Some Thoughts Concerning Education*. For the philosophic young gentleman Locke's education is only incompletely and perhaps propaduetically suited. For the philosophic nature Locke's *Thoughts* is incomplete, an invitation elsewhere, to the *Essay* and a later return to the *Two Treatises* perhaps. For the non-philosophic however *Some Thoughts* is the civic education suited to their nature, it is a second order education, participating incompletely in reason but fully in civic virtue. Its character further confirms that education is predicated on inclination and nature and that its absence renders any attempt to teach "against the grain" futile.[50]

---

[48] Locke, *Thoughts*, sec. 195.

[49] Locke, *Some Thoughts*, 215.

[50] Of course Locke differs dramatically from Cicero and Plato in arguing that such an education may be futile and pointless but not explicitly concluding that it is dangerous, barefaced, and unremitting ignorance and not an incomplete and imperfect schooling is for Locke a much greater threat to civil society.

4 Locke's Education for Ordinary Life and Liberal Citizenship

This concluding declaration points towards a series of critical sympathies between the Lockean and Platonic accounts of education. The first and most explicit of these is the undeniable diaretic character of education. Leaving any account of philosophic education till the concluding sections of *Some Thoughts* and placing it after the conclusion of formal education by default sorts out those for whom it is not suited. Admittedly this default mechanism lacks the rigor of Platonic diaresis. This absence is justified by the account of the person offered in *Essay Concerning Human Understanding*. The borders of a distinctly human nature and therefore the necessarily more obscure borders of philosophic nature have become blurred, these latter borders perhaps to a much greater extent. As such no trustworthy mechanism, one akin to those presented in Plato's *Republic*, is possible. Beyond reliance on natural inclination, presenting as an apparent existential tension towards the philosophic, is all that remains for Locke.[51] However, the absence of a fine tool does not establish the superfluity of such a tool.

The explicit substance of *Some Thoughts* points to substantial sympathies with Plato's *Republic*. Locke complements these initial sympathies in the structure of his conclusion. That conclusion evokes Plato's *Laws* albeit in uniquely modern and even domestic tones. The abruptness of the conclusion of *Some Thoughts*, the sudden turn to marriage, powerfully recalls the sudden turn to hunting in Book VII of *Laws*. The discussion of marriage brings the account of education to a definitive end. There are no husbands in the classroom. They have new concerns which preclude the pursuit of further learning. If we consider the venue of their respective enterprises the connection between *Laws* and *Some Thoughts* and between hunting, marriage, and the account of civic education further illuminates the break between the modern and the ancient. In the discussion of hunting and the implications for war Plato's *Laws* suggests the necessity that education both continue and possess an extramural element. Civic education for Plato must address the literally extra-civic contexts in which its subjects will inevitably find themselves.

---

[51] This remains a problem that bedevils the classrooms of liberal democracies in particular when it comes to the practice of "streaming" the necessity of which only the most radical and ideological reject and the problematic and potential biased character of only the willfully blind deny.

The contrast in pedagogic imperatives with the modern could not be more profound. Locke's education concludes with an allusion to the most intramural setting of all. In ending education not with the departure of the citizen for the field of Ares but for Hera's connubial hearth Locke points to the new challenge to civic education, the ever-expanding presence of the private. This new presence, this new concept of liberty as Benjamin Constant would later formulate it, presents distinct challenges to civic education. The teacher can travel outside the walls of the city and indeed does in both Cicero's *De Oratore* and Plato's *Phaedrus*. Where Locke's civic student is headed no teacher can follow, at least until Rousseau arrives unblushing at the side of Emile.

Civic Education and the Non-Philosophic Citizen

In tracing in outline Locke's philosophic education, the discrete existence of a non-philosophic education emerges in relief. This education, a specifically and solely civic education, is as determined in its content by the nature of the student as its philosophic counterpart. However, it is at this point that the similarities between the education of the two types of pupils ends. Locke's civic education is marked in its methodology by three key elements, a full recognition of the role of habit and experience in civic education, a rejection of abstract learning, and an acknowledgment of a range of aptitude among students. Out of this tripartite foundation, Locke shapes a conception of civic education aimed at constructing a citizen suited for civic life.

The necessary starting point in a discussion of the education of the non-philosophic citizen is Locke's terrible declaration at the end of *The Reasonableness of Christianity*. The working classes, Locke appears to contend, are the polar opposite of the philosophic citizen. They are incapable of reason. They may not arrive at true knowledge, gained through careful deduction.

And you may as soon hope to have all the day-labourers and tradesmen, spinsters and dairymaids, perfect mathematicians, as to have them perfect in ethics this way: hearing plain commands, is the sure and only course to bring them to obedience and practice. The greatest part cannot know, and therefore they must believe.[52]

Discerning the outline of education of the philosophic student and his selection from among the sons of gentlemen drains a great deal of acidity from Locke's declaration. Nonetheless in *The Theory of Possessive Individualism* C.B. Macpherson seizes upon this passage to conclude that Locke endorses a two-tiered and class-based conception of human reason. Macpherson contends that Locke held the laboring classes as a specific caste apart. For Macpherson the Lockean bifurcation entailed two key claims.

> These are (1) that while the laboring class is a necessary part of the nation, its members are not in fact full members of the body politic and have no claim to be so; and (2) that the members of the laboring class do not and cannot live a fully rational li.[53]

It is undeniably the case that there are ample citations within Locke to support this view of the laboring class's ability.[54] Nonetheless, in order for Macpherson's assertion to be correct there must be a corresponding assertion that the gentlemanly class can be, *as a class*, credited with a fully rational life. More precisely still, beyond an assumed class-wide rationality Locke must contend that full rationality is a sine qua non of civic life. This is a much more difficult case to make. Macpherson's argument makes clear the need to discover precisely whose education Locke is describing in *Some Thoughts*. The discussion above concerning the philosophic student hopefully served to illustrate that the primary division between students, between the philosophic and the civic nature, even occurring within the pages of a text concerning the education of

---

[52] John Locke, *Reasonableness of Christianity*, ed. L.T. Ramsey (London: Adam & Charles Black, 1958), 67.
[53] C. B. Macpherson, "The Social Bearing of Locke's Political Theory," *The Western Political Quarterly* 7, no. 1 (1954): 4.
[54] For instance, Locke, *Essay*, IV.xx.2.

the gentlemanly classes, precludes at least the primacy of the class division that Macpherson maintains. Instead, the division is not between rich and poor but between philosophic and simply civic natures. It is not across classes but within one, the gentlemanly.

Turning now to the education of the non-philosophic character two complementary elements emerge. First, there is the new centrality of character and difference within the civic educational cohort. Second is Locke's subtle and intricate assessment of the limited role of reason in civic life. While there is a clear division in the intellectual capacity of the philosophic versus non-philosophic student, a corresponding distinction *within* the non-philosophic civic cohort is much more difficult to locate. This is not to argue that nature ceases to play any role in education among this cohort, rather it is simply to suggest that differences in education are less profound than those between the two natures. Less is at stake among the intramural distinctions in pedagogy within the cohort of civic students. The differences are differences not in type but in degree. This is hinted at most strongly in the opening sections of Locke's *Some Thoughts* when, in discussing the ideal education of the children of gentlemen, the first laudatory comparison he makes among ways of educating is to the methods of child-rearing practiced by "honest farmers and substantial yeoman."[55]

Within Locke's civic education much more room is made for education and for environment to draw out distinctions than that implied in his division of the civic from the philosophic. Within the former the possibility for minimizing, if not altogether removing the differences among people through education seems much more plausible. In the *Essay* Locke hints at the same differences of condition as opposed to kind.

> And had the *Virginia* King, *Apochancana*, been educated in *England*, he had, perhaps, been as knowing as a Divine, and as good a Mathematician,

---

[55] Locke, *Some Thoughts*, sec. 3. Of interest for the discussion of Rousseau below is the early placement of a near identical sentiment in *Emile*. "Let us, then, choose a rich man. We will at least be sure we have made one more man, while a poor person can become a man by himself." J.J. Rousseau, *Emile*, trans. Allan Bloom (New York: HarperCollins, 1979), 53.

as any in it. The difference between him, and a more improved *English-man*, lying barely in this, That the exercise of his Faculties was bounded with the ways, Modes and notions of his own Country, and never directed to any other, or farther Enquiries.[56]

The difference in status between *Apochancana* and the *English*-man is a direct consequence of the conditions in his country, including his education. The relative economic impoverishment of the American king in *Two Treatises* is twinned with a similar intellectual impoverishment in the *Essay*. Of central importance the impoverishment is contingent on condition and not fundamental nature. The Virginia chief can just as easily become a prosperous property holder as an educated citizen, nothing fundamental to him rules it out. At the same time, it is clear that he is not the preeminent man of the *Two Treatises*[57] who needs no teacher and whose nature allows him to rise above mere rule and become a lawgiver. In this sense, while much less may be intellectually at stake in the education of citizens much more is at risk in their schooling in terms of their character and its social and political consequences. The intellectual development of the philosophic student seems to emerge inevitably out of his nature; for the ordinary student much more depends on his receiving the right education. In civic education Locke reveals a subtle double movement: the range and potential for education contracts as the consequences of a bad education expand. More precisely, within the limited purview of civic education the range of consequence is much more dependent on education. This contraction of potential combined with expansion of consequence explains Locke's suspicion of "book-learning," his emphasis on habit and custom as the primary method of education, and ultimately the recalibrating of the goals of education to focus on character and virtue.

---

[56] Locke, *Essay*, I.iv.12.
[57] Locke, *Two Treatises*, II.94.

The Non-Philosophic Student and the Uniform Pedagogy

The peculiar contrapuntal motion between education's scope and its significance for the teaching of the two natures must dictate a profoundly different pedagogy for each. Locke remains prudently silent on what exactly the preferred pedagogy is for the philosophic student. Within the pages of *Some Thoughts Concerning Education* at least, Locke hints that the education commences only in adulthood and requires the careful discernment of a philosophic nature. Further it may follow and expand on a civic education, but such an education is not ontogenetically essential to the philosophic nature.[58] In contrast to Locke's taciturn treatment of the philosophic student *Some Thoughts Concerning Education* is a remarkably detailed working out of the ideal pedagogy and curriculum for the non-philosophic student who is also a member of the gentlemanly class.

It is the peculiarly focused character of Locke's *Some Thoughts* and the absence of matching works of similar singular dedication and equal significance for the lower classes that suggests the mistaken conclusion that the method of education in *Some Thoughts*, as opposed to the specific curriculum, is distinct from that offered the lower classes. Close examination of Locke's admittedly briefer treatments of education for the lower classes reveals the opposite. Even a perfunctory examination of texts like Locke's *Board of Trade* papers reveals that the differences in education between the classes are minor and primarily involve the selection of curricular material. The similarity in the approach to delivering that material is striking. That commonality of method strongly suggests a common human nature if not a common social destiny. Unlike the stark differences between the philosophic and the non-philosophic, the intramural distinctions among the non-philosophic arise not out of nature but habit.

---

[58] Recall the 'men of pre-heminency' *Two Treatises*, II.94.

4 Locke's Education for Ordinary Life and Liberal Citizenship 131

> As it is in the body, so it is in the mind; practice makes it what it is, and most even of those excellences which are looked on as natural endowments will be found, when examined into more narrowly, to be the product of exercise and to be raised to that pitch only by repeated actions.[59]

With these remarks Locke describes the difference between those who are not among the preeminent, the unbidden, and spontaneously emerging intellectual elite. Instead, with the emphasis on habituation, the attempt to clarify the distinction between ascriptive and acquired characteristics clearly points to those of a non-philosophic nature, these students, unlike the preeminent, will become only what they can be taught.

In the handful of allusions within Locke to the teaching of the philosophic nature he consistently alludes to the role of nature, inclination, and development. Philosophic education clearly involves an interconnected ascent through ideas and beyond the habituation to rules. For the education of the non-philosophic the emphasis is not on linear development but on repetition and practice, not on discovery of the unknown but on mastery of the readily attainable. The pedagogical claim implies an equally significant ontological claim about the non-philosophic cohort. Locke's deliberate connection of physical education and mental education (with the important caveat 'most') increases the plausibility that intellectually, as is certainly and observably true physically, most difference is based on practice and habit not nature. Further by drawing in the physical and employing in illustration ploughmen, country hedgers, rope dancers, and tumblers[60] Locke further confirms that he is describing the ordinary, those who live primarily in and by their physicality, and not the intellectually exceptional. Practice, the settling of habit and custom, is the heart of education for the non-philosophic regardless of the task they are called to.

> Nobody is made anything by hearing of rules or laying them up in his memory; practice must settle the habit of doing without reflecting on

---

[59] John Locke, *On the Conduct of Understanding*, ed. Francis W. Garforth (New York: Teachers College Press, 1966), 42.
[60] Ibid.

> the rule, and you may as well hope to make a good painter or musician extempore by a lecture and instruction in the arts of music and painting as a coherent thinker or strict reasoner by a set of rules showing him wherein right reasoning consists.[61]

Locke attributes the same method to the learning of right reasoning, painting, and music as he does earlier to rope dancing and country-hedging.[62] I will return again to the importance of habit and custom below my aim here is merely to indicate the presence of a uniform pedagogy across both trade and class.

Locke forcefully illustrates the necessity, as opposed to merely the prudence, of a uniform pedagogy across the social strata with his account of the common sources of decline in the character of the poor, the working classes, *and* the young gentleman who are the ostensible object of *Some Thoughts*. At the miserable bottom of the social ladder Locke's oft quoted and admittedly brutal depiction conceals within its brutality an understanding of the fundamental nature of most decline in character. In his study of the poor laws, part of his *Board of Trade Papers*, he attributes the growing numbers of poor wholly to the circumstances in which their children are raised. Locke locates the source of adult poverty in the failures of child-rearing and education among the poor.

> The growth of the poor must therefore have some other cause, and it can be nothing else but the relaxation of discipline and corruption of manners; virtue and industry being as constant companions on the one side as vice and idleness are on the other.[63]

Moving past the admittedly callous tone and some of the brutal provisions advocated this passage matters because of the utter absence of any essentialist account of either the sources of poverty or its growth. Poverty,

---

[61] Ibid., 44.
[62] Right reasoning I take here to mean not true reason but a prudential calculus. Locke acknowledges as much when he suggests that such an ability can be "made" and simultaneously rejects the idea that any benefit can be gained from "reflecting on a rule" which is surely the very heart of a full and complete reason.
[63] Locke, "Board of Trade Papers," in Fox Bourne, *The Life of John Locke*, vol. II (London: Henry S. King & Co., 1876), 378.

4 Locke's Education for Ordinary Life and Liberal Citizenship

for Locke, bears no meaningful connection to nature. The poor possess no natural inferiority that would serve to both explain and justify their economic and social inferiority. In fact, Locke's report on the poor laws continues on to suggest that by bringing children into charity schools and exposing them to both religion and industry they might be improved to the same extent that the absence of the experience of religion and industry corrupted them.[64] Here Locke takes the political next step from claims first seen in Cicero's assertions concerning a birth for justice. Now, the claims to a fundamental if not perfect equality are first attached to a program aimed at its realization.

Locke argues nothing less than that the profound intellectual, social, and political significance of habit and custom upon character is so great that we can imagine scenarios in which an entire population becomes, by virtue of external conditions, immiserated. In the *Essay* Locke imagines an England in which critical cultural sources of salutary custom were suddenly lost. Speaking only (and perhaps somewhat bizarrely) of metallurgy, leaving out more obviously and potently formative social forces as religion, Locke considers a post-metallurgic as post-apocalyptic England. In just a few generations, civilization is all but lost.

> I suppose, it will appear past doubt, that were the use of *Iron* lost among us, we should in a few Ages be unavoidably reduced to the Wants and Ignorance of the ancient and savage *Americans*, whose natural Endowments and Provisions come in no way short of those of the most flourishing and polite Nations.[65]

Locke makes the same assessment of all of English society that he attributes in the *Board of Trade Papers* to the increase in poor children. It is not any innate let alone national character but the salutary effects on character of an emerging industrial and commercial society, with the habits and customs it engenders, that explains the lion's share of England's lack of both ignorance and want. The sources of poverty then are social and contingent more than individual and essential, they reside

---

[64] Locke, "Trade Papers," 385.
[65] Locke, *Essay*, IV.xii.11.

in condition not nature. As such Locke's observations suggest a potentially broad range of those who would benefit from civic education if not for accidents of circumstance. Of course, all of this does not suggest that contingencies are easily or even with great difficulty overcome. That the poor are consigned to their misery by contingencies and not nature does not necessarily render their relief more ready. The contingent can be just as intractable as the natural.

Returning to individual classes Locke baldly states in *Reasonableness of Christianity* that the conditions of working-class existence confine their character and intellect to that roughly bounded and "cooped in close by the laws of their country."[66] If not to the same extent at least in similar fashion to the poor, the American and the imagined post-metallurgic Briton, the laboring classes suffer from the absence of access to salutary habit and custom. However, for the laboring classes the absence is less dire. It is not an absence of industry or virtue but rather of the necessary habits of temperament and intellect for full citizenship. This is an accident not of nature but of condition. Locke will argue, ultimately, that the difference in the intellectual condition and civic character of the poor and laboring, as between the laboring and the gentlemanly classes, is rooted in habit and custom not nature.[67]

It is clear that for Locke scaling the social ladder improves the intellectual condition and civic character. Upward social mobility broadens the boundaries of experience, improves access to formal education and frees the character from its cooped-up condition. Nonetheless, for the gentlemanly classes, as for all save the philosophic and men of preeminence, the powerful educative effects of negative and positive habit and custom continue to define character. This explains Locke's concerns in *Some Thoughts* with boarding schools.

> But till you can find a school wherein it is possible for the master to look after the manners of his scholars and can show as great effects of his care of forming their minds to virtue and their carriage to good breeding as of forming their tongues to the learned languages, you must confess that

---

[66] Locke, *Essay*, IV.xx.4. Recall here the absence of reflection on rules described in *Of the Conduct of Understanding*, 44.
[67] Locke, *Essay*, IV.xx.4.

4 Locke's Education for Ordinary Life and Liberal Citizenship

you have a strange value for words, when preferring the languages of the ancient Greeks and Romans to that which made them such brave men, you think it worthwhile to hazard your son's innocence and virtue for a little Greek and Latin.[68]

Locke rejects boarding schools on grounds pedagogically identical to those he offers in explanation of the character of the poor. Boarding school education and particularly the company of boys, servants, and perhaps unscrupulous tutors provides a potentially corrupting set of experiences. The early expectation of service and the early exposure to servants corrupts in ways that outweigh any benefit gained within the classroom. For Locke questions of curriculum remain secondary to the establishing habit and custom. Particular classroom curricula may be complementary to habit and custom, even taught through them but the damage done by bad habit and custom can never be remedied by an allegedly civilizing curriculum. A corrupting habit and custom, for rich or poor, learned from fourth form school chums or Fagan & Co. exerts the same pernicious pressure on character. Locke's pedagogical position brings the children of the poor off the streets but also keeps the children of the wealthy out of boarding schools. The intractable differences of condition not nature determine the different loci and substance of teaching, but the common nature demands an underlying unity of approach.

In the relative paucity of advice regarding literary education Locke offers his strongest hint that he places little faith in the allegedly civilizing qualities of a literary education. Locke implicitly admits that the education of gentlemen, suited to their nature, remains an education through habit, practice, and custom. The lack of a significantly broad literary education in *Some Thoughts* suggests not only that erudition plays an insignificant role in cultivating civic virtue but equally that gentlemen specifically are unlikely to be meaningfully educated through reading. This places Locke in striking contrast to both his immediate contemporary Milton and more distant predecessors such as Erasmus in his

---

[68] Locke, *Thoughts*, sec. 70.

Education of a Christian Prince. Returning to Milton's *Of Education* fruitfully illuminates the commonality of nature across the non-philosophic classes that Locke maintains and the relegation of reading equally advocated. For Milton it simply follows from a literary education that the lessons learned through study will manifest, by means unknown, in the character and conduct of the erudite gentleman.

> By this time years and good general precepts will have furnished them more distinctly with that of reason which in ethics is called proairesis, that they may with some judgment contemplate upon moral good and evil.[69]

The education Locke offers the non-philosophic nature rejects Milton's mysterious moral formation by rote. Locke remains deeply suspicious of the independent force of moral ideas. Indeed, a careful examination of the education even of the gentlemanly classes calls into question whether for Locke moral ideas on their own, as for instance when offered as simple curricular lessons, can ever inform action. The condition of the greatest part of humanity, Locke makes clear in *The Reasonableness of Christianity*, must be persuaded by fear and longing for reward and not the simple justice and truth of a given proposition.[70] Locke relegates reading because of its inability to inform character and shape conduct.[71] Obviously Locke acknowledges that gentlemen must be taught to read. Nonetheless within the remarkably limited range of literary education Locke proposes he presents consistent approach that aims to convince the student rather than inform him.[72] Nowhere is this more evident than in Locke's highly circumscribed approach to Bible study. Rather than a study of the Bible Locke recommends the memorization of a short catechism of biblical questions *and answers*. Locke's teacher directs his efforts at encouraging a habit of belief rather than a comprehending faith

---

[69] Milton, *Of Education*, 66.
[70] Locke, *Reasonableness of Christianity*, sec. 243.
[71] Locke, *Some Thoughts*, 147.
[72] Michael Zuckert, "Fools and Knaves: Reflections on Locke's Theory of Philosophical Discourse," *Review of Politics* 36 (1974): 560.

let alone a robust theological curiosity.[73] Literary education and erudition for the gentleman differ little from the habits and practices of the laboring classes, they provide in the memory useful habits and lessons for application. Like the means of country-hedging or animal husbandry they serve not to develop the range of understanding but to furnish the intellect with the habits necessary for life. In so arguing Locke again places himself in sympathy with Plato. The aim of civic education, as opposed to its philosophic alternative, is to settle true opinion and to develop the capacity for a civic *logismos*.

Habit and Custom: The Civic Education of Gentlemen

Locke willing concedes that for better or worse habit and custom are the central forces that determine the character of the non-philosophic citizen. However, this concession does not lead to the conclusion that because all non-philosophic students may be taught the same way that they should be taught the same things. *Some Thoughts Concerning Education* concerns the education of young gentlemen and that education has both peculiar demands and a unique set of civic obligations. What it does not appear to have is the same implied intellectual superiority over the education of the lower classes that the education of the philosophic citizen has over all others. The education of gentlemen is not structurally unique what is unique is its peculiarly civic character. Locke offers a specifically and solely civic education to gentlemen in recognition of their social location and not, as Macpherson would have it, out of a misguided belief in their capacious propensity for reason. As a result of their social location the education, uniform in its pedagogy, focuses first and foremost on civic virtue. The civic virtue to be learned, ironically considering Locke's admonition to parents in the final sentence of *Some Thoughts*,[74] is founded on habit and custom. Locke closes out the treatment of the

---

[73] Lee Ward, *John Locke and Modern Life* (Cambridge: Cambridge University Press, 2010), 186.
[74] Locke, *Some Thoughts*, sec. 216.

civic education of gentlemen with a turn towards the larger social significance of that education. Recognizing the prominent place the intended objects of his education occupy Locke considers the extent to which the public character and conduct of gentlemen in itself constitutes a broader form of social education. The gentleman student *in his person* serves both as the subject of education and an element in the education of others a degree removed. As such, the cultivation of virtue in the gentleman has both his character and the character of those with whom he has conduct as its dual concern.

The central element of Locke's program of civic education is the teaching of virtue. Indeed, the goal of civic education simply *is* virtue. All other ends of an individual's education are secondary. Virtue's primacy reveals a great deal about the character of Lockean civic virtue but also about the ideal educated character of the citizen Locke aims at.

> Tis' virtue then, direct virtue, which is the hard and valuable part to be aimed at in education, and not a forward pertness or any little arts of shifting. All other considerations and accomplishments should give way and be postponed to this. This is the solid and substantial good which tutors should not only read lectures and talk of, but the labour and art of education should furnish the mind with and fasten there, and never cease till the young man had a true relish of it and placed his strength, his glory, and his pleasure in it.[75]

The pupil for whom virtue is the central aim of their schooling is the student both suited for and socially placed to receive an education in civic virtue. Locke's education in virtue is constructed on a tripartite foundation of countervailing passion, deep ingrained habit of character, and ethical hedonism. Each facet of Locke's program for teaching buttresses the others. In conjunction they educate a citizen whose passions, rooted in habit lead him to desire a reputation for reason and a concomitant belief that reason's object is happiness. However, Locke subtly implies that such a reputation is guaranteed not by the presence of reason but the deep-seated visceral virtue of fortitude, a

---

[75] Ibid., sec. 70.

virtue occasionally emboldened by hope of reward or chastened by fear of punishment.

Indeed, the very ambiguity surrounding reason suggests a central element of Locke's civic education. Early in *Some Thoughts* Locke suggests the virtue his education aims at is such that it creates a character able and inclined to act upon the dictates of reason.

> As the strength of the body lies chiefly in being able to endure hardships, so also does that of the mind. And the great principle and foundation of all virtue and worth is placed in this, that a man is able to *deny himself* his own desires, cross his own inclinations, and purely follow what reason directs as best though the appetite lean the other way.[76]

Locke's ordering of the process of virtuous deliberation is telling. The presence of reason indubitably plays a role in right conduct however most of the difficult work occurs before reason has gained the field. Rather than reason, Locke suggests that the "great principle and foundation" of virtue is the strength of character that allows hostile inclinations to be checked. Save reason, all the stages in the deliberative process are spoken of in the possessive: It is the self explicitly that is denied, it is *his* desire that is checked, *his* inclinations crossed. Reason on the other hand is to be *followed*, wherein reason dwells and the precise character of its leadership and relationship to the person Locke leaves deliberately vague. Here, albeit formulated differently, we have Locke reiterating the relation of reason to the self first promulgated by Plato. The qualities of character inhere in the ordinary citizen unlike the content of reason which is applied to and guided from without.

Locke is remarkably obscure, *even for Locke*, about the precise relationship of reason to virtue. He employs phrases such as "true gaurantor" (sec. 115) "true principle" (sec. 56) and "true principles of morality" (sec. 200) to describe the well spring of virtue. Locke deliberately cultivates imprecision in countenancing the relationship of virtue to reason.

---

[76] Ibid., sec. 33.

In the imprecision Locke equally avoids committing to a set definition of educations object or end beyond the formation of virtue.[77] In avoiding a precise account of that relationship Locke avoids the need to provide a measuring stick, a bar against which citizens might be ranked and ordered, a means that is for reintroducing the deep difference his civic education so assiduously undermines. Ultimately the ambiguity concerning reason's role, scope, and possibility explains Locke's democratizing claim that fortitude and not reason is virtue's true guarantor.

> *Fortitude* is the guard and support of the other virtues; and without courage a man will scarce keep steady to his duty and fill up the character of a truly worthy man.[78]

Fortitude is the unique virtue of the civic-minded citizen, especially the liberal civic-minded citizen of *Some Thoughts*. Fortitude is Locke's uniquely modern substitute for both the heroic reason of the philosopher that he only hints at and the heroic valor of the soldier that he never mentions.[79] Fortitude represents the modern motion within the person that parallels the political settlement Locke presents in *Two Treatises*. Fortitude does more than simply ensure the other virtues it shapes their very character. Fortitude engages the objectives of civic virtue and infuses it with a civil constancy. Equally, the centrality of fortitude to virtue further suggests the negligible force of reason in civic life. Recalling and rejecting the modern moral rote of Milton's *On Education*, Locke maintains that knowledge of the right cannot guarantee its pursuance. For Locke rational knowledge seems incapable of decisively informing or sustaining ethical action.

In a civic character imbued with ethical constancy by fortitude reason fails even to meaningfully exercise itself in settling upon virtue's object. The object instead avails itself only of reason's ability to strategically

---

[77] While at one point in *Some Thoughts* reason is described as the fullest perfection of man the range, number, and likelihood of its realization is left conspicuously undeclared. See *Some Thoughts*, sec. 122.

[78] Ibid., sec. 115.

[79] Pangle and Pangle, *Learning*, 59.

navigate under the steam of fortitude on a course determined by an appetite for virtue.[80] Reason, in its limited and inchoate civic incarnation, serves solely as a strategic and calculative faculty. Locke further confirms reason's lack of motive force through a description of the role of desire and aversion in conduct. Locke embraces a sort of ethical hedonism that conceives of human conduct as profoundly informed by the desire for reward and the concomitant fear of punishment.[81] However, in an important distinction from the surface coarseness of Hobbes' pairing of appetite and aversion, Locke suggests a particular set of desires and fears that are of use to a specifically civic education. Central to Locke's understanding of civic education is the pleasure that children take in esteem and the distress they experience when shamed. The careful application and impression of these two, Locke contends, allows for the conduct of children to be shaped into a salutary civic form.

> If you can once get into children a love of credit and an apprehension of shame and disgrace, you have put into them the true principle, which will constantly work and incline them to the right.[82]

Shame and disgrace then and not reason incline children towards the just. Pulled and pushed by desire and aversion and shored up by fortitude, for Locke's pupil reason stands reduced to little more than a strategic and calculative tool for scouting the route through peril and towards happiness. Locke repeatedly suggests that as the pupil nears the age of discretion this diminished reason will develop and take a more dominant role. Despite such claims Locke never delivers the promised account of reason's transformation and completion of man's perfection in reason.[83] Instead, such an account is left, like the philosophic education promised Kleinias and Megillos, just the other side of a threshold which serves more as destination than gateway.

The ambivalence between reason and conduct in the education of the Lockean gentleman explains the importance of habit and custom to his

---

[80] Tarcov, *Locke's Education*, 173.
[81] Locke, *Some Thoughts*, sec. 54.
[82] Ibid., 56.
[83] Tarcov, *Locke's Education*, 107.

conception of civic virtue. As noted above, Locke pointedly asserts in *The Conduct of Understanding* that lessons and lectures even those that forcefully convey precepts of civil conduct, cannot guarantee just action. This contention when combined with the ambiguity surrounding reason leaves Locke with only one strong resource for founding civic virtue: habit.

> The great thing to be minded in education is what *habits* you settle: and therefore in this, as all other things, do not begin to make anything *customary* the practice whereof you would not have continue and increase.[84]

This "great thing" explains the relative absence of questions of curriculum from the education Locke describes. Rather than focusing on rules, precepts, and principles acquired in the classroom Locke's civic education is carefully founded on a shaping of temper, sentiment, and inclination through practice and repetition.[85] Indeed the prerational even nonrational character of education recurs as the consistent pedagogic theme of *Some Thoughts*. Locke's education aims to settle patterns and principles of conduct so deeply and subtly in the character that they function independently of reason.

> But pray remember, children are *not* to be *taught by rules*, which will be always slipping out of their memories. What you think necessary for them to do, settle in them by an indispensable practice as often as the occasion returns; and if it be possible, make occasions. This will beget habits in them, which, being once established, operate of themselves easily and naturally without the assistance of the memory.[86]

Locke's education via habituation is most remarkable in and to the extent that it functions tacitly. Locke would guide the character without necessarily informing the intellect. This vision of education recalls powerfully

---

[84] Locke, *Some Thoughts*, sec. 18.
[85] John Yolton, *John Locke and Education* (New York: Random House, 1971), 69.
[86] Locke, *Some Thoughts*, sec. 66.

his description of innate ideas in *Essay Concerning Human Understanding*, those ideas acquired before the age of recollection.[87] That the habits taught dictate conduct without the aid of memory is critical, even more critical is the way in which they are experienced and held by pupils. First lessons and habits learned early *"grow up to the dignity of Principles."*[88] Those lessons acquire the dignity of innate principles without actually being innate. In Locke's civic education these habits of civility and citizenship take on this character in the experience of them by the citizen despite their true nature. Moreover, such principles more than simply subsisting in the character fundamentally inform action with a force and to an extent not possible through the simple teaching of rules.

"Innate" principles carefully woven into the character of the civic pupil simulate the experience of principled conduct and to the extent that the habits are wisely instilled may indeed act in consonance with true principles of reason even though the civic pupil never completely discerns those principles with his own limited rationality. Here Locke again finds himself in deep agreement with Plato in conceiving of a second order education that is taught to act in a manner consonant with reason's dictates even though such teaching, the weaving of principles into the soul, is achieved independent of the pupil's reason.[89]

Good Breeding, Good Example, and Social Replication

Locke's *Some Thoughts Concerning Education* begins with conflicted, if not outright contradictory, admonition, and advice to parents of young gentlemen. Locke asserts both that the responsibility for their education is a specifically private duty and at the same time of that this duty possesses profound public consequence.[90] For Locke, the private setting in which education engages with morality splits its nature. In dividing essential origins from ultimate consequences Locke's education

---

[87] Locke, *Essay*, I.ii.12.
[88] Locke, *Essay*, I.iii.22.
[89] See Plato, *Laws* 653b-c, from Pangle, *Locke* n265.
[90] Locke, Epistle Dedicatory to *Some Thoughts*, 8.

mirrors the essential split between private and public that characterizes so much of liberalism after him. This division between public and private is further echoed and even inverted in Locke's account of the consequence of his education both with others and for others. Locke first acknowledges that the civic consequences of the gentlemen's education rest first and foremost with the pupil and yet they are only fully realized in the company of others. Locke then goes on to add a critical political nuance. The social position of the gentleman imbues his education, and in consequence his character, with a particular and pressing civic significance. Recalling Cicero's Scipionic tableau, the education of Locke's pupil is in important ways deliberately *for* others.[91] As he says in the dedication to *Some Thoughts* "for if those of that rank are by their education once set right, they will quickly bring all the rest into order."[92] *Some Thoughts Concerning Education* is double in its intent, it beholds young gentlemen and considers them as both subjects and objects of education, both to be taught and in turn to teach by example.

It is natural that Locke's educational writings concern gentlemen. Lockean society, as opposed to its feudal and aristocratic precursors, is founded on and for the protection of property[93] and therefore the central and most politically directed education must have as its object the propertied class.[94] But the import and significance of the class is not so singular as to occlude from view others. Rather the unique status and location of the gentlemanly class renders its relations with others of first order importance. Locke emphasizes the importance, for any parent of a young gentleman, of educating their son in much more than the careful possession and retention of his estate. In particular and beyond an education in inward and personal virtue Locke seeks to encourage the socially correlative virtue of good breeding. Good breeding serves the external and explicitly social function that fortitude provides internally; it shapes and reinforces virtue in dealings with others. This is of particular importance for the gentleman placed in a class conspicuously above some and

---

[91] Ibid.
[92] Ibid.
[93] Locke, *Two Treatises*, II.94.
[94] Robert Horwitz, "John Locke and the Preservation of Liberty," *American Political Science Reviewer* 6: 340.

below others. Breeding, necessary for the civil coexistence of disparate citizens and classes, teaches respect and civility for others.

> For the very end and business of *good breeding* is to supple the natural stiffness and so soften men's tempers that they may bend to a compliance and accommodate themselves to those they have to do with.[95]

This is an explicitly civic education of character in Lockean terms. Note that the well-bred gentleman is disposed by the softening of his temper, and not by a consultation of his reason, to the restrained and peaceable existence of Locke's state of nature. This is precisely the habituation of civic character necessary for the limited government of the *Two Treatises*.[96]

But the social and educational significance of good breeding is almost as great for the classes that the gentleman deals with as it is for the gentleman himself. More than good neighborliness the importance of breeding arises out of the Lockean understanding of example as a pedagogic tool. Locke suggests that among the young example is perhaps second only to habituation as a means of teaching conduct. Unlike habituation, example works on the student both before and after the age of recollection with a depth and a degree of subtlety that renders its lessons often imperceptible to the student in their administration at any age.

> Nay, I know not whether it be not the best way to be used by a father as long as he shall think fit, on any occasion, to reform anything he wishes mended in his son: nothing sinking so gently and so deep into men's minds as *example*.[97]

Locke draws attention to the educational question first identified by Cicero in lamenting a "shortage of men." Now though, as with so much of his education, the heuristic horizon narrows from the public into the private. Locke makes it clear that the subtle influence of example is best, and perhaps most deliberately used by a father in the teaching of his

---

[95] Locke, *Some Thoughts*, sec. 142.
[96] Pangle and Pangle, *Learning of Liberty*, 72.
[97] Locke, *Some Thoughts*, sec. 81.

son. But the pedagogic power of example stretches beyond intimate relationships. Throughout life and especially across social classes learning by example seems to Locke a hallmark of humanity; "We are all a sort of chameleons that still take a tincture from things near us."[98] As a result good breeding provides in the conduct of gentlemen a model and lesson for the lower classes. In all the gentlemen's conduct that has a public aspect there is pedagogic possibility.

Broad social example and imitation add a third level to the educational superstructure of *Some Thoughts*. At the highest level Locke only hints at the nature of the philosophic student, and by scattered implication the structure of his education. In the middle ranks, among students destined not for philosophy but citizenship, the education in civic virtue that Locke describes at such length trains and shapes the character through habit, custom, and example towards a conduct that outwardly expresses civic virtue. This education, instantiate in the public dealings and comportment of the gentleman, then translates downwards by the powerful human inclination to imitation. Those to whom a fuller civic education is closed by the accidents of class and circumstance, come to possess through observation a portion of that virtue embodied in those virtuous citizens who they live alongside.

The virtuous gentleman/citizen stands in a social and pedagogical positioned akin to that occupied by Cicero's sublunar Scipio. Locke's civic education and its subject embody and express the median point between simple mimesis and the fullness of wisdom. Locke's civic education focuses above all on virtue while subtly acknowledging the distinction between a nature capable of its embodiment and one suited to the comprehension of that embodied. The multiple lives shaped by Locke's civic education are thus guided by rules deeply held but only ever incompletely comprehended.

---

[98] Locke, *Some Thoughts*, sec. 67.

5

Rousseau and the Redefinition of Nature and Education

> The lessons of history, confirmed by the evidence immediately before me, show conclusively that continued dependence upon relief induces a spiritual and moral disintegration fundamentally destructive to the national fibre. To dole out relief in this way is to administer a narcotic, a subtle destroyer of the human spirit.
>
> Franklin Delano Roosevelt, *Annual Message to Congress*, January 4, 1935[1]

Introduction

John Locke's *Some Thoughts Concerning Education* revolutionized educational philosophy. Unsatisfied, Jean-Jacques Rousseau revolutionized human nature. Rousseau set out to challenge not only the popular assumptions concerning education but the popular prejudices

---

[1] Franklin D. Roosevelt, *Annual Address to Congress*, http://www.presidency.ucsb.edu/ws/index.php?pid=14890.

© The Author(s), under exclusive license to Springer Nature Switzerland AG 2022
G. C. Kellow, *The Wisdom of the Commons*, Palgrave Studies in Classical Liberalism, https://doi.org/10.1007/978-3-030-95872-5_5

concerning the pupil. So far, I have attempted to trace a deep connection across Plato, Cicero, and Locke. All three see in the diversity of human nature, in the range of intellectual ability, profound consequences for both pedagogy and politics. In their own ways, with more or less openness or subtlety, they insisted that these differences in nature should inform the substance of schooling and inevitably shape the structure of politics. This deep connection is challenged, amended, reformed, and restored at different moments but the core contention that a pupil's distinct nature should inform his education endures. Rousseau, by exploding the idea of a knowable, distinct, and discrete human nature specific to the pupil renders permanently problematic the connection between nature and education.

Rousseau's revolution in education and human nature commenced with a reassessment of the relationship of education to human nature. This assessment began, as it must, with an epistemological survey. Rousseau conceded that principles of education may legitimately be informed by facts about human nature. However, he noted that this concession fails to establish the veracity of the traditional conception of human nature upon which such principles are founded. More radically still, Rousseau questioned whether a pedagogically foundational knowledge of human nature was even possible. According to Rousseau, the question of education, like the question of inequality's origins, suffers from a profound paucity of evidence. To inquire into either was to confront the obscured and elusive character of our true nature. The modern student, as much as the modern citizen riddled with *amour-propre*, resembled the marine Glaucus.

> Like the statue of Glaucus, which time, sea and storms had disfigured to such an extent that it looked less like a god than a wild beast, the human soul, altered in the midst of society by a thousand constantly recurring causes, by the acquisition of a multitude of bits of knowledge and of errors, by changes that took place in the constitution of bodies, by the constant impact of the passions, has, as it were, changed its appearance to the point of being nearly unrecognizable.[2]

---

[2] Jean Jacques Rousseau, "Discourse on the Origin of Inequality," in *The Basic Political Writings*, trans. Donald A. Cress (Indianapolis: Hackett Publishing Company, 1987), 33.

5 Rousseau and the Redefinition of Nature and Education

Rousseau's reflections on the marine Glaucus provide grounds for both hope and despair. Rousseau concluded that to whatever degree human nature is transformed by life in society, a degree so great that the subject becomes unrecognizable, to that degree it may also be positively shaped by education. Society's vast potential to corrupt encourages Rousseau; it shows the dramatic extent of human malleability toward good or ill. It remains only for education to take up this force and either construct the moral citizen or neutralize its acidity and in so doing retain the natural goodness of man.

The profound malleability of man explains why Rousseau repeatedly describes his star pupil, the eponymous hero of his philosophic bildungsroman *Emile*, as by nature ordinary. In order to emphasize the power and potential of education rightly conducted Emile must be typical. Emile's ordinariness is Rousseau's most powerful claim for the force of education, a force so powerful that it may trump rank and fortune. Whenever Rousseau describes this triumph, he testifies to both the force of right education and the corruption of traditional schooling, a schooling which is only fit for, and furthermore the well spring of, men "only vain, rascally, and false: they do not even have enough courage to be illustrious criminals".[3] The vital and natural Emile stands in marked contrast to the enervated subject of traditional education. This difference, born of schooling not of character, testifies to the power of the former over the latter, a power Rousseau envisages as just as equally influential as pedagogic principle and social fact.

> No matter how little birth and fortune had done for Emile, he would be that man if he wanted to be. But he would despise these young men too much to deign to enslave them.[4]

Passages such as these have encouraged a reading of Rousseau's educational thought, at least as represented in *Emile*, which claims a total triumph of nurture over nature. As Allan Bloom writes in *Love and Friendship*

---

[3] Jean Jacques Rousseau, *Emile*, trans. Allan Bloom (New York: HarperCollins, 1979), 335.
[4] Ibid.

So much power does Rousseau attribute to nurture or education over nature that this ordinary man, properly educated, can be seen as a harbinger of Nietzsche's Superman. Here one also finds the roots of the Marxist's great expectations for socialist man.[5]

Rousseau may be the unwitting harbinger of both Marx and Nietzsche. But it is important to recall that Emile's potential supremacy is a consequence of the forces countenanced in *Emile* and *Discourse on the Origins of Inequality*. Emile stands out because he is healthy, ordinarily healthy, against a background of men who have institutionalized and normalized illness, he is no Superman he is only natural man living among social man.

This is where we find the deep break between Rousseau and both his ancient and early modern precursors. Rousseau insists on the potential that education presents to overcome human social nature. If Emile's supremacy is at least partly premised on the miseducation of others that doesn't preclude the wider education of other ordinary citizens. Rousseau envisions an education that could potentially either ameliorate or displace altogether social differentiation. As Rousseau argued so forcefully in his *Second Discourse*, such differentiation was previously assumed to be natural and both pedagogically and politically intractable. Rejecting this, Rousseau presents the possibility of a society made up of men like Emile. Obstacles exist, but these obstacles concern practicalities of delivery and not irremediable facts of nature.

Rousseau makes explicit his rejection of nature as a principle of pedagogic and political differentiation as early as the preface to the *Emile*. Presaging his rejection of careful discrimination among students, a hallmark of all three of the philosophers so far considered, Rousseau opens the *Emile* to all comers.

> It is enough for me that wherever men are born, what I propose can be done with them; and that, having done with them what I propose, what is best both for themselves and for others will have been done.[6]

---

[5] Allan Bloom, *Love and Friendship* (New York: Simon & Schuster, 1993), 93.
[6] Rousseau, *Emile*, 35.

5 Rousseau and the Redefinition of Nature and Education

It looks like we have come a long way from the Socratic silence of Plato's *Cleitophon*. Both Rousseau's prose and his proposals open themselves to readers and pupils independent of time, place, or ability. The warnings of Plato about the teaching of dialectic through Cicero's complementary concerns about oratory to the carefully crafted balance between innate ideas and different natures of Locke's *Essay* stand as the first foes of Rousseau's revolution.

Despite this break Rousseau praises Plato's *Republic* as "the most beautiful educational treatise ever written."[7] But Rousseau makes clear that beautiful though it is Plato's *Republic* lacks pedagogic courage, imagination, and most of all confidence. Rousseau is an ambitious and self-assured teacher; he is the uncommon tutor able to transform the common pupil. Unlike Socrates' pupils Rousseau's intended need not be the gifted, politically placed, and potentially philosophic. Rousseau's pupils are ordinary men and his self-described pedagogy is defined by its predicted efficacy.[8] Rousseau's confidence banishes the careful and discriminating speech of Socrates, hallmark of Platonic pedagogy, a legacy carried forward, as I have argued above, in the educational thought of both Cicero and Locke.

What are the sources of Rousseau's tremendous confidence in education's potential? Answering this question requires that we chase down connections not always made obvious by the author. Alongside a discussion of Rousseau's lack of faith in the claims to nature made by rank and difference, we must unpack his radical re-assessment of nature itself. Rousseau rejects nature's previous role as a pedagogically and politically relevant principle of differentiation. No longer a principle, *nature* becomes *the* principle. For Rousseau nature becomes both source and benchmark. Critically, nature ceases to be understood as the combination of specific and determinative elements of each individual character. Rousseau transforms nature into a universal principle, common in character and degree across humanity. An education founded either on its

---

[7] Ibid., 40.
[8] Joseph Cropsey, *Political Philosophy and the Issues of Politics* (Chicago: University of Chicago Press, 1977), 316.

retrieval or rejection, the two educational options Rousseau describes,[9] must therefore also have at its heart a similar commonality. Such an education for "men wherever they are born"[10] has political consequences whose revolutionary nature is hard to fully measure, save by a survey of history from 1789 to the present.

Duty and Inclination: Nature at the Crossroads

The reconceptualization of nature, as both source and benchmark, constitutes Rousseau's defining educational principle. The precise character of this principle is what makes Rousseau's educational philosophy truly remarkable. Having discerned nature in human beings Rousseau draws out of this universal source two diametrically opposed possibilities for education. Education can nurture and retrieve nature, educating the pupil to be a natural man within an unnatural society or education can seek to radically denature the pupil, creating a citizen wholly defined by his duties and removed completely from nature. No middle ground exists. Education must serve one of two masters, inclination, or duty.[11]

The necessity of choice speaks to the heart of Rousseau's critique of both modern political life and education. Rousseau considers division and its concomitant sense of incompleteness as the defining characteristics of modern civic identity. Torn between duty and inclination, turned ever inward in desire and outward for its satisfaction the modern citizen is both divided and disorientated.[12] He can neither tell what nor where he is. Nowhere is this enfeebling inner division more completely realized than in the bourgeois, of whom Rousseau offers an infamous account early in *Emile*.

---

[9] I am suggesting that his teaching is fully expressed only in two ways, the radically denatured citizen of *The Government of Poland* and *Discourse on Political Economy* and the natural education of the ordinary man in and towards nature described in *Emile*. Of a potential education of the philosophic and natural man I would suggest Rousseau offers observations but no program. I take seriously his claim in *Emile*, "All rare cases are outside the rules." Rousseau, *Emile*, 245.

[10] Rousseau, *Emile*, 35.

[11] Strauss, *Natural Right*, 253.

[12] Judith Shklar, *Men and Citizens* (Cambridge: Cambridge University Press, 1969), 5.

5 Rousseau and the Redefinition of Nature and Education 153

He who in civil order wants to preserve the primacy of the sentiments of nature does not know what he wants. Always in contradiction with himself, always floating between his inclinations and his duties, he will never be either man or citizen. He will be good neither for himself nor for others. He will be one of these men of our days: a Frenchman, and Englishman, a bourgeois. He will be nothing.[13]

The bourgeois is as much nowhere as nothing, as much lost as empty. In response, Rousseau offers two educations, one seeks to place the student, the other seeks to preserve him, both seek to reconcile the internal schism. This over-arching goal explains the apparent contradiction between the radically collectivist education of *The Government of Poland* and *Discourse on Political Economy* and the individualist education of *Emile*. The ultimate educational goal in both cases is a curative teaching that removes men from the disorientating bifurcated existence of selfish selflessness, of living for oneself through others that Rousseau captures so powerfully in the *Discourse on the Origins of Inequality*. A complete education, either in duty or nature is the only cure for men who only "know how to be happy and content with themselves on the testimony of others rather than their own."[14] Moreover an education in completeness, an education aimed not at drawing the soul upward but rather at resolving division sits outside the preceding ordinal and diuretic conception of education.

The obvious and radical differences between the education of the moral citizen and Emile tempt the reader to conclude that Emile's education is superior to that of the citizen of either the *Constitution of Poland* or *The Social Contract*. The celebration of natural goodness might suggest that the collective is inferior to the individual pupil. The temptation to rank the two educations leads to an equally erroneous conclusion that the collective education of the virtuous citizen is Rousseau's vision of a specifically civic education whereas *Emile* is a singularly natural even rustic education. However, the criterion of completeness provides only for a horizontal appraisal. Unlike his predecessors, Rousseau conceives of

---

[13] Rousseau, *Emile*, 40.
[14] Rousseau, *Discourse on the Origin of Inequality*, 80.

nature as a broad principle that through education or cultivation may be either nurtured or uprooted. For Rousseau nature is not a ladder but a fork in the road.[15] The education of the moral citizen is the education of the man *of* society (albeit a society defined by duty not *amour-propre*). Emile's education also possesses a strong civic element, but he is nature's citizen, schooled in its lessons and living among but not of society.

This chapter focuses primarily on the educational project described in Rousseau's *Emile*. It is the most fully realized of Rousseau's educational writings and Rousseau possesses a faith in its practicality largely absent from the discussion of the moral citizen. Nonetheless this duality makes Rousseau unique. His presentation of two distinct but not philosophically discrete accounts of civic education appears on first pass to provide the reader with a contradiction and a choice. However, Rousseau insists that he is a systematic thinker, the writings are an intended unity.[16] Taking him at his word suggests that a full understanding of one education can reasonably be supposed to rest at least partially on an understanding of the other. The other in question is the radically denaturing education of the citizen that Rousseau offers most explicitly in *The Government of Poland* and *The Discourse on Political Economy*. Rousseau offers in these two loci a totalizing vision of education complete in its effort to displace nature and its inclinations with a love of the state and to re-found individual identity on the artificial ground of civic duty. The totalizing character of this education makes itself most apparent in the breadth of its intention and the early age in which it commences.

> The newly-born infant, upon first opening his eyes, must gaze upon the fatherland, and until his dying day should behold nothing else. Your true republican is a man who imbibed love of the fatherland, which is love of the liberty, with his mother's milk.[17]

---

[15] Arthur Melzer, *The Natural Goodness of Man* (Chicago: University of Chicago Press, 1990), 103.
[16] Melzer, *Natural Goodness of Man*, 9.
[17] Jean Jacques Rousseau, *The Government of Poland*, trans. Willmoore Kendall (Indianapolis: Library of the Library of the Liberal Arts, 1972), 19.

5 Rousseau and the Redefinition of Nature and Education

The conjunction of politically paternal and domestically maternal imagery points to the ultimate displacement of the latter by the former. While the initial period of complete neo-natal dependence must necessarily come to an end no such political weaning is necessary or even desirable for the education of the denatured citizen. The pairing of these two at the outset points to a key element of education for both duty and inclination: the careful nurturing and guiding of instinct and eros. In the case of instinctual filial affection that instinct is, for Rousseau's citizen, carefully shepherded away from the ground of nature and toward the new country of duty.[18] It is utterly transformed, all that is retained of the original is its locus and force, its expression and object are wholly artificial and introduced by education.

This is not to suggest that the denatured citizen is somehow free of individual drive and identity. The new citizen still feels his existence as occurring within him, but in important ways it is not his to own, nor is it primarily about him. It is *his* concern, but it concerns only others. For Rousseau the transformation of *amour-propre* comprises the most powerful example of this change of sentiment's character and object. This previously anti-social passion for distinction undergoes a profound metamorphosis becoming a patriotism that seeks the conspicuous distinction not of the individual but the collective identity.[19] Rousseau describes this transformation of sentiment most succinctly in *The Social Contract*, a text which in many ways works out the institutional arrangements best suited to the denatured citizen.

> This passage from the state of nature to the civil state produces quite a remarkable change in man, for it substitutes justice for instinct in his behavior and gives his actions a moral quality they previously lacked. Only then, when the voice of duty replaces physical impulse and right

---

[18] Allan Bloom, "Rousseau's Critique of Liberal Constitutionalism," in *The Legacy of Rousseau*, eds. Clifford Orwin and Nathan Tarcov (Chicago: University of Chicago Press, 1997), 148.
[19] Ibid.

replaces appetite, does man, who had hitherto taken only himself into account, find himself forced to act from other principles and to consult his reason before listening to his inclinations.[20]

This passage first strikes the reader in its remarkable influence and anticipation of Kant. In the interaction between the inclinations and the sense of duty we begin to see the outlines of the hero of the *Groundwork of the Metaphysics of Morals*. Rousseau's ideal is freedom from selfishness, the freedom to choose rightly. Rousseau's citizen counters selfishness at every opportunity and is defined by an education premised on such countering of the natural self. This education, effectively independent of the citizen's nature, by rendering it operationally ineffective erases natural difference. In suppressing nature Rousseau institutes a denatured equality. The virtuous citizen's education is the mirror image of the education of Emile to be discussed below, Emile's education is for everyone because it is premised on the development of sentiments shared by all and not the more meagerly apportioned reason.[21] The virtuous citizen's education is equally for all by dint of the common ability to educate and sublimate, if not fully eradicate, those same common sentiments.

The lingering presence of inclination represents Rousseau's concession to the intractability of nature. Nature can be transformed, sublimated, and redirected but it may not be wholly removed. The citizen may never be wholly denatured, but his lingering idiosyncratic inclinations can be rendered irrelevant to his considerations. Nature endures, like the faint recollections of the virtuous citizen's neotany. It endures in echoes of the vacated grounds of his initial existence no longer informing his actions or possessing the vitality to divide his self.[22] In this regard too Rousseau's virtuous citizen is Emile's opposite number. Emile is the natural man who lives among and unmoved by society and its prejudices. The virtuous citizen is the converse, wholly a creature of society he lives among his vestigial inclinations but remains unmoved by them.

---

[20] Jean Jacques Rousseau, "*On the Social Contract or Principles of Political Right*," in *The Basic Political Writings*, ed. Donald Cress (Indianapolis: Hackett Publishing, 1987), 150–151.

[21] Masters, *The Political Philosophy of Rousseau* (Princeton: Princeton University Press, 1968), 93.

[22] Melzer, *Natural Goodness*, 103.

A Savage for the City: The Education of Emile

The perdurability of inclinations in the virtuous citizen of *The Government of Poland* and *The Social Contract* implies the need to transform that which cannot be excised. For the moral citizen certain aspects of his individuality fit this description; in *Emile*, the education is civic to the extent that Rousseau recognizes a similar intractability of social fact. Emile must live among men, but Emile may be prepared in his nature for that experience, tempered in such a way that when he inevitably moves into society its corrosive Glaucusian effects can be checked. In this regard Emile becomes the romantic hero of Rousseau's bildungsroman as the noble savage constitutes the tragic hero of the *Discourse on the Origins of Inequality*.

To the extent that the education of the moral citizen involves dissolving nature Emile's education contains an equally powerful element of prophylaxis. The shielding of his nature is as fundamental to Emile's education as its displacement is to the moral citizen of *The Government of Poland*. Preserving nature, and its role as the guiding principle, is ever present in Rousseau's mind as he educates Emile. He is guided by it as surely as he placed it at his back in *The Government of Poland*. Rousseau draws out the tragic and inevitable social element shared with *Discourse on Inequality* when he resigns himself to the necessity of Emile living in society.

> But consider, in the first place, that although I want to form the man of nature, the object is not, for all that, to make him a savage and to relegate him to the depths of the woods. It suffices that, enclosed in a social whirlpool, he not let himself get carried away by either the passions or the opinions of men, that he see with his eyes, that he feel with his heart, that no authority govern him beyond his own reason.[23]

This passage is critical to understanding the education Rousseau presents in *Emile*. By acknowledging that Emile's education prepares him for life among men Rousseau makes evident the practical intent and immediacy

---

[23] Rousseau, *Emile*, 255.

of the work. Rousseau sets this against his pessimistic acknowledgment early in the *Emile* that the alternative education, that of the virtuous citizen, is fatally dependent on broad social and institutional transformations no longer possible. Rousseau laments that the very words *fatherland* and *citizen* no longer contain plausible meanings, the triumph of Christianity and the advent of mass society has proscribed both such a conception of the state and of the citizen.[24] These factors constitute the most immediate and critical difference between Rousseau's two educations. Emile's education does not require societal transformation as either a necessary condition or an ultimate consequence. Emile may be formed in nature's image despite society; he requires only a good teacher, not a good society.[25]

Rousseau's assertion that Emile's education may occur within and despite a corrupting social order serves to do more than simply increase the chances of such an education's successful execution. Emile's education is aimed at fitting him to live in society but not *of* society. As a result, Emile's education takes on an almost Augustinian tone, Rousseau's student moves among men and alongside politics while remaining unaffected by the corrosive effects of either. At first glance Emile seems to occupy a position in relation to his fellow citizens not unlike that of the philosophic student and indeed the philosopher as described by Plato, Cicero, and Locke. Emile stands outside the city in every sense, suggesting obvious sympathies between the House of Cephalus and Rousseau's rustic retreat. However, Emile is not, as Rousseau continually reminds the reader, an ideal student. Emile's privileged position is solely a result of education. Emile is not intellectually elevated, his education is not contingent as much on nature as teacher; instead, Emile is morally elevated, an elevation consequent on a common nature's contact with uncommon education.[26]

The remarkable consequences of the conjunction of uncommon teacher with common student render Rousseau's revolution in education every bit as dramatic as Locke's. Such a conjunction and outcome

---

[24] Rousseau, *Social Contract*, 225, *Emile* 40, n. 8.
[25] Roger Masters, *Political Philosophy of Rousseau*, 93.
[26] John Plamenatz, "Rousseau: The Education of Emile," *The Proceedings of the Philosophy of Education Society of Great Britain* (July 1972): 179.

5 Rousseau and the Redefinition of Nature and Education 159

are premised on a single, central assertion. Rousseau states simply and unambiguously: "Everything is good as it leaves the hand of nature."[27] The preservation of this natural goodness is the object of Emile's education. The central pillar of Emile's civic education is just translation of natural goodness, by means of its carefully guided development into an authentic sociality and a natural citizenship. Rousseau, in his account of natural goodness shares some common ground with the Ciceronian seminal imagery of the *inchoata intelligentia* and its explicitly ontological imperative toward the just. Two important differences set Rousseau off from Cicero. First and most crucially Rousseauan man is born with a natural goodness and not a natural propensity for justice. Emile and all others on Rousseau's account are born with a faculty that does not require the city for its development. To be born for justice is to be born for politics in a way that innate goodness need not be. The teleological character of Cicero's account represents a further distinction between the two accounts. The natural goodness of Rousseau's man does develop and expand but it does not possess the specific teleological arc that being "born for justice" must.[28]

It is by no means obvious to Rousseau how he might achieve this latter goal, the preparation of the naturally good student for life in society. Rousseau's *Second Discourse* is in part an account of how easily and almost invariably such a project fails. This failure starkly illuminates the educational structure of the *Emile*. In the *Discourse on the Origins of Inequality* Rousseau presents an account of the various moments in the history of man in which his nature has accreted new social corruptions, moving from a being almost devoid of ego, through *amour de soi* and into *amour-propre*. The *Emile* charts a converse course, that of nature carefully shepherded. Emile's sentimental education runs nature's intended course, from a simple newborn, through sentience and sensitivity, to reason, sociality, and finally full humanity defined by deep sentiment inclined positively toward both individual and species.[29]

---

[27] Rousseau, *Emile*, 37.
[28] *De Leg.* I.x.28.
[29] David Owen, "History and Curriculum in Rousseau's *Emile*," *Educational Theory* 32 (1982): 129.

It is critical to establish the similarity between the Rousseau's more explicitly political *Discourse on Inequality* and the *Emile* because the structural similarity of the two accounts of human development powerfully inclines the reader toward the civic component of the "natural education" of *Emile*. Rousseau provides further testimony to the deep similarity between the two educations, more than a little ironically, through the similarities in the means by which Emile is educated and the noble savage corrupted. It is in society that the savage learns *amour-propre* and it is in a wholly manufactured and stage-managed artificial society that Emile receives his natural education.[30] Both men experience their education as a series of experiences and sensations and not as a set of lessons and maxims. Both learn in spite of themselves, both are shaped gradually and almost imperceptibly.

The root of Emile's natural education is the recognition that as much as the moral citizen must be estranged from his nature, Emile must ever be drawn back into it. To preserve Emile's natural and original goodness it is essential to affirm first and foremost its boundaries and to teach him to be content within them. As Rousseau more broadly implores:

> O man, draw your existence up within yourself, and you will no longer be miserable. Remain in the place which nature assigns to you in the chain of being. Nothing will be able to make you leave it.[31]

This is Rousseau's cardinal injunction and Emile is forever drawn back to it. In contrast the bourgeois man is moulded in the rejection of the principle, in its perfect corruption. Defined by *amour-propre* modern man represents the fullest incarnation of man living outside himself, lost to the grounds of his existence.

Pedagogically the moral citizen of the *Government of Poland* and the *Discourse on Political Economy* represents the salutary transformation of *amour-propre:* the citizen virtuously estranged from himself. Nonetheless he too lives outside of himself. Emile's education, hinged to nature, seeks

---

[30] Judith Shklar, *Men and Citizens*, 148.
[31] Rousseau, *Emile*, 83.

instead a naturally good resignation. Emile's education allows him to retain his nature and thus his independence. It aims at creating a decent citizen who is primarily at home in nature, at home in himself.

After Locke: Rousseau's Education in Sense and Experience

The revolutionary character of his naturalistic pedagogy of retrieval and prophylaxis can obscure the extent to which Rousseau seeks to educate, to cultivate, and even transform Emile. The importance of preserving the pupil's natural and original goodness does not suggest to Rousseau an education meant to freeze the pupil in prelapsarian innocence. Rousseau founds Emile's education on the natural rather than against it, in so doing he seeks to encourage rather than stifle instinct, inclination, and sentiment. Rousseau's pedagogy balances the forces of nature and teacher, of Emile's natural progress and his tutor's careful and constant attention. Ultimately this leads Rousseau to take on Locke's conclusions regarding childhood and the centrality of experience and sensation to education but to reject the mechanism of habituation as the means to the good citizen.

In introducing the question of education in the preface to *Emile* Rousseau observes that countless books have been written on the subject with, in his estimation, very little useful being said. Those who have written on education before remain unnamed with one exception.

> In spite of so many writings having as their end, it is said, only what is useful for the public, the first of all useful things, the art of forming men, is still forgotten. After Locke's book *my subject was still entirely fresh*, and I am very much afraid that the same will be the case after mine.[32] (my italics)

---

[32] Ibid., 33.

Rousseau's all too typical dismissal of Locke conceals the deep sympathies between the two authors on the question of education. Counter to expectations Rousseau engages with Locke, in *Emile* at least, on a level and with an intensity matched perhaps only by his engagement with Plato. Despite Rousseau's initial dismissal, this encounter is more complex than it first appears, colored by both divergence and concurrence. Centrally, and still remarkably novel at the time of *Emile's* composition, is the shared belief in the principle and idea of childhood, a belief that owes a conceptual if not a substantive intellectual debt to Locke. Both philosophers consider childhood as an ontologically distinct period in a human life, one whose unique and transitory essence is of unparalleled import to the conduct of education. Nonetheless, later in the same passage, so initially dismissive of Locke, Rousseau suggests: "Childhood is unknown."[33] The indictment is clear: even after all of Locke's efforts childhood *remains unknown*. As such Rousseau both affirms and condemns Locke. Along with Locke he acknowledges the centrality of childhood to teaching while denying that Locke understood the true nature of that acknowledged. Locke has asked the right question, but provided the wrong answer. In this opening salvo Rousseau restates the critique of Locke first offered in the *Discourse on the Origins of Inequality*.[34] According to Rousseau, Locke no more correctly identifies the natural in man in the *Two Treatises* than he identifies the true nature of childhood in *Some Thoughts Concerning Education*.

Rousseau's initial and profound difference concerning the specific nature of childhood does not preclude a later identification with several of Locke's most primordial assertions. Early in Book I of *Emile* Rousseau clearly echoes Locke's critique of both innate ideas and the role they play in education. Rousseau adopts Locke's strong sensationalist position and as such is equally concerned with even the most minor details of neonatal care. Like Locke, Rousseau regards these as nothing less than first lessons.

---

[33] Ibid.
[34] Consider in particular the critique of private property and the labour theory of value that commences Part Two of *The Discourse on Inequality* and marks a high point of Rousseau's rhetorical brilliance.

5 Rousseau and the Redefinition of Nature and Education 163

> I repeat: the education of man begins at his birth; before speaking, before understanding, he is already learning. Experience anticipates lessons. The moment he knows his nurse, he has already acquired a great deal. One would be surprised at the knowledge of the coarsest man if one followed his progress from the moment of his birth to where he is now.[35]

Rousseau goes so far as to calculate a rough estimate of the amount of our learning so characterized. Roughly half of all human learning, Rousseau contends, occurs either before the age of recollection or after in the form of imperceptible "lessons" of sense experience never formally propounded or encountered as explicit instruction.[36] Humans, as sentient beings, are constantly learning and it is our sentience and not our reason that provides for this constant education. So, Rousseau's apparent obsessions with swaddling, like Locke's fascination with the movements of the human digestive tract, were not oddities but inevitable lessons. Here Rousseau, though he remains revolutionary in most other aspects, moves back, past Locke. He moves all the way back to his other educational source, back to Plato. As in *Republic* so too in *Emile*, from birth intellectual lessons are taught by way of the handling of the body. Plato teaches order and law through the rhythm (*nomos*) of neo-natal rocking. Rousseau takes the technique but rejects the lesson. Instead of teaching order through the rhythm of Plato's rocking Rousseau encourages liberty through the rejection of swaddling. Despite Rousseau's earlier contentions concerning the epistemic status of infancy he accepts a central pedagogic contention of both Locke and Plato: education begins before reason's emergence and the intellect may be shaped by lessons administered to the body.

The consensus between Locke and Rousseau specifically concerning the role of the senses as the constant teacher of childhood doubtless comprises the point of their deepest agreement. This sympathy leads Rousseau to concern himself, very much as Locke does, with controlling and even fabricating the experiences of childhood. The sensationalist tutor recognizes in each experience a potential lesson. This recognition,

---

[35] Ibid., 62.
[36] Ibid.

along with others, leads Locke to recommend against boarding schools and toward the careful supervision of childhood experience. For Locke, the experiential education demands attention to the arena of learning. Rousseau takes the principle even further. For Rousseau, education in experience demands more than a sound arena, it demands a careful script, a stage. Rousseau moves education from carefully constructed lessons and the restriction of certain sorts of activities and relations into a thoroughly controlled and almost theatrical early existence.[37] Rousseau's Emile lives in a sort of pedagogic bubble, the most quotidian encounters, as apparently trivial as a dispute over beans and melon seeds, invariably turn out to have been wholly contrived for his education.[38] Rousseau, playing the role of tutor in *Emile*, is extremely reluctant to offer explicit lessons. Instead, the role of tutor seems to require a careful attention and tracking of his charge's natural curiosity and the careful construction of experiences that are then placed in the path of that curiosity.[39]

In terms reminiscent of Locke, Rousseau characterizes the course of education as entailing the construction of a cognitive chain of learning, drawn into conjunction one rung at a time by the pupil's natural curiosity.

> There is a chain of general truths by which all the sciences are connected with common principles out of which they develop successively. This chain is the method of philosophers. We are not dealing with it here. There is another entirely different chain by which each particular object attracts another and always shows the one that follows. This order, which fosters by means of constant curiosity the attention that they all demand is the one most men follow and, in particular is the one required for children.[40]

The role of Emile's tutor is to ever orient his gaze a little farther up the ladder and make sure that the appropriate experience is at hand

---

[37] Amelie Oksenberg Rorty, "Rousseau's Educational Experiments," in *Philosophers on Education*, ed. Amelie Oksenberg Rorty (London: Routledge, 1998), 250.
[38] Rousseau, *Emile*, 99.
[39] Julia Simon, "Natural Freedom and Moral Autonomy: Emile as Parent, Teacher and Citizen," *History of Political Thought* 36 (1995): 24.
[40] Rousseau, *Emile*, 172.

5 Rousseau and the Redefinition of Nature and Education 165

for Emile when his curiosity naturally leads him to reach for the next rung. Admittedly, it may be fairly charged of such an education that it possesses a dubious authenticity.[41] If natural curiosity has as its experiential substance only the unrecognized simulacra of nature how does such an education create a natural pupil? In part the answer, as we will discuss below, is that Emile's experiential education is primarily propaduetic, it prepares and initially protects him from the full and necessarily less manageable experiences of love, desire and even philosophy and even geometry. Speaking carefully only of the last while subtly suggesting the full range of childhood experience directed at adult character Rousseau contends

> To bound from one end of the room to the other, to judge a ball's bounce while still in the air, to return it with a hand strong and sure-such games are less suitable for a grown man than useful for forming him.[42]

The lessons may be simulacra but inevitably they draw the pupil toward nature's truth, whatever the motions in question. Always Rousseau attends the pupil's progression, aware that a sudden leap forward can scupper the tenuous chain of natural knowing drawn from experience. At the same time, Rousseau's reader is led to wonder whether Jean-Jacques' student or Rousseau's reader is shown, can reach for or even read of the final rung on the ladder of learning.

Implicit in Rousseau's pedagogic vision of a carefully shepherded and ever developing curiosity is a strong conception, again in common with Plato, Cicero, and Locke, of age-appropriate teaching. The chain of learning is not merely an epistemic account it is also an ontological account. Rousseau facilitates each step taken by natural curiosity not only by education but with constant attention to the unbidden and yet inevitable progress of nature. Locke, by Rousseau's lights, may not have

---

[41] Simon, "Natural Freedom and Moral Autonomy," 24 n9.
[42] Rousseau, *Emile*, 147.

comprehended the true nature of childhood but he nonetheless recognized the principle that a child's education must always be informed by his development.[43]

Rousseau contends that the attempt to teach children beyond their age produces not prodigies and precocious intellects rather it results in studied mimicry and distorted natures.[44] Moving quickly on from the banal Rousseau reveals that there is more to educational principle than the simple and modern educational idea of age appropriateness or "readiness."[45] Rousseau sees a critical lesson in the very limits of development. Emile is to learn at the pace dictated not only by the chain of his curiosity but also by the dictates of nature's necessity. Rousseau, Emile's constant tutor, ensures that the boy's curiosity never chases past what it is possible at his age to know. Emile's experiences are carefully constructed to appeal to both his natural curiosity and to necessity as those develop over the course of his childhood. Emile is educated to be curious only about that which is within the boundaries of his slowly expanding existence.

> A child knows that he is made to become a man; all the ideas he can have of man's estate are opportunities of instruction for him; but he must remain in absolute ignorance of ideas of that estate which are not within his reach. My whole book is only a constant proof of this principle of education.[46]

Rousseau justifies this principle above all else by asserting that the ground of Emile's education is an undivided existence. Stopping Emile's curiosity from leaping too early into adulthood, Rousseau wishes to preclude the fatal step outside of self that initiates an internal longing and concomitant sense of absence. Untrammeled curiosity violates Rousseau's fundamental injunction: "O man, draw your existence up within yourself, and you will no longer be miserable."[47] As such Emile's curiosity is

---

[43] Locke, *Some Thoughts*, sec. 195.
[44] Rousseau, *Emile*, 89–90.
[45] R.S. Peters, *Essays on Educators* (London: Allen & Unwin, 1981), 19.
[46] Rousseau, *Emile*, 178.
[47] Ibid., 83. This critique of curiosity per se will have real consequences for both character and politics that we will return to in the closing of this chapter.

5 Rousseau and the Redefinition of Nature and Education

not merely guided it is deliberately restricted. Curiosity is never allowed to turn to fancy and imagination, to move beyond the realms of the possible. The same can not be said for the reader. As he draws Emile and Jean-Jacques into imaginative existence the very structure of the work insists on an existence outside itself, a perspective unavailable to either student or teacher, reserved only for Rousseau and his readers.

Rousseau's debt to Locke, especially concerning the primacy of experience and the uniquely transitory status of childhood patently defies his initial assertion that Locke had contributed nothing of use to the understanding of education. Rousseau differs as profoundly with Locke in the substance and object of the pedagogy he recommends as he does in his assessment of the character and relevance of human nature. For Rousseau, at its most basic, Locke's education proposes means that cannot serve their educational end. This contention, that Locke proposes a crude pedagogical alchemy, remains the essential element of Rousseau's critique, the aspect that informs all others. Locke, Rousseau maintains, vainly imagines that out of a mechanistic education he can form a rational subject.[48] Rousseau accuses Locke of misconstruing the developmental nature of childhood and of ignoring reason's place in that development. Reasoning with children, Rousseau contends, confuses the end of education with its means. Reasoning with a child merely teaches him the phrases and affectations of reason without inculcating the faculty itself, it is to misconstrue the nature of reason as a mere habit acquired and not the realization at education's completion of a distinct faculty.[49]

Rousseau's critique of Locke attacks both the perceived attempt to prematurely cultivate rationality and the reliance on habit as the central pillar of his pedagogy. On the question of habit Rousseau opposes Locke absolutely. Rousseau goes so far as to suggest that "The only habit that a child should be allowed is to contract none."[50] Rousseau's rejection of habit rests on the belief that habit inevitability transforms itself into dependence. Habituation, he contends, first constructs and then reifies

---

[48] Cropsey, *Political Philosophy and the Issues*, 323.
[49] Rousseau, *Emile*, 89. It is important to point out that Rousseau's interpretation of Locke's pedagogic position on education is controversial to say the least. For an alternate interpretation of the role of rationality in Lockean pedagogy see the previous chapter.
[50] Rousseau, *Emile*, 63.

the needs of the student within an artificial framework of expectation. The pupil's identity becomes inextricably sewn up with a pattern of actions. Inevitably a pupil so educated begins to demand that the world comply with his internal patterning and when, as it must, the world fails the pupil experiences this failure as privation. Habit breeds expectation and expectation moves the self beyond his natural borders, into a future he cannot wisely depend upon. Habit extends need forward in time, making us dependent on that thing most we can last count upon, that which does not yet exist.[51]

Rousseau eschews habituation for a second pedagogic and, more significantly, a moral reason. To the extent that regularity inculcates in the pupil a routine-based sense of self it convinces the pupil of the permanence of his place. Routine and habit encourage a mistaken belief in fortune's predictability. Such a lesson encourages both a temporally expansive imprudence and a concomitant constriction of empathy's scope. Politically and pedagogically Rousseau rejects habituation on grounds that echo and reaffirm his rejection of Plato. Rousseau discerns in habituation a substitute principle of social differentiation intended to replace the now disqualified nature. Rousseau charges Lockean education, education through habituation, with preparing men for one role, one job, one rank just as surely as the twinned conceptions of nature and the noble lie in Plato's *Republic*.[52]

For Rousseau, to the degree that it defines the horizons of one's experience on a moral level, habituation defines the central moral sentiment: empathy. Rousseau understands empathy as the moral sentiment that allows us to have concern for others through the identification with their suffering. Most essentially, in an insight he shares with Adam Smith, Rousseau recognizes that at its heart empathy involves an imaginative act of identification with the condition of others. Where one cannot imagine, one cannot empathize.

---

[51] Tracy Strong, *Jean-Jacques Rousseau, The Politics of the Ordinary* (London: Sage Publications, 1994), 115.

[52] Cropsey, *Political Philosophy and the Issues*, 329.

Why are kings without pity for their subjects? Because they count on never being mere men. Why are the rich so hard toward the poor? It is because they have no fear of becoming poor. Why does the nobility have so great a contempt for the people? It is because a noble will never be a commoner.[53]

In Lockean terms, Rousseau maintains, to be a king, to be a rich person, a noble, is to practice a series of habits, to grow accustomed to a specific set of ways of being in the world, and to give them a status and permanence that masquerades as nature. Each of the groups Rousseau identifies possess identities hinged on future expectations. These are then, inevitably, attached to assessments both about themselves and others. Somewhat counter-intuitively Rousseau draws the opposite conclusion about those who live under tyrannical, arbitrary, or unstable forms of rule. Such individuals, by dint of the precarious nature of their existence, are more readily able to identify with the misfortune of others because they cannot rule out such misfortune for themselves. Precariousness, the very anti-thesis of a habit driven life, encourages empathy, furthermore it encourages the central tenet of Rousseau's education of Emile, an informed attention to necessity. An awareness of future risk encourages charity and discourages the thoughtless assumptions of permanence that cultivate unconscious forms of dependence.

To contract no habits is both a pedagogic and a moral imperative for Rousseau. The only habit Emile may acquire is versatility, in essence the habit of having no habit at all. The absence of habit trains him for the vicissitudes of fortune and teaches him to empathize with others, to identify with humanity in all its variety rather than with the narrow ways shared in common within a given class. Ultimately the refusal to settle habits in the soul of the student allows for sentiment and character to grow and expand along lines and on a schedule consistent with the imperatives of nature not society.

---

[53] Rousseau, *Emile*, 224.

The Lesson of Necessity

The ability to recognize the capriciousness of fortune and the strength to reject the temptations of routine prepare Emile for the full encounter with the defining external fact of his education: Nature. Nature plays a dual role in the education of Emile. Nature appears as the essential and primordial element of Emile's person. But nature also appears as an external fact or facet of his existence, nature *is* the primary world that Emile inhabits and the apparent source of his experience. In particular, Emile's experience of nature leads him to see in it equally the origins of necessity and the sources of limitation. In revealing nature to Emile in these terms, Rousseau offers an almost perfect inversion of the earlier considered tradition in education. While previously the student's unique nature provided the limits to teaching now nature reconceived as a fact about the world provides the limits and potential of his education. It is not the facts of Emile's nature which constrain his education but rather the facts of the world he finds himself in. This informative principle of Rousseau's pedagogy appears early in Emile's education, in the distinction drawn between dependence on others and dependence on things.

> Keep the child in dependence only on things. You will have followed the order of nature in the progress of his education. Never present to his undiscriminating will anything but physical obstacles or punishments which stem from the actions themselves and which he will recall on the proper occasion. Without forbidding him to do harm, it suffices to prevent him from doing it. Experience or impotence alone ought to take the place of law for him.[54]

Following the order of nature, Rousseau makes clear, is both an admonition to right pedagogical technique and a distinct lesson in itself. Following the order of nature not only allows for a natural education but it provides Emile with a daily confirmation of the limits of his existence. Allowing nature and natural causes to both restrain and punish Emile teaches an appreciation of and a healthy resignation toward nature's

---

[54] Ibid., 85.

5 Rousseau and the Redefinition of Nature and Education 171

multivariate inevitabilities.[55] By presenting to Emile this lesson early and often Rousseau highlights both the potential civic content and the undeniable sympathy between the structure of Emile's education and the education of the moral citizen. Where Rousseau's virtuous citizen is from birth nourished with and raised to gaze upon the fatherland and its laws, Emile is raised and nourished by and in his own nature and taught early its laws. Emile's gaze is deliberately restricted. He lifts his eyes only to those significant others that surround him and of course to his own growing reflection.

The fundamental "law" of nature that Emile is taught by being so exposed to both necessity and natural consequence is the law of resignation. Rousseau argues that in nature human beings, like animals, are naturally inclined toward resignation.[56] In nature, Rousseau contends, we are constantly reminded of our finitude; as there is no apparent remedy at hand for this condition, we learn early to accept it. Rousseau commends the careful translation of this belief into educational practice advising that children, especially young children, should never have things beyond their reach retrieved for them. On the most rudimentary of level Rousseau founds the lesson of necessity: in all things in life, including life itself, man may not have that which is beyond his reach.[57]

Reach comprises both a primary instructional tool and the central metaphor for Rousseau's pedagogy. It first appears in the education of young children, but the lesson once learned appears later as a principle of Emile's life in society.

> The only one who does his own will is he who, in order to do it, has no need to put another's arms at the end of his own: from which follows that the first of all goods is not authority but freedom. The truly free man wants only what he can do and does what he pleases.[58]

---

[55] Masters, *Political Philosophy of Rousseau*, 18.
[56] Rousseau, *Emile*, 82.
[57] Ibid., 66.
[58] Ibid., 84.

Emile's civic education aims at this principle above all others. External nature and necessity put things beyond his grasp, his education teaches him to accept this. The young child is ever taught that there is no more so that as an adult he may only want that which there is.[59] This unity of intention, the resignation of Emile to the existentially defining force of nature echoes a similar resignation of the citizen in the face of the people, laws and force of the *volonte generale* Rousseau describes so dramatically in *On the Social Contract*.[60]

Self-sufficiency's centrality to Emile's education explains the unique and deeply ironic hostility that Rousseau repeatedly directs toward books and book learning. Lest his point be missed by the inattentive reader Rousseau proclaims unequivocally "I hate books."[61] Text based education, Rousseau contends, is the unhealthy alternative to his experiential pedagogy. His animosity originates in the relatively uncontroversial connection he descries between the reading of books and the expansion of the imagination. Rousseau contends that every such expansion is inevitably accompanied by an attendant expansion of desires and expectations, and with it a potential increase in the distance between desire and nature, an increase which inevitably vitiates both contentment and completion.[62] Considering the young Emile, Rousseau concludes that he will appear less well read than some but that "Reading is the plague of childhood and almost the only occupation we know how to give it."[63] What Emile lacks in erudition he more than compensates for in vitality and versatility.

Rousseau initially and perhaps least effectively, condemns books for what he sees as their dubious moral content. Children's stories and in particular fables, Rousseau argues, teach children crude, simplistic and often downright immoral lessons and even when the lessons appear moral the inchoate comprehension of childhood often leads to their unwitting subversion.[64] *Prima facie* this critique appears most amenable

---

[59] Mary Nichols, "Rousseau's Novel Education in the *Emile*," *Political Theory* 13 (1985): 538.
[60] Rousseau, *Social Contract*, 161, 163.
[61] Rousseau, *Emile*, 184.
[62] Ibid., 81.
[63] Ibid., 116.
[64] Ibid., 115.

5 Rousseau and the Redefinition of Nature and Education 173

to remedy. However, Rousseau's attack deepens to condemn not merely the content of reading, but the lesson taught by reading itself, especially in comparison to those lessons taught through the experience of nature and necessity. Rousseau first criticizes the very practice of reading on developmental grounds. He insists that teaching reading to children too early provides them with a corrupting lesson far beyond the tedium of mastering one's ABCs. Too often, Rousseau declares, parents and teachers force reading on children before they could have any possible need of it and before their developing intellects are ready for it.[65] In forcing the child to read before he has need of literacy the tutor inculcates a conception of learning's advantages beyond what is simply useful from the vantage of their own experience. What is worse, that which students have "learned" through reading possesses no real meaning as a lesson in itself, learning becomes merely a way to dazzle the salon and please the tutor.[66] More significantly still, Rousseau worries that reading beyond the limits of the experientially possible, learning from words what cannot be learned yet from the world, encourages appeals to authority. The pupil so educated comes to rely first for his beliefs but inevitably later for his desires on a will and understanding other than his own. Though innocuously delivered by the written word, such learning inevitably leads to dependence on others.

Of course, the absence of reading, or rather by adulthood the absence in Emile of excessive reading, informs not only his character but also his intellect.

> The sphere of his knowledge does not extend farther than what is profitable. His route is narrow and well marked. He is not tempted to leave it, and so he remains indistinguishable from those who follow it. He wants neither to stray from his path nor to shine. Emile is a man of good sense, and he does not want to be anything else. One may very well try to insult him by this title; he will stick to it and always feel honored by it.[67]

---

[65] John Darling, "Rousseau as Progressive Instrumentalist," *Journal of Philosophy of Education* 27 (1993): 28.
[66] Rousseau, *Emile*, 119.
[67] Ibid., 339.

Rousseau's linked imagery of the man of common sense and the possibility of insult place Emile firmly within society and both bounds Emile's intellect and locates him socially. Within society Emile's education acts in a way remarkably different from the education in refinement and ornamental erudition Rousseau so obviously loathes. Emile's education teaches him both contentment within the limits of his existence and more importantly it provides no opportunity for artificial distinctions that might incline Emile toward pride and ostentation.

Rousseau's education focuses on ordinary experience and sensation rather than erudition because he recognizes in conventional students a cultivated carriage that quickly transforms into a principle of social differentiation. Education tends to transform itself into little more than the willing costumer for the all-encompassing masquerade of social existence. Education as ornamental and affected erudition instead of countering ends up aggravating and deepening the effects of *amour-propre*.

> The man of the world is whole in his mask. Almost never being himself, he is always alien and ill at ease when forced to go back there. What he is, is nothing; what he appears to be is everything for him.[68]

The intellectual modesty of Emile's education not only holds his inclinations close to nature it encourages equality by leaving unrealized the artificial differences brought out by higher learning.[69] Emile need not, indeed cannot, attain rank by appeal either to his education or to learned authority. Nature's law of necessity, as expressed in Emile's experiential curriculum, completes its transformation from an agent of differentiation into the common principle of humanity.

---

[68] Rousseau, *Emile*, 230.
[69] Shklar, *Men and Citizens*, 45.

Politics, Citizenship, and Philo-Sophie

Both explicitly and implicitly Rousseau presents his Emile with an education that prepares him to live in society and to weather its politics. At the very heart of *Emile* Rousseau recasts the incompatibility between inclination and duty and between a solitary existence and life in society that he captured so compellingly in his *Second Discourse*. Rousseau mitigates the terrible starkness of the *Discourse on Inequality* with *Emile* by providing for the possibility of two sorts of natural man. He contends that Emile and the Noble Savage are both equally, though differently, men of nature.

> There is a great difference between the natural man living in the state of nature and the natural man living in the state of society. Emile is not a savage to be relegated to the desert. He is a savage made to inhabit cities. He has to know how to find his necessities in them, to take advantage of their inhabitants, and to live, if not like them, at least with them.[70]

Rousseau reveals here the explicitly, though of course not solely, civic intention of Emile's education, and restates the first justification of all education in necessity. Rousseau's intention is informed by three distinct but interconnected, mutually reinforcing imperatives. These are simple necessity, internal natural necessity and external natural necessity. Further Emile's education must countenance his growing desire for intimacy with one particular other. As Emile grows into adolescence an irresistible desire that is inextricably connected to both internal and external necessity, a desire that connects the natural to the conventional inevitably emerges and gains strength. Slowly Rousseau reveals a deeper more fully realized portrait of the natural man in society than that drawn of the noble savage; he is as complete as his sylvan counterpart but hued in colors beyond the bucolic. He is colored by and stands against a more complex horizon. Rousseau explains and informs Emile's social education with the essential inextricability of the roles of owner, husband, father, and citizen. In this inextricability Rousseau reveals that these final lessons

---

[70] Rousseau, *Emile*, 205.

prepare Emile for an explicitly civic education, for the education of an intellect already well-shaped by the sentiments.

Nonetheless Rousseau fundamentally qualifies these connections. The sort of civic life and the sort of city that Rousseau imagines Emile dwelling in are most definitely not the decadent and cosmopolitan cities of *ancien regime* Paris or sprawling London. Rather it is closer to the Calvinist Geneva or perhaps better still Clarens, the outlying mountain village of his epistolary romance, *Julie, ou La Nouvelle Heloise*. Rousseau's contempt for the modern metropolis was complete. Arthur Melzer captures this contempt so perfectly in *The Natural Goodness of Man* that his description bears quoting in its entirety.

> He [Rousseau] is suspicious of liberal cosmopolitanism, wary of the arts and sciences, opposed to pluralism, against technology and industrialism, appalled by commercialism, disgusted by urbanization, revolted by the bourgeoisie, and dead set against "extending the sphere."[71]

Rousseau's contempt for modern living within the city and indeed within politics itself does not lead him, or rather lead him to lead Emile, into the mountains and into the life of a solitary wanderer. Instead, Rousseau resigns himself to the necessity of living among wicked men, men of government, church, court, and marketplace, who will seek to take advantage of Emile. Emile's frankest civic education, if not his first or most profound, will be in the arts of defending both his status and his property against such interlopers.[72] Of particular importance for Emile's civic education is the peculiar ontological status of what he learns to this end. Unlike all the natural and experiential education he received in childhood and early adolescence Rousseau makes it clear to Emile that in learning the defense of his property he is finally learning the ways of convention and artifice essential to social existence. Emile is carefully schooled to understand that the laws and systems he uses are

---

[71] Melzer, *The Natural Goodness of Man*, 109–110.
[72] Rousseau, *Emile*, 457.

5 Rousseau and the Redefinition of Nature and Education

mere shadows of true law, he is taught to live justly engaging them only defensively. But even this requires a degree of worldly education.[73]

> In any event, he [Emile] has lived tranquilly under a government and the simulacra of laws. What difference does it make that the social contract has not been observed, individual interest protected him as the general will would have done, if public violence guaranteed him as the general will would have done, if public violence guaranteed him against individual violence, if the evil he saw done made him love what is good and if our institutions themselves have made him know and hate their iniquities? O Emile, where is the good man who owes nothing to his country?[74]

Rousseau sounds almost Augustinian[75] in his admonishment to Emile. Emile is to live a virtuous life and perhaps if necessity calls to offer his services to his country, but his primary duty is to himself and later to his own. The institutions and affectations of the state that possesses only the "simulacra of laws" affect Emile only in a supervening manner, only on occasions when they are coincident with necessity. The only laws that truly and invariably bind Emile are those of nature and necessity.[76]

That Emile must learn the laws, or at least their simulacra, is perhaps the least significant of the reasons that Jean-Jacques teaches Emile the conventions of civic virtue and city life. Of much greater importance for Rousseau is the inextricable connection between civic virtue and social virtue and Emile's search for a mate. The fundamental principle of Emile's education has been self-sufficiency, at every turn to assiduously eschew dependence on persons, to accept only the limits of nature. But inevitably, albeit postponed as long as possible, Emile comes to long

---

[73] Geraint Parry, "*Emile*: Learning to be Men, Women and Citizens," in *Cambridge Companion to Rousseau*, ed. Patrick Riley (Cambridge: Cambridge University Press, 2001), 260.

[74] Rousseau, *Emile*, 473.

[75] "Hence, even the heavenly city uses the earthly peace on its journey, and it is concerned about and desires the orderly arrangement of human wills concerning the things pertaining to mortal human nature, insofar as it is agreeable to sound piety and religion" St. Augustine, *City of God*. Book XIX, Chapter 17 in *Political Writings*, trans. M.W. Tkacz and D. Kries (Indianapolis: Hackett Publishing, 1994).

[76] Rousseau, *Emile*, 472.

for another. This is perhaps the moment when the incredible influence of his tutor is most obvious. Rousseau has carefully removed all longing for things beyond himself from Emile and ultimately, even appropriately, it is the tutor who introduces Emile to longing that most essential longing beyond oneself, to Sophie.

Rousseau introduces Emile to romantic attachment and then founds civic virtue upon it. The final stage of his education is to extend his concern for himself to concern for another, to in essence draw another up into his existence. What is truly remarkable is not the inevitability of Emile's desire for Sophie but the transformation of that singular and often selfish desire, through Jean-Jacques' careful tutelage, into a concern for all others and a form of civic virtue.[77] As Rousseau remarks "Observe how the physical leads us unawares to the moral, and how the sweetest laws of love are born little by little from the coarse union of the sexes."[78] This is perhaps the single most remarkable pedagogic "rope trick" of Emile's education. In providing Emile with an object for his affections Rousseau appears to teach his charge the ways of a good husband while in reality teaching him the ways of the just citizen. In learning to love, Emile discovers first himself, then the conventions of civic life, and finally the grounds of justice and the social contract.

Rousseau carefully introduces Emile to the idea, truly the ideal, of Sophie in terms that make it clear that the unknown Sophie is to be for Emile a woman like no other. The extraordinary role she must play in Emile's education demands nothing less. Rousseau implies as much when he describes the delicate first conversation with Emile concerning love.

> I shall begin by moving his imagination. I shall choose the time, the place and the objects most favourable to the impression I want to make. I shall, so to speak, call all of nature as a witness to our conversations.[79]

In this first exposition of erotic passion to Emile the central verb is *witness*. It is in the role of witness to his conduct that the actual Sophie

---

[77] Bloom, *Love and Friendship*, 127.
[78] Rousseau, *Emile*, 360.
[79] Ibid., 323.

5 Rousseau and the Redefinition of Nature and Education

most profoundly informs Emile's education. Carefully trained, his education in nature has prepared him finally to live in the eyes of another, he is ready to be witnessed. However, this living in the eyes of another is not that of *amour-propre*, rather it is the final developmental step of Emile's intellect and sentiment. Through the desire to be seen as just in Sophie's eyes Emile completes his own development, he becomes self-conscious.[80]

The content of Emile's self-consciousness, the demands it will make on his conduct, are also implied in the very first conversation about love that Emile has with his tutor. From the first discussion of erotic passion Emile recognizes a singular object but a multiplicity of witnesses. First in priority of these witnesses is Rousseau himself.

> I shall press him [Emile] to my breast and shed tears of tenderness on him, I shall say to him, "You are my property, my child, my work. It is from your happiness that I expect my own. If you frustrate my hopes, you are robbing me of twenty years of my life and you are causing the unhappiness of my old age."[81]

The combination of Sophie and Jean-Jacques weaves a powerful skein around Emile's conduct. It informs in a way structurally similar to *amour-propre* but in substance of a nature diametrically opposed. The expectations of Sophie and the beloved tutor lead the newly self-conscious Emile to consider his actions from their perspective. This is not the living in the eyes of another of the *Discourse on Inequality*; when Emile acts, he considers not what he desires in recognition but what he owes in duty and obligation. Rather than the hopelessly divided conduct of *amour-propre*, the selfish selflessness, Emile's love of both teacher and wife leads to a self-conscious and sentimental selflessness. Emile's selflessness is not born of an ascetic nature or an autonomous reason that concludes on the good independent of sentiment, quite the contrary, inclination draws Emile to duty. It is his affection for both tutor and beloved that inclines Emile toward virtue, because they are worthy he must be worthy. This worthiness quickly takes on broader proportions

---

[80] Bloom, *Love and Friendship*, 133.
[81] Rousseau, *Emile*, 323.

than the trivial challenges of courtship. Inevitably if Emile is to remain worthy of the worthy it must. At the same time, and especially in what follows, the reader cannot help but note that in his continued control of Emile, Jean-Jacques imagines a student who is worthy of but never equal to his teacher. When Emile stops overnight to attend to a pregnant woman and a wounded man and thus misses an appointment with Sophie, she is at first piqued upon his arrival at her home a day late. After explanations are offered Emile implores his beloved:

> Sophie you are the arbiter of my fate. You know it well, you can make me die of pain. But do not hope to make me forget the rights of humanity, They are more sacred to me than yours. I will never give them up for you.[82]

Counter-intuitively perhaps it is the very depth and force of Emile's sentiment for Sophie that leads him to this gentle rebuke. Emile's most profound sentimental inclinations, carefully cultivated by his teacher, now lead him away from selfish action. Translated from the intimate to the civic the same transformation of inclination will lead Emile or others so educated to seek the esteem of their fellow citizens not through personal aggrandizement but its opposite.

Unlike the love, duty, and obligation that Emile feels for his tutor, his love for Sophie possesses a further unique element (beyond the obvious) important to Emile's civic education. At one point Emile, in courting Sophie, is made to walk two leagues from where he stays to her home to see her. In walking this great distance Emile is tempted to stay over but his tutor refuses, reminding Emile of the importance of safeguarding Sophie's reputation. Reputation, Rousseau argues, is central to women's existence in a way wholly different from men. "Opinion is the grave of virtue among men and its throne among women."[83] Setting aside the fairness of Rousseau's contention,[84] the undeniable importance of reputation to Sophie, and of Sophie to Emile, brings to the young pupil an

---

[82] Ibid., 441.
[83] Ibid., 365.
[84] Allan Bloom, *Love and Friendship*, 99.

acceptance of and an attention to convention.[85] Emile develops social acumen in order to safeguard Sophie's reputation, not to expand his. Through a careful education of Emile to her interests Sophie provides Rousseau a way to teach Emile to attend to the ways of society without succumbing to them, to recognize and be sensitive to the effects of *amour-propre* at a safe degree of removal from their influence. Emile will attend to the conventions of society carefully but not selfishly.

Rousseau draws the final civic lessons from Emile's encounter with Sophie, somewhat ironically, out of this forced absence from his beloved. In both the sharpness of its initial realization and the education offered by travel the absence from Sophie undergirds the explicitly civic curriculum of Emile's education. Emile's departure, demanded by his tutor, tests his ability to abide by his word, an abiding that is first understood not in terms of the moral citizen's laws of duty but under the maxim of self-sufficiency. Rousseau establishes as much when as a prelude to enforcing his contract with Emile, a contract whereby Emile consented to be guided without question or objection by Jean-Jacques, he tells the young man that his beloved Sophie has perished. Emile's impassioned reaction, his uncontrolled initial dismay and then indignant anger at being deceived, convince Jean-Jacques that in teaching Emile to love he has failed to fully enshrine the maxim of self-sufficiency. Protecting Sophie from death is beyond Emile's reach, taught to always accept necessity and finitude he has forgotten all in the case of Sophie. Rousseau rebukes Emile in the harshest terms for forgetting his first lesson. "Nature had enslaved you only to a single death. You are enslaving yourself to a second. Now you are in the position of dying twice."[86] Rousseau demands that Emile learns to love Sophie without being enslaved to her; Sophie is worthy of a free man and not a slave, even one enslaved to her. Emile must go, complete his education, and in his absence prove his fidelity, that she may give herself to him "not as an act of grace but as a recompense."[87] To truly love Sophie he must not utterly

---

[85] Joseph Cropsey, *Political Philosophy and the Issues*, 328.
[86] Rousseau, *Emile*, 444.
[87] Ibid., 448.

depend upon her, she cannot be the *sine qua non* of his existence if he is to be free.

> You must be able to tell Sophie that you are leaving her in spite of yourself. Very well be content; and since you do not obey reason, recognize another master. You have not forgotten the promise you made to me. Emile, you have to leave Sophie, I wish it.[88]

Rousseau has both shown that Emile is ready to learn and how much he has already learned. Emile learns the importance of keeping his word, of honoring the obligation he has to his tutor, he has learned to contract.[89] At last Emile is ready to learn about the social contract. Emile's tutor hints that this will be Emile's final lesson, "You believe you have learned everything, and you still know nothing. Before taking a place in the civil order, learn to know it and to know what rank in it suits you."[90] Emile does not assent in his reason but in his sentiment, in his newly acquired self-consciousness. But he has in assenting opened up the final ground for his reason, he can discern between his inclinations, for Sophie and for his tutor. He can weigh and evaluate his inclinations, in so discerning sentiment has borne him to the threshold of reason.

Rousseau makes clear from the outset that the social contract will be the final lesson of Emile's travels with his tutor. The objects and locales of Emile's travels suggest studies of comparative government and not mere sightseeing. Rousseau soon reveals that to this end Emile's travel guides will not be *Baedecker* or *Fodor's* but *Discourse on the Origins of Inequality* and *On the Social Contract*. Emile experiences various types of rule: monarchies, aristocracies, mixed rule and democracy and all are carefully considered, weighed, and evaluated. Eventually Emile's travels bring him to the original context of his departure. The lesson of his departure, imperceptibly drawn out of his character by experience of tutor and beloved, is carefully translated and brought before his intellect in the explicit language of Rousseau's political philosophy.

---

[88] Ibid., 449. Compare with the reasoning process of the moral citizen in *On the Social Contract*, 151.
[89] Strong, *Jean-Jacques Rousseau*, 137.
[90] Rousseau, *Emile*, 448.

5 Rousseau and the Redefinition of Nature and Education

Inasmuch as the essence of sovereignty consists in the general will, it is also hard to see how one can be certain that a particular will always will agree with this general will. One ought rather to presume that the particular will will often be contrary to the general will, for private interest always tends to preferences, and the public interest always tends to equality.[91]

Emile learns the political philosophy of his tutor while traveling. Rousseau's pedagogy demands that these lessons be taught to Emile through travel, his knowledge must always be tied to his experience, to debate questions of government and sovereignty he must experience them. Recalling the earlier condemnation of reading Jean-Jacques eschews the reading even of *The Social Contract* the appeal to its substance even its authority may be made only in conjunction with experience.[92] Emile draws his political principles only from the experience of them in fact. The origins of states, the nature of inequality, the nature of man even the elusive state of nature are taught to Emile only in the context of actual and immediate experiences of the forms of rule generated by institutional appeals to political right.[93]

When Emile returns to Sophie his education appears complete. In his journey he has covered geographic distance and achieved the final essential sentimental distance necessary for civic virtue. Unlike the moral citizen he does not return to a fatherland but merely to a country, one he lives in but not for.[94] His inclinations have been so formed that politically this is enough. His civic education begins when his sentiments are ready for it; his experience of government is the final lesson, appropriate to a grown man rightly educated. Returning to Sophie his education is complete, he understands where he stands and has drawn up into his existence, husband, citizen, owner, and soon father. He returns to the countryside, virtuously, even joyfully, resigned to the life his nature

---

[91] Rousseau, *Emile*, 462–463 compare with *Social Contract*, 203.
[92] It is perhaps useful in this context to consider the closing aphorism of Nietzsche's *Beyond Good and Evil*.
[93] Rousseau, *Emile*, 458.
[94] Ibid., 473.

demands of him. He has no more ambitions, he is satisfied that in politics as in all else, there is no more. Moreover, Rousseau concedes, in the world of *amour-propre* men who are educated both in their nature and in resignation to the finitude of that nature are unlikely to either have cause or opportunity for political adventure. "As long as there are men who belong to the present age, you are not the man who will be sought out to serve the state."[95]

Rousseau's Revolution

Rousseau exploded the traditional connection between the nature of the student and the potential for his education. In their own ways, Plato, Cicero and Locke all embraced this distinction in their careful discriminating between the philosophic education and the civic education. This distinction further belies the epistemologically privileged status of the philosophic student's education. This privilege obviously need not translate into a concurrent political privilege, indeed for different reasons each philosopher suspects that perhaps it is best if it doesn't. Nonetheless, the variegated character of student's natures demanded this distinction and each philosopher embraced it as a fact both intractable and ordinal with the philosophic always superordinate. Rejecting this, Rousseau transformed nature from a principle of distinction into a principle of unification. Instead of focusing on nature's variety he emphasized its commonality. The double movement of natural goodness and natural necessity, of common facts internal and external about humanity and the world led Rousseau to reject the ladder of learning to which Plato, Cicero, and Locke clung. He appears to be the first modern advocate of a deeply democratic and radically egalitarian pedagogy. Whether it is the common education of the radically denatured moral citizen or the natural education, founded on sentiments common to all men of the *Emile*, there seems little room in Rousseau for a naturally superordinate education. But there is a wrinkle, one Rousseau saves for the final page of *Emile*. Emile, married now to Sophie, attends to his ever-present tutor

---

[95] Ibid., 475.

5 Rousseau and the Redefinition of Nature and Education

with news of Sophie's pregnancy. Assuring him that he need not fear that now he must raise his progeny, Emile strangely implores his tutor to stay, and more importantly to stay as his tutor.

> But remain the master of the young masters. Advise us and govern us. We shall be docile. As long as I live, I shall need you. I need you more than ever now that my functions as man begin. You have fulfilled yours. Guide me so that I can imitate you. And take your rest. It is time.[96]

In this singular and final passage Rousseau reasserts the hierarchy between the philosophic and the civic that he appeared to eschew in dividing the healthy pedagogic possibilities for human nature in terms either of duty or inclination. In a very real sense Rousseau returns the status of the philosopher, in relation to his civic student, to a pre-Lockean period. Recall that, as Rousseau himself reminds, Locke leaves his pupil when it is time for him to marry, "But the young gentleman being got within view of matrimony, 'tis time to leave him to his mistress."[97] Rousseau, the philosopher tutor, never leaves his Emile. Moreover, he stays on in the role of *governor*, and governor to a citizenry self-described as docile. He is needed not only to found Emile's character but to keep founding it, forever. Rousseau implies the permanent (if not established as natural) superordinate status of the tutor not only in the use of the language of governance but in the final verb that Emile uses to describe his future relation to his tutor. Emile will *imitate* Jean-Jacques, here the language resembles nothing so strongly as the mimetic language of the *Republic*.[98] Emile appears to be happily reconciled to inherit the true opinions of his tutor, who suddenly reveals himself as not only indispensable but epistemologically privileged. In so doing Rousseau dramatically reinstates the division between knowledge and belief discerned in the other philosophers discussed above. Jean-Jacques takes on the role of Athenian stranger and lawgiver; Emile and Sophie simply "keep the wheel rolling."[99]

---

[96] Ibid., 480.
[97] Locke, *Some Thoughts*, sec. 215.
[98] Plato, *Republic*, 590c–d.
[99] Bloom, *Love and Friendship*, 140.

Rousseau waits till the final page of *Emile* to confess that his education is truly for the ordinary, and that it retains the privileged place of the naturally extraordinary. Concealed at the heart of the *Emile* Rousseau warns the reader as much, both explaining his silence on the superordinate status of the philosopher and dismissing attempts to criticize his silence, "All rare cases are outside the rules."[100] Emile, filled with a civic education but denied that ultimate education in philosophy itself, stands alongside Kleinias and Megillos. The education of Emile admits as much when it identifies as its object both an affirmation of nature and a resignation to it. Striving beyond what may appear possible, no matter how noble, to the extent it rejects necessity and inevitability, appears to Rousseau as a form of dependence and incompleteness. Emile's education prevents him from becoming the bourgeois *nothing* ever seeking after material goods that Rousseau so detests but Emile is also prevented from being the doomed hero contending in a hopeless but honorable enterprise or a saint reaching up to an ever elusive and mysterious God.[101] He is ordinary. His education is predicated on and completed in that ordinariness, "he is a man of common sense."[102] The reader, closing the book, notes the distinction between Jean-Jacques and Rousseau, between the former's studied silence at *Emile's* end and the torrent of philosophy that continued to flow from the latter and which calls from beyond to the philosophic reader.

---

[100] Rousseau, *Emile*, 245.
[101] Nichols, *Rousseau's Emile*, 555.
[102] Rousseau, *Emile*, 339.

6

Adam Smith's Sentimental Education

> Economics are the method; the object is to change the heart and soul.
> Margaret Thatcher, May 1, 1981[1]

Introduction

Until quite recently, scholars most especially economists and historians of economic ideas, have overlooked the unique contribution to the philosophy of civic education that informs both the first and the final books of Smith's monumental *Inquiry into the Nature and Causes of the Wealth of Nations*. This neglect is surprising. The most perfunctory examination of Smith's classic reveals a deep engagement with ancient and modern political philosophy and education; a careful reading of Smith's famous text reveals a work that constantly alludes to the presence of the political and pedagogic in all aspects of economic development. Indeed, in a whole

[1] Cf. John Campbell, *The Iron Lady* (London: Penguin, 2009), 116.

© The Author(s), under exclusive license to Springer Nature
Switzerland AG 2022
G. C. Kellow, *The Wisdom of the Commons*,
Palgrave Studies in Classical Liberalism,
https://doi.org/10.1007/978-3-030-95872-5_6

host of ways the culmination of Smith's argument and account, the fifth and final book of *The Wealth of Nations*, speaks more emphatically and more explicitly to the prerogatives of power than to the imperatives of the marketplace. Book Five culminates in a discussion of politics and the role of government a full third of which is dedicated to the question of education. The significance of Smith's contribution to educational theory in *Wealth of Nations* compelled John Maynard Keynes to comment that it "contains passages which ought to be prefixed to the statutes of every University and College."[2]

Of course, any serious account of Smith's moral and political philosophy must also include an appreciation of the relationship between Smith's two major works, *The Theory of Moral Sentiments* and *The Wealth of Nations*. In this instance, in discussing Smith's thoughts on education I plan to reflect the superstructure of Smith's own philosophy: *The Theory of Moral Sentiments* sits at the center rendering an account of human beings as passionate creatures who long both for the society and the sympathy of others. *The Wealth of Nations* politically and perhaps even tragically brackets this account of how these passionate beings live together and how they are educated and socialized into a society and an economy that shows a dangerous predilection to reduce and mutilate their deeper desire for sympathy and society into a crude and dominating self-interest. It is easy to misconstrue the relationship and even discern a false antipathy between Smith's two texts. Superficially at least, *The Theory of Moral Sentiments* appears to be a work of ethics and *The Wealth of Nations* a work of economics. However, especially when read with an eye to Smith's enduring concern with education and politics they reveal themselves as a set piece of moral and political philosophy. They combine to offer a full and complementary account of the sources of both civic character and corruption in the citizen's passions.

Two reasons, one rhetorical and one philosophical, demand that a contemporary consideration of *The Wealth of Nations* address question of civic education. Rhetorically, Smith is invoked knowingly by the

---

[2] John Maynard Keynes, *Economic History* IV, cf. C.E. Dankert "Adam Smith, Educator," *Dalhousie Review* 47 (1967): 13.

popular proponents of not only liberal capitalism but also by the advocates of an almost uniquely modern critique of liberal education. In brief this critique, the technological or utilitarian critique, argues that as a result of liberal education's failure to conspicuously prepare the pupil for economic life under free-market capitalism it remains ill-suited to the new and novel pedagogical needs of a free-market citizenry and ought therefore to be replaced by vocational and specifically technical training. It is of particular political import today than to show that such a position stands at odds not only with Smith's teaching in *The Theory of Moral Sentiments* but equally at odds with the new science of *The Wealth of Nations*. Rebutting this claim not only recovers Adam Smith for liberal education, an important symbolic act, but also brings back into view Smith's deep insight and profound misgivings about the relationship between commerce, liberty, and citizenship. Ultimately in the larger context of the development of economic and political thought reading Smith as he intended, and thereby grasping the broad scope and significance of *Wealth of Nations*[3] seems an unambiguous and unqualified good in itself.

All of this is not to say that there is nothing at all to the appropriation of Smith by the technological critique both of education and of politics. There is no doubt that the commonly held contention that Smith and the other key figures of the Scottish Enlightenment began the process whereby political economy eclipsed political philosophy bears a great deal of truth.[4] While this is a phenomenon in which Smith participated it is far from obvious that this result represents the author's full intention. As I shall argue, Smith may have been the herald of the new political economy, but he was far from its unambiguous champion. To the contrary, throughout *The Wealth of Nations* we find Smith trying

---

[3] It is for this reason that I deliberately avoid citing or even to some degree considering the notes of Smith's students which comprise the *Lectures on Jurisprudence*. To do so is to erroneously and irresponsibly equate the personae of educator and philosopher. As I will discuss below to use the *Lectures* in this way contradicts authorial intent as revealed in Smith's remarkably scrupulous maintenance and editing of his literary legacy. See Jeffrey Lomonaco, "Adam Smith's 'Letter to the Authors of the Edinburgh Review,'" *Journal of the History of Ideas* 63 (October 2002): 672.

[4] Joseph Cropsey, "Adam Smith and Political Philosophy," in *Essays on Adam Smith*, eds. A.S. Skinner and T. Wilson (Oxford: Clarendon Press, 1975), 132.

to bring politics, virtue, and moral philosophy back in, not to buttress but to temper the enthusiasm for both the new social science and the new economy. A careful examination of Smith's thought reveals a philosophy closely connected and indeed attempting to reconcile the ideas of Locke and Rousseau that went before. Reaching farther back still, at key moments, especially around questions of wealth and virtue, Smith reaches farther back, to Cicero. Smith's efforts at continuity and reconciliation so characteristic of his philosophical temperance, first seen in this great engagement with contemporaries and predecessors is nowhere more keenly felt than in his treatment of education and character in the emerging market economy and liberal polity.

A Civic Reading of the *Wealth of Nations*

Smith was a meticulous author and editor.[5] He wrote and published with a prudence and reserve without doubt learned from the example of John Locke whose influence on both the structure and substance of *Wealth of Nations* is conspicuous throughout. Biographically nothing testifies to Smith's Lockean prudence more than his destruction of hundreds of pages of manuscripts before his death.[6] In his two key works Smith also followed Locke's example in constantly editing new editions throughout his life; at his death he had just completed no less than the sixth revision of *Theory of Moral Sentiments*.[7] In the case of the *Wealth of Nations* the first edition alone was the product of twelve years of work.[8] Smith wrote with tremendous care and attention especially to the architecture of the text, an architecture that is as full of meaning as the words themselves. Helpfully, Smith placed the hermeneutic key to this architecture

---

[5] For an overview of this aspect of Smith's writing see Geoffrey Kellow, "Things Familiar to the Mind: Heuristic Style and Elliptical Citation in *The Wealth of Nations*" *History of the Human Sciences* 24 (2011): 1–18.

[6] Charles Griswold offers an excellent discussion of the genesis and contours of Smith's literary corpus see Griswold, *Adam Smith*, 29–39.

[7] Of course a great deal can also be drawn from the fact that it was *Sentiments* and not *Wealth* which occupied Smith's last years.

[8] Dankert, "Adam Smith", 18.

and philosophy at the very center of *The Wealth of Nations*. The brisk definition of statesmanship and its relation to political economy conspicuously placed at the beginning of Book IV contains the central tension of the work and bears witness to its careful construction.

> Political Economy, considered as a branch of the science of a statesman or legislator, proposes two distinct objects: first, to provide a plentiful revenue or subsistence for the people, or more properly to enable them to provide such a revenue of subsistence for themselves; and secondly, to supply the state or commonwealth with a revenue sufficient for the publick services. It proposes to enrich both the people and the sovereign. (*Wealth*, IV.i.1)[9]

Smith's classification of the relationships within the definition is key. Political Economy is only a "branch" of the science of the legislator. It occurs within, and in pressing the arboreal metaphor, depends upon the other aspects of the science of a legislator. It has no independent existence. Setting aside the clearly stated dependence of political economy on the science of statesmanship the structure of the definition itself reflects and reveals the larger structure of *Wealth of Nations*. By listing the individual and independent subsistence of the citizenry as the first task of government Smith positions *The Wealth of Nations* in the liberal and specifically Lockean camp. The state is no longer directly concerned with ensuring the virtue of either citizen or state it is concerned instead with, as Locke famously defines it, "liberty, health and indolency of the body; and the possession of outward things, such as money, lands, houses, furniture, and the like."[10] Political society is instituted in the name of preservation and not of virtue.[11] The structure of Smith's entire text mirrors the ordering present in his definition. It commences with a

---

[9] Adam Smith, *An Inquiry into the Nature and Causes of the Wealth of Nations,* eds. R.H. Cambell and A.S. Skinner (Indianapolis: Liberty Fund 1981).
[10] John Locke, *A Letter Concerning Toleration* (Indianapolis: Hackett Publishing, 1983), 18.
[11] Joseph Cropsey, *Polity and Economy: An Interpretation of the Principles of Adam Smith* (The Hague: M. Nijhoff, 1957), 40.

lengthy description of the sources of wealth and only after having established these does Smith's definition go on to explain which services this wealth will be drawn upon to provide for.

The text as a whole broadly follows this pattern. However, within the definition and within the text itself lurks an essential contradiction. The definition of Political Economy presents the science of the legislator as prior to its means, the legislator first governs in a way that provides for revenue and only then receives revenue with which to govern. It appears then that the economic originates in the political which is dependent for its existence on the economic; Smith's ontogenetic principle remains deliberately unclear. The same equivocality appears in Smith's account of economic development and in the superstructure of the text itself. *The Wealth of Nations* begins with a relatively unambiguous endorsement of the division of labor and concludes with a condemnation of that division's impact on the character of the citizenry and the nature of liberal capitalist polities. The careful reader discovers a work bracketed by antipathetic (but not ultimately incompatible) assessments of the division of labor, a discovery that leaves the reader with a tragic sense of liberal capitalism. It is this tragic vision that fundamentally informs Smith's treatment of polity, pedagogy, and economy.

Nothing more succinctly reveals the character of Smith's subject than the subtle assessment offered by the title read in full. In choosing to characterize his work as *An Inquiry into the Causes and Nature of the Wealth of Nations* Smith telegraphs a philosophic and epistemic hesitancy starkly *opposed* to the view from the frontispiece of his earlier work in moral philosophy, *The Theory of Moral Sentiments*.[12] Smith's title suggests the incomplete, aporetic, and ultimately tragic character of politics and its study. Inquiries may be ambiguous, they may contain contradictions even incompatibilities; theories on the other hand live and die by their consistency.[13] Even his choice to abjure the definite in favor of the indefinite article places his effort among others, the work is a sortie not a final

---

[12] For an interesting treatment of the title of *The Theory of Moral Sentiments* see Griswold, *Adam Smith*, 44.

[13] A.D. Megill, "Theory and Experience in Adam Smith," *Journal of the History of Ideas* 36 (1975): 90.

statement. Tellingly, this titular ambivalence provides a powerful prelude to the ambiguities in Smith's account of the relation and priority of the economic and the political, a recurring theme present most powerfully in his treatment of character and civic education.

The Division of Labor

Smith marvels at the dynamism and productive potential of the specialization of labor. In almost breathless prose he begins the first chapter of Book I by declaring

> The greatest improvement in the productive powers of labour, and the greater part of the skill, dexterity, and judgment with which it is any where directed, or applied, seem to have been the effects of the division of labour. (I.i.1)

From the outset Smith recognizes that the division of labor possesses significance far beyond the walls of the new and growing manufactures. It is the singular engine transforming the rank, role, and status of the common people.[14] Moreover, Smith clearly believes that at least *materially* the division of labor profoundly improved a lot of the lower classes (I.viii.36). According to Smith, in broader economic terms the division of labor tends to improve not only the lives but the productive character and even the total number of the laboring classes. Tying the division of labor to its material benefits Smith contends that "The liberal reward of labour, as it encourages the propagation, so it increases the industry of the common people" (I.viii.42). On Smith's own account there remains little doubt he holds to the contention that the division of labor is salutary for the economic character of the citizenry, however so holding never

---

[14] Smith uses the terms 'inferior ranks', 'common people' and 'labouring classes' loosely and almost interchangeably to imply what would now be understood as the non-professional working class.

implies that economic character is the total or even primary characteristic of the person.[15]

It is clear from the outset of Smith's discussion that the division of labor is much more than an economic phenomenon. The deeper significance lies in its impact on the structure of society and the status of this new and industrious common people. This import is implied in Smith's closing remarks to the chapter that introduces the concept.

> Compared, indeed, with the more extravagant luxury of the great, his accommodation must no doubt appear extremely simple and easy: and yet it may be true, perhaps, that the accommodation of an European prince does not always so much exceed that of an industrious and frugal peasant, as the accommodation of the latter exceeds that of many an African king, the absolute master of the lives and liberty of ten thousand naked savages. (1.i.11)

The import of this passage is two-fold. First it clearly attaches the transformation of market and production relations to political relations. The common people working in industry are not merely materially better off than the "naked savages." It is clear that the degree to which laborers material conditions exceeds that of "naked savages" is accompanied by an implicit and consonant transformation in political status even civil liberty.[16] The commerce between classes, in all senses, draws the conditions of those classes closer together. That closeness, combined with the cooperation and interdependence that characterize commercial society, herald ever greater economic but also cultural and political improvement.

Smith's remarks reveal the true foundational significance of the return of an economic argument to its origins in the political. Smith the

---

[15] The importance of this distinction is critical to understanding Smith. The economic character is never described as more than one of the 'original principles' or 'whether, as seems more probable, it be the necessary consequence of the faculties of reason and speech' (*Wealth* I.ii.21). Economic Man, as a totalizing definition cannot be construed from Smith's account in *Wealth* setting aside the fuller account offered in combination with *Theory of Moral Sentiments*.

[16] Smith's precise conception of civil liberty is beyond the scope of this essay, it appears to range from negative liberty and non-interference to full political participation. However, the definition is not absolutely central to an argument (I would and do contend this is Smith's position) that posits that the conditions that give rise to this new liberty simultaneously undermine its full expression.

political economist consciously returns to political philosophy and in particular to John Locke's *Two Treatises of Government*. Locke's account of the increased productive capacities of labor consequent on its division and the resulting improvement in the condition of the common people results from the move away from subsistence and toward a specialized market agriculture.[17] Smith clearly follows Locke in recognizing that the transformations in the nature of rule are intimately connected to changes in the nature of economy. To make their point both Locke and Smith invoke visions of an impoverished rustic monarch who is then negatively contrasted with a British laborer. The only real difference in their respective accounts is the locus of the regal seat. The critical connection between them resides in the character of material improvement: an improvement fundamentally unequal in degree but universal in dispersal. Every member of society is, according to both philosophers, materially improved at the same time that society becomes increasingly unequal. However, Smith, unlike Locke, suspects that the compromise has non-economic consequences for the character of the common people that may severely mitigate the material benefits of the bargain.

Civic Character and the Division of Labor

Smith's primary political disagreement with Locke concerns the compromise at the very heart of liberal capitalism. Smith breaks with Locke over evidence and ideas not available to the seventeenth century. Locke did not live to see the eighteenth-century development of complex manufacturing, nor could he read Rousseau's revolutionary account of character formation and deformation. However, Smith was separated from Locke he shared deeply one common source: Cicero. Smith, Locke and the majority of the liberal tradition in education, indeed the majority of the Western tradition of the previous millennia drew heavily on Cicero.[18]

---

[17] John Locke, *Two Treatises of Government*, ed. Peter Laslett (Cambridge: Cambridge University Press, 1994), sec. 41.
[18] Cicero, *On the Commonwealth and On the Laws*, trans. James Zetzel (New York: Cambridge University Press, 1999), *De Leg.* I.30.

In wildly different ways, earlier thinkers as deeply opposed as Machiavelli and Erasmus drew on Cicero, most especially *De Officiis,* as the textual model for their respective enterprises in princely pedagogy. Smith may not have adopted the Ciceronian model of epistolary education, but he shared his central educational contention, that education is the decisive element in civic character. Arguing to this effect in *Theory of Moral Sentiments* Smith contends.

> There is scarce any man, however, who by discipline, education, and example, may not be so impressed with a regard to general rules, as to act upon almost every occasion with tolerably decency, and through the whole of his life to avoid any considerable degree of blame. (III.v.1)[19]

Here Smith draws deeply on the Ciceronian tradition, on the assertion of an *inchoata intelligentia,*[20] the idea of a seed within each person that education cultivates. Smith implicitly evokes Cicero's assertion that human beings are "born for justice."[21] Smith's language lacks the explicit teleological assumptions of Cicero, but it echoes the tension between essential nature and propensity, the same tension with which Smith begins *The Wealth of Nations.*[22]

In Book V of *Wealth of Nations* Smith explicitly recognizes that the division of labor's consequences extend far beyond the simply economic. Smith admits that the division of labor is an educating and socializing force; it constitutes an unceasing, unbidden, and corrosive social pedagogy that fundamentally transforms the character of citizenry. It undermines and displaces the conditions of "discipline, education, and example" necessary for at least "tolerable decency." But as early as Book I, in fact as early as the very first discussion of the division of labor, Smith hints at the problematic even tragic character of the division of labor. Smith's selection of pin manufacturing as archetypal example strongly

---

[19] Adam Smith, *The Theory of Moral Sentiments*, eds. D.D. Raphael and A. Macfie (Indianapols: Liberty Fund, 1984).
[20] Maryanne C. Horowitz, "The Stoic Synthesis of Natural Law in Man: Four Themes," *Journal of the History of Ideas* 35 (1974): 14.
[21] Cicero, *De Leg* I.28.
[22] Smith, *Wealth*, 13.

suggests that the new economic order is not founded on necessity but on the caprice of human passions and in the case of pins of the relatively minor passions for adornment and luxury.[23] Indeed the tension between need and desire and Smith's placement of the tendency to conflate the two at the outset of *The Wealth of Nations* provides the first of two tragic brackets to the entire work to which I will return later.

Smith recognized in pin manufacturing the perfect conjunction of innovations in production and economic responses to all too human passions. Pin manufacturing broke down a complex task into as many as eighteen discrete steps. Each step was the responsibility of a single worker. One worker was responsible for drawing the wire, another for pointing, yet another for grinding and so on. The resulting exponential explosion in production was a modern industrial marvel (I.i.3). In the original description, by way of a number of subtle literary techniques and no small amount of irony in his depiction of "the important business of making a pin" Smith suggests that the products, especially the unexpected externalities, are not solely salutary (I.i.3). To the careful reader then it comes as no surprise when in Book V of *The Wealth of Nations* Smith's critical attention to the returns to the selfsame division of labor now shifts to questions of character and discerns not productive dynamism but enervating monotony and simplicity. Now Smith laments explicitly the costs that come with the benefits, most especially for the youngest workers in the new world of divided labor. Smith famously enumerates and condemns the deleterious consequences of stultifying labor that are exacerbated by the growing rate of child labor.

> As soon as they [child labourers] are able to work, they must apply to some trade by which they can earn their subsistence. That trade too is

---

[23] Griswold, *Adam Smith*, 297n. Griswold draws out with the examples of both brewing and pin manufacture the element of luxury in Smith's account but considering pin making alone as the chosen example of the new form of labour a second element emerges. Pin making speaks to luxury and more specifically to the crafts of adornment which constitute the very first labour of any kind engaged in by Adam and Eve in Genesis 3:7. Moreover this labour is turned to immediately after the eating of the fruit of the Tree of Knowledge of Good and Evil. Smith example, placed at the outset of the work points to the tragic nature of both his *Inquiry* and perhaps even inquiry per se. See Leon Kass, *The Beginning of Wisdom* (New York: Free Press, 2003), 90.

generally so simple and uniform as to give little exercises to the understanding; while at the same time, their labour is both so constant and so severe, that it leaves them little leisure and less inclination to apply to, or even to think of anything else. (Vi.f.53)

There is an awful lot of "anything else" out there. Civic virtue, citizenship, literacy, the simple conscious conduct of an ethical life, all these are corroded by the institution of child labor. Smith's unblinking account of the emerging industrial reality throws into doubt the fundamental viability of the compromise at the heart of liberal capitalism. Smith's depiction of the new labor suggests that the emerging inequality, made tolerable by improvements in the material conditions of all, may not in fact be tolerable if that improvement is solely material. Indeed, Smith makes this explicit, reading his account of the common industrial laborer one wonders if *any* amount of material improvement would justify the reduction in character and merit the division of labor entails.

> A man, without the proper use of the intellectual faculties of a man, is, if possible, more contemptible than even a coward, and seems to be mutilated and deformed in a still more essential part of the character of human nature. (V.i.f.60)

Note that Smith's account in no way precludes the possibility that the "contemptible coward" is better off materially, indeed references to material condition are conspicuous by their absence. What is present by implication is a robust account of the person that explicitly eschews wealth as the sole measure of merit.[24] Smith hearkens back again to Cicero's preference for "a man that lacks money to money that lacks a man."[25]

---

[24] Note that Smith is considering the consequences not of luxury but simply commodious living. Contrast this with the political economy of Hume, see especially David Hume "Of Refinement in the Arts" in *Political Writings,* ed. Stuart Warner (Indianapolis: Hackett Publishing, 1994) 238.

[25] Cicero, *De Officiis,* translated and edited by M. Griffin and E.M. Atkins (New York: Cambridge University Press, 1991), II.71.

The Theory of Moral Sentiments: Sympathy as the "Essential Part"

Smith's account of civic character and the division of labor in *The Wealth of Nations* offers an almost singularly negative vision of character formation. Smith begins the discussion of education's import early in the work when he suggests that the main differences among people, even between people as diverse as the philosopher and the street porter, "arise not so much from nature, as from habit, custom, and education" (I.ii.4). Once this principle has been asserted the implications for civic character in Book V seem inevitable. The habit, custom, and education of a proto-industrial society and the accompanying division of labor, for the laboring classes at least, seem irredeemably corrosive to character and incompatible with full citizenship. Reading *The Wealth of Nations*, we can only discern darkly the contour of a positive vision of character education based on habit, custom and education. For its explicit exposition we must look elsewhere. It is within the pages of *The Theory of Moral Sentiments* that Smith offers a full exposition of the "essential part," that part that the division of labor so deforms.

The Theory of Moral Sentiments is unique in its discussion of civic character and virtue in the extent of its focus on the character and virtue of the ordinary citizen to the almost complete exclusion of either philosopher or statesman. Smith found this exclusion on a distinction between virtue *qua* virtue, a quality of exceptional individuals, and propriety the universally dispersed second-order social and political virtue.

> There is, in this respect, a considerable difference between virtue and mere propriety, between those qualities and actions which deserve to be admired and celebrated, and those which simply deserve to be approved of. (I.v.7)

Smith reserves the category of virtue and the virtuous for the truly exceptional both in deed and person, those who have a degree of wisdom, self-command, and prudence far greater than that of the bulk of mankind.[26] The remainder of mankind possesses only the second-order virtue of propriety. Propriety, Smith makes clear, owes much to the Platonic notions of proportion and order within the non-philosophic soul so clearly outlined in Plato's *Laws*.

However, no sooner has Smith acknowledged the innate superiority of virtue to "mere propriety" than his full attention turns to the second order, from the sublime to the prosaic. Curiously, Smith locates the justification for *The Theory of Moral Sentiments*' conspicuous focus on the ordinary in *The Wealth of Nations*. There Smith insists that the emerging democratic politics will be defined in large part by the character and judgment of the ordinary citizenry. A prudential accounting of the emerging concept of public opinion demands that the philosopher and statesman cast their gaze downward on those whose estimation they increasingly depend upon (V.i.f.60). Politically *The Theory of Moral Sentiments* constitutes the inquiry into the character of the citizen that *The Wealth of Nations* counsels.

In passages that echo Jean-Jacques Rousseau, Smith accounts for propriety in terms eerily similar to the *amour de soi-meme* and *amour-propre* of the *Second Discourse*. In *Moral Sentiments* Smith imagines a solitary man brought suddenly into society, no sooner do others surround him than the mode whereby he estimates his actions is fundamentally transformed.

> Bring him into society, and he is immediately provided with the mirror he wanted before. It is placed in the countenance and behavior of those who he lives with, which always mark when they enter into, and they disapprove of his sentiments; and it is here that he first views the propriety and impropriety of his own passions, the beauty and deformity of his own mind. (III.i.3)

Smith's account reveals two critical facets of propriety. Foremost of these is the obvious social nature of propriety: man's actions only manifest

---

[26] Norbert Waczek, "Two Concepts of Morality: A Distinction of Adam Smith's Ethics and its Stoic Origin", *Journal of the History of Ideas* 45 (1984): 593.

propriety or its opposite within society.[27] This is central to the second-order justice that the ordinary citizen is capable of. True virtues are, by Smith's lights, exist wholly independent of the influence of others. Here Smith again draws on a distinction, in his definition of propriety, which he first locates in the Greek tradition of Plato, Aristotle, and Zeno. Unlike the highest virtues of the ancients, those perhaps experienced by the Philosopher freed from the cave, standing in the sunlight, inevitably alone, propriety can exist only within the city. Understanding propriety to consist of and exist only in our encounters with others, he declares "According to Plato, to Aristotle, and to Zeno, virtue consists in the propriety of conduct, or in the suitableness of the affection from which we act to the object which excites it."[28]

Moreover, the lesser "virtue" of propriety appears to be fully realized not simply in our conduct but in the approval of that conduct by others. Here Smith seems to be deliberately diminishing civic virtue, stripping it of any heroic component, and transforming it into a social virtue above all, one characterized primarily by harmonious living within narrowly defined limits of just conduct.[29] More essentially still the reactions of others to conduct and expressed sentiment conduce to ethical development and inculcate the sense of propriety by revealing to the formerly solitary man aspects of his personhood previously concealed by his solitude, especially the "beauty and deformity of his own mind" (III.i.3). The society of others not only permits an inward estimation of outward conduct it also creates the conditions of interiority necessary for any inquiry into one's own motives, sentiments, and conduct.

Smith's account of the introduction of a solitary man into society obviously possesses strong pedagogic overtones. In describing the experience of children new to the schoolroom Smith dramatically illustrates the connection. Prior to contact with others, save understandably partial

---

[27] Consider in this light Pierre Bayle, "Ninth Letter" *Various Thoughts on the Occasion of a Comet* (Albany: SUNY Press, 2000), 200.
[28] Smith, *Theory*, VII.1.i.
[29] Istvan Hont and Michael Ignatieff, "Needs and Justice in the *Wealth of Nations*: An Introductory Essay," in *Wealth and Virtue*, eds. Hont and Ignatieff (Cambridge: Cambridge University Press, 1985), 44.

parents and caregivers, the child's experience of his passions and interests is defined by egocentricity. The classroom, the first encounter with true peers, offers a rough tonic to the infant's ego and his overwhelming partiality in his own cause.

> When it is old enough to go to school, or to mix with its equals, it soon finds that they have no such indulgent partiality. It naturally wishes to gain their favour, and to avoid their hatred or contempt. Regard even to its own safety teaches it to do so; and it soon finds that it can do so in no other way than moderating not only its anger, but all other passions, to the degree which its playfellows and companions are likely to be pleased with. (III.Iii.22a)

The central lesson originates not with the teacher but with the peers. Like the previously solitary man the child learns to gauge the worth of his actions and sentiments by their reception among his equals.

The critical civic and social element of education eventually develops beyond the lessons of the schoolyard and moves into the public square. Even the more subtle and explicitly political lessons given to young men, and in particular ambitious young men, retain a common core of truth with the first rough lessons of the schoolroom. Smith illustrates by rendering the eternal political problem of youth who espouse licentiousness, court scandal, and proudly extol that which should be eschewed "sometimes from corruption, but more frequently from the vanity of their own hearts" (II.Iii.8).[30] Such young men, Smith argues, consequent upon their passionate, proud and partial characters, are rarely susceptible to an explicitly moral education in the error of their ways. Instead, Smith suggests that the substance of their first lessons in temperance emerges through the hard knocks offered by first their classmates then their fellow citizens. Such students are first taught not through the invocation of moral principle but through the cruder appeal to consequence. Smith expresses his own iteration of an old lesson as a civic imperative that is substantially proto-Kantian in nature.

---

[30] Smith, *Theory*, 128–129. Consider also Saint Augustine, *Confessions*, trans. E.B. Pusey (New York: Modern Library, 1949), Book II.

> Upon this account we generally cast about for other arguments, and the consideration which first occurs to us, is the disorder and confusion of society which would result from the universal prevalence of such practices. (II.iii.8)

As in its first incarnation in the classroom, the lesson is not expressed in terms of political or moral philosophy, the appeal is to civic efficacy and consequence not moral verity. In an ethical echo of his market arguments, the first appeal is not to the student's soul but his self-interest. In so arguing Smith reveals a deep and insistent suspicion of the capacity for ever more education and greater erudition to cultivate civic virtue. In its place, Smith depends not on the latest lesson but that "which first occurs to us." Civic education involves tending to the chain of observation and response, to the work that character does, the work of bringing the right thing, almost as if unbidden, to the mind as that which occurs first. Smith's reliance on childhood experience to ground adult dispositions toward civic life suggests that this work on character is both best taught and best practiced as a settling of temperament as opposed to a sophistication of intellect. Smith relies on teaching right response and rejects dependence on right reason.

> If we examine the different shades and gradations of weakness and self-command, as we meet with them in common life, we shall very easily satisfy ourselves that this control of our passive feelings must be acquired, not from the abstruse syllogisms of a quibbling dialectic, but from that great discipline which Nature has established for the acquisition of this and every other virtue; a regard to the sentiments of the real or supposed spectator of our conduct. (III.Iii.21)

Smith's description of education reveals a process that begins, but only begins, with socialization. The ordinary citizen, first as a child then as a young man, is forced to consider the reactions of actual others to his actions. If this were the sum total of Smith's account it would appear that civic education amounts to scarcely more than socialization, merely a heightened sensitivity to the impressions of others. Setting aside its obvious limitations this also seems to set up conditions for a deep relativizing of ethical conduct. To the contrary, Smith sees this initial purely prudential civic virtue (if such a term is not oxymoronic) as only the first step in the development of civic character. This first step creates the conditions for an internalization of the experience of actual others, which is followed upon by an act of ethical imagination both commonplace and extraordinary. Smith suggests that education turns inevitably from a code of conduct based on the responses of others to one predicated on an ideal imagined other.

This ideal other, the impartial spectator, is the imaginative extension of the perceived impartiality of the multitude of mankind in its evaluation of the agent's conduct and sentiments.[31] Smith distills the abstract "mankind" and its impartial perspective in the imagination into a single impartial spectator, who dwells within the agent and with whom he consults to receive an impartial estimate of his conduct. He consults this impartial spectator in much the same way that he imagines himself in a third, ideal position and perspective when he assesses the size of objects at varying distances (III.i.4). Through an act of ethical imagination the citizen moves beyond mere strategic considerations of conduct and toward a coherent ethical and civic faculty of judgment. This development is not accomplished through explicit instruction, nor is it comprehended even in its newfound possession in explicitly civic or ethical terms. Instead like the ability to discern magnitude at varying distances it exists almost in spite of attempts to render it explicit. The evaluation of the impartial spectator becomes that "which first occurs." Smith suggests as much when he describes the subtle inculcation of the sense of magnitude and distance.

> Habit and experience have taught me to do this so easily and so readily, that I am scarce sensible that I do it: and a man must be, in some measure, acquainted with the philosophy of vision before he can be thoroughly convinced how little those distant objects would appear to the eye, if the imagination, from a knowledge of their real magnitudes, did not swell and dilate them. (II.iii.3)

---

[31] See D.D. Raphael, "The Impartial Spectator," in *Essays on Adam Smith,* eds. A.S. Skinner and T. Wilson (Oxford: Clarendon Press, 1975), 88.

Ethical estimation is acquired in the same way as sense of proportion, almost insensibly; yet Smith leaves no doubt that propriety is learned not only as rules but (unlike proportion) as a very specific mode of reasoning about those rules. Moreover, as in Smith's optical metaphor, nothing precludes a later higher order comprehension of what is at work, but that understanding is not essential to its functioning. In this way, again, Smith's account seems to place ordinary understandings of ethics, the ordinary workings of the impartial spectator in a category structurally similar to the true opinion and the virtuous character of Plato's *Laws*.

The move from contemplation of the perspective of actual others to the imaginative impartial spectator instills within the person not only a set of social rules but an operative principle which allows the individual to apply these learned ethical and civic rules. This operative principle is the impartial spectator understood as the "man within the breast."

> When I endeavour to examine my own conduct, when I endeavour to pass sentence upon it, and either approve or condemn it, it is evident that, in all such cases, I divide myself, as it were, into two persons; and that I the examiner and judge, represent a different character from that other I, the person whose conduct is examined into and judged of. (III.i.2)

Essentially, the impartial spectator within tries the case of the considered conduct or expressed sentiment. In what form the perspective of philosophy and ethics may seem a counter-intuitive move, Smith captures the experience and essence of impartial reasoning by personifying it, rendering impartiality as a perspective. This is possible because Smith does not equate impartiality with perfect knowledge (or, as with Rawls, the converse).[32] Instead Smith suggests that the impartiality of the interior judge is based upon the judge having access to the same knowledge available to the agent.[33]

As an operative principle the impartial spectator informs not only the course of future actions but also our reactions to the reception our past actions have received from actual others. To the extent that this is so

---

[32] Raphael, "The Impartial Spectator," 96.
[33] V.M. Hope, *Virtue by Consensus* (Oxford: Clarendon Press, 1989), 102.

Smith protects himself from the charge that his moral philosophy is a solely social construct. Smith then goes on to address the suggestion that the practice of propriety is desirable because pleasurable, that its ultimate criteria are hedonistic. Smith asserts that the experience of being praised by others for our actions is pleasurable only if that praise is consistent with our own internal estimation of those action's praiseworthiness. Emphatically and unequivocally Smith asserts "The most sincere praise can give little pleasure when it cannot be considered as some sort of proof of praiseworthiness" (III.Iii.4).

The impact of the ethical principle of the impartial spectator on the civic character of the citizen is profound. The force of the principle arises out of its dual function as evaluative mechanism for our own conduct and sentiment and as a gauge for our responses to the actions and sentiments of others. Smith observes in human beings a fundamental longing to have others share in our passions and a concomitant propensity to participate in theirs. This dual sentiment Smith designates as sympathy. According to Smith, sympathy with the suffering of another is so basic to human nature that while the great may be defined by a surfeit of this sensibility even the criminal and villainous, the "most hardened violator of the laws of society, is not altogether without it" (I.i.1). The universal nature of sympathy creates and is complemented by a reciprocal desire among humans to be the object of sympathy. As a result, the longing for sympathy is accompanied by a sense of outrage and injustice when the expected sympathy or fellow-feeling is not proffered (I.Ii.4).

As the preeminent social faculty sympathy substantially mirrors the impartial spectator. In Smith's account sympathy entails a division of self akin to the imaginative splitting at the heart of the impartial spectator but with two crucial differences. First the imaginative act of division is directed outward rather than inward. We imagine ourselves as if we were, to adopt Smith's language, within the breast of the person with whom we sympathize. Through an act of imagination, we place ourselves not in an objective position within but outside in the subjective position of the other. Sympathetic fellow-feeling on Smith's account is vicariousness transformed into ethical and civic virtue.

> When we see a stroke aimed, and just ready to fall upon the leg or arm of another person, we shrink and draw back our own leg or our own arm: and when it does fall, we feel it in some measure, and are hurt by it as well as the sufferer. (1.i.3)

It is this imaginative act that allows for our estimation of other people's conduct to be evaluated as we evaluate our own. Our sympathetic participation leads us to commiserate, to remain unmoved, or even repudiate the conduct and experience of another and as such serves as the foundation of our moral and political judgment.[34]

For Smith, the ability to see oneself in others is central to democratic political life.[35] Smith conceives of this centrality in two distinct ways, the first and most obvious is the moral and political faculty of evaluating both the claims and responses of others through acts of sympathetic imagination. This learned ability to evaluate the legitimacy or lack thereof of another's perspective is obviously a key element of political life and decision-making. However, Smith places this functional benefit on the surface, the core significance of sympathy resides in its status as a fundamental social demand, a *sine qua non* of communication and social existence.

> But if you have either no fellow-feeling for the misfortunes I have met with, or none that bears any proportion to the grief which distracts me; or if you have either no indignation at the injuries I have suffered, or none that bears any proportion to the resentment which transports men, we can no longer converse upon these subjects. *We become intolerable to one another.* (Emphasis added) (I.Iv.5)

More than an expectation, sympathy is a necessary condition for communication and ultimately society.[36] Sympathy implies not merely fellow-feeling but a shared sense of proportion: indeed the necessary condition of commensurability is prior to the most basic acts of identification and

---

[34] Morrow, *Adam Smith*, 32.
[35] Compare with Jean Jacques Rousseau, *Emile,* trans. Allan Bloom (New York: HarperCollins, 1979), 224.
[36] Morrow, *Adam Smith*, 28.

the very possibility of solidarity. In complexes of interlocution the individual learns what the marketplace of sympathy will bear; the individual discerns common values and acquires the mutual sense of proportion through a process akin to bargaining.[37] Sympathy emerges in an obviously intersubjective context that both informs and ultimately satisfies or fails to satisfy our need for it. The experience of other's demands and expectations and the act of ethical imagination of other's perspectives train our passion for sympathy to conform itself to a proportion and mode of expression likely to generate the desired response.

> If he would act so as that the impartial spectator may enter into the principles of his conduct, which is what of all things he has the greatest desire to do, he must upon this, as upon all other occasions, humble the arrogance of his self-love, and bring it down to something other men can go along with. (II.Ii.1)

The natural desire for sympathy is an essential and original element of social existence and "getting it right" generates positive consequences for social and political cooperation.[38] We are led to moderate our individual passions and our partial estimation of events as a result of a deeper passion: the longing for sympathetic response. In our most basic cause and desire we are transformed from tyrants of self-love into creatures of compromise, from anti-social and self-interested partiality into potential citizens adept at tempering our passions to render them fit for social existence.

Smith's account of the development and training of the passions through human interaction rests heavily on a conception of varied social intercourse as the primary source of meaningful social and civic education. By internalizing and embodying impartiality and combining it with the sentimental primacy of consonance between inwardly recognized truth and outward reality Smith's account of the development of both faculties of moral and ethical judgment and a genuinely civic character

---

[37] Griswold, *Adam Smith*, 297.
[38] Douglas J. Den Uyl and Charles Griswold Jr., "Adam Smith on Friendship and Love," *Review of Metaphysics* 49 (1996): 617.

avoids being reduced to simple socialization. Smith does not doubt that human passions need such education and equally rejects the belief that its provision occurs inevitably in all social forms and encounters. Turning from *The Theory of Moral Sentiments* back to *The Wealth of Nations* we find Smith rendering an account of how the division of labor and the emerging economy serve to corrupt, disorder and mutilate essential social and civic faculties.

Sympathy, Variety of Experience, and Civic Character

To understand why the consequences of the division of labor are so grave for the character of the citizenry it is necessary to recall one final aspect of sympathy. The combination of sympathy and imagination gives rise to the central social passion of fellow feeling. Defining the social role of sympathy and imagination at the very outset of *Moral Sentiments* Smith writes.

> As we have no immediate experience of what other men feel, we can form no idea of the manner in which they are affected, but by conceiving what we ourselves should feel in the like situation. Though our brother is upon the rack, as long as we ourselves are at our ease, our senses will never inform us of what he suffers. They never did, and never can, carry us beyond our own person, and it is by the imagination only that we can form any conception of what are his sensations. (I.i.2)

From here Smith goes on to describe how our nascent senses develop "from their ease" into a faculty of ethical and political judgment rooted in internal impartiality and external fellow-feeling. *The Wealth of Nations* then describes how this process, essential to social and civic life, can be stunted or thwarted altogether.

In the context of sympathetic imagination in particular Smith worries that the singular and simple tasks which define the newly divided labor smother the imagination by denying its experience of others, of social contact, and of mental exercise. This intellectual and imaginative isolation renders the laborer incapable of identifying with the causes, complaints, and interests of his fellow citizens. Like the preschool age child, the new laborer lacks sufficient experience of others. He lacks the educational experiences that generate both the experience and capacity for impartiality and the ability to imagine sympathetically. He is estranged from the worlds of evaluation and imagination essential for social and civic life. This mutilation matters particularly in a democratic society as "the safety of government depends very much upon the favourable judgment which the people may form of its conduct."[39] Smith makes clear that certain types of labor, types increasing every day in number and range are rendering whole segments of society not only unable to render favorable judgment but unable to render any judgment at all. He paints a bleak picture of the isolation such workers face and of its consequences.

> His condition leaves him no time to receive the necessary information, and his education and habits are commonly such as to render him unfit to judge even though he was fully informed. In the publick deliberations, therefore, his voice is little heard and less regarded. (I.xi.p.9)

As Nicholas Phillipson poignantly remarks, such people are "lost to the world of sympathy and could look forward to lives which were governed by the principles of empathy and dependence."[40] The laborer is not only unable to sympathize with others but those selfsame others upon contemplating the strange crudeness of his character cannot sympathize with him. The nature of his labor limits his contact with the larger social context of sympathy that renders passions commensurate.[41] He remains utterly alien and as Smith warns, inevitably the crisis of incommensurability makes citizens mutually intolerable.[42]

---

[39] Smith, *Wealth*, 740.
[40] Nicholas Phillipson, "Adam Smith as Civic Moralist," in *Wealth and Virtue,* eds. Istvan Hont and Michael Ignatieff (Cambridge: Cambridge University Press, 1985), 193.
[41] For an excellent discussion of the problem of commensureability in politics see Alisdair MacIntyre *After Virtue* (South Bend: Notre Dame University Press, 1982).
[42] Ryan Hanley, *Adam Smith and the Character of Virtue* (Cambridge: Cambridge University Press, 2009), 47.

In response to this emerging crisis Smith offers some rudimentary proposals for public education both for the general population and also for education for those who wish to hold public office. These ideas seem wholly inadequate when applied to the corrosive effects on character that Smith goes to such length to describe. Indeed, the sheer inadequacy of Smith's educational proposals points to the possibility that Smith is tacitly acknowledging the futility of the enterprise. This possibility is further borne out by both the discussion of the structure of the modern state and its defense and the carefully placed allusions, both biblical and classical, that Smith uses to indicate the inevitable arc of the new economy.

If the nature of their work provides the common laborer with few opportunities to develop civic faculties the nature of mass government under liberal capitalism further exacerbates the condition. Recalling the second element of Smith's "science of the legislator," the provision of services, the "service" most singularly responsible for civic character in the ancient world is found to be almost completely absent from liberal capitalism. This most crucial "service" is the maintenance of a popular militia with its consequent inculcation within the citizenry of a martial spirit. Describing the citizenry lacking both militia and martial spirit Smith gloomily opines

> Even though the martial spirit of the people were of no use towards the defense of the society, yet to prevent that sort of mental mutilation, deformity and wretchedness, which cowardice necessarily involves in it, from spreading themselves through the great body of the people, would still deserve the most serious attention of government; in the same manner as it would deserve its most serious attention to prevent a leprosy or any other loathsome and offensive disease. (V.i.f.60)

Note that Smith advocates the creation of a militia *independent* of the presence of a specific threat or enemy to justify it. Smith justifies the expense of a militia primarily by pointing to the salutary influence on the citizenry before it is ever justified or even if it is *never* justified on the battlefield. A militia is justified because it provides opportunities to tune and temper our passions to a greater degree than the mundane bustle and business of commercial society. It offers educational opportunities to the passions, to the impartial spectator, to our capacity for fellow-feeling, far beyond those of the market square or even the best of classrooms. In a tone more closely associated with Romanticism than the Scottish Enlightenment *The Theory of Moral Sentiments* evokes the consequences of conflict on character.

> Under the boisterous and stormy sky of war and faction, of public tumult and confusion, the sturdy severity of self-command prospers the most, and can be most successfully cultivated. (III.Iii.37)

The educational rationale for a militia, for the experience of conflict, is utterly devoid of an economic element indeed it is to a great degree inimical to it. From an economic point of view the great virtue of liberal capitalism, the ever-increasing prosperity and dimension of the free market, provides adequate resources to provide for a standing and professional army. This is not an accident but an archetypal expression of liberal capitalist polities, a standing army provides for preservation, a militia provides for the martial virtues.[43] Smith seeks with his arguments for a citizen militia to mitigate the consequences of a tragic contrapuntal movement unique to modern market society. Smith fears that ever greater economic development coincides with ever-decreasing development and education of character and the practice of civic virtue.[44] Smith's declarations place him squarely, if perhaps with a certain tragic resignation, within the Ciceronian camp that praises virtue over commerce, that prefers the man to the money, and struggles to discern a route to their civic reconciliation.

This suspicion of economic justification defines another element of Smith's more specific recommendations concerning education. Smith proposes a system of primary education that the state should supply even if the state "was to derive no advantage from the instruction of the

---

[43] Donald Winch, *Adam Smith's Politics* (Cambridge: Cambridge University Press, 1978), 113.

[44] In the treatment of the relationship between commerce, character and martial virtue Smith places himself squarely in the context of the Scottish Enlightenment and in particular Adam Ferguson, see J.G.A. Pocock, *The Machiavellian Moment* (Princeton: Princeton University Press, 1975), 503.

inferior ranks of people" (V.i.f.60) which of course he contends it does. As with the maintenance of a militia, Smith maintains that the benefits of education paid out of the public purse are justified independently of economic rationale. Turning back to the definition of Political Economy at the center of *The Wealth of Nations* what emerges is not an ontogenetic ambiguity but a tragic contradiction. The sovereign should provide services to the people for their improvement beyond mere preservation. The state depends on the prosperity of the citizens to provide services aimed at ensuring that prosperity, but this dependence may undermine institutions that would promote other equally essential ends especially civic virtue.[45] In many ways this is the story of Adam Smith in the two centuries that follow his death. His essential insights into the other branches of the science of the legislator, even his other principle work, *The Theory of Moral Sentiments*, are overwhelmed by the disciplinary and material prerogatives of economics.

Smith's project to inculcate civic virtue in spite of the new science places him at the headwaters of a discussion almost unique to modernity concerning liberal education: the argument from utility. This is one of the true marvels of *The Wealth of Nations*. In his discussion of the yeomanry[46] and even of the educational class, estimations of value, virtue and social significance trump economic considerations. In discussing the moral and intellectual character of the yeomanry Smith describes in detail how the mental habits demanded by husbandry are second only to a few liberal professions in their demands on the intellect. Agricultural science, Smith contends, "has never been regarded as a matter very easily understood" (I.x.c.24). In contrast industrial trades are almost singularly defined by the ease with which they are learned. Smith opines

---

[45] For disparate interpretations of this element in Smith see Winch, *Smith's Politics*, 118–120 and Cropsey, *Polity,* 98–101.

[46] Smith, *Wealth*, (I.x.c.24). The passage concerning the yeomanry bears quoting in full: The common ploughman, though generally regarded as the pattern of stupidity and ignorance, is seldom defective in this judgment and discretion. He is less accustomed, indeed, to social intercourse than the mechanick who lives in town. His voice and language are more uncouth and more difficult to understood by those who are not used to them. His understanding, however, being accustomed to consider a greater variety of objects is generally much superior to that of the other, whose whole attention from morning till night is commonly occupied in performing one or two very simple operations.

that hardly a single trade requires more than a simple pamphlet of a few pages with illustrations to explain it fully (ibid.). Nonetheless, rarely do the wages of the yeomanry surpass those of the industrial laborer. Worse still is the case of the "men of letters" whose swelling number are so great "as commonly to reduce the price of their labour to a very paltry recompence" (I.x.c.37). Smith posits a radical disconnect, even an inverse relationship between the inherent difficulty and the implicit merit of a task and its economic reward. Ironically, considering his place in the pantheon of liberal economics, Smith champions civic virtue and its requisite education not only independent of economic rationale but in spite of it. As the discussion of the emerging modern trades and the mastery thereof indicates the circumstances conducive to prosperity are not merely irrelevant but may be hostile to the conditions conducive to both civic and intellectual development.

"Things Familiar to the Mind"

As I suggested at the outset of my discussion of Smith, I have consciously attempted to mirror a particular relationship between *The Theory of Moral Sentiments* and *The Wealth of Nations*. The philosophical and ethical account of the development of the person provided by the former is only fully realized when combined with the philosophical, political, and economic account of the development of society in the latter. A similar structure emerges within the context of *The Wealth of Nations* itself wherein Smith tempers the account of political and economic development with philosophic and ethical concerns. These concerns, present at commencement and conclusion in the form of explicit description and muted allusion, leave the careful reader with a tragic sense of the nature and causes into which Smith has inquired.

It is only very late in modernity that inquiry becomes disconnected from aporia and ultimately from tragedy. Smith, like the others I have discussed, stretching all the way back to Plato's Socrates, remains all too aware of the intractable consequences of the inevitable limits on our understanding. Smith indicates in the account of the growth of knowledge through education and inquiry, that *The Wealth of Nations* is deeply informed by a premodern sensibility that retains the poignant connection between inquiry and tragedy and calls back to an insistent concern with the relationship of knowledge to virtue. Smith acknowledges that the economic consequences of the absence of moral, martial, and civic education seem negligible or perhaps even materially beneficial. He leaves conspicuously open the possibility that the material improvement of the common people is connected, perhaps inextricably, to their moral corruption.[47] Smith illustrates his reservations most explicitly with the account of the evils of child labor and the monotony of the emerging trades with which he concludes *The Wealth of Nations*. However, an even deeper sense of tragic moment emerges through a careful consideration of Smith's deep reliance on classical and primarily republican sources of metaphor, parable, and example.[48] A particularly illuminating ancient source for Smith is Cicero's *De Officiis*. The use Smith puts *De Officiis* in one instance in particular appears to equate Cicero's position with his own and *initially appears to* suggest that their shared position endorses simple self-interest. Quoting in his own translation the last great Roman republican Smith writes

> To feed well, old Cato said, as we are told by Cicero, was the first and most profitable thing in the management of a private estate; to feed tolerably well, the second; and to feed ill, the third. To plough, he ranked only in the fourth place of profit and advantage. (I.xi.b.12)

What Smith has left out and what in his own time and now the educated reader would have recognized as absent in this famous passage from Cicero's epistle on duty is that the quoted text does not conclude with the fourth interrogation of Cato. To the contrary it reads radically different when taken in full.[49]

---

[47] John Salter, "Adam Smith on Feudalism, Commerce and Slavery," *History of Political Thought* 13 (1992): 234.
[48] Of Roman sources alone Smith refers to or directly quotes Cicero, Columella, Cato, Livy, Seneca, Plutarch, Varro and Virgil among others.
[49] For a lengthy treatment of Smith's use of this passage see my "Elegant Ellipsis," 9–13.

Externals are compared, on the other hand, when glory is preferred to riches, or urban income to rural. The words of the Elder Cato belong to this class of comparison. Someone asked him what was the most profitable activity for a family estate. He replied, "To grace herds well" "And what next" "To graze them adequately" And what third? "To graze them, though poorly" and what fourth? "To plough" Then when the question was asked, "What about money lending?" Cato's reply was "What about killing someone?" (Ibid.)

Smith does identify with Cicero but not in the manner the text seems initially to imply. Rather Smith like Cicero finds himself at a moment of profound social and political disruption and transformation. He beholds a particular set of virtues and a particular vision of state and citizen being displaced and ultimately discarded. Upon a careful reading *The Wealth of Nations* reveals a philosopher convinced that the economic goods derived from the division of labor are never completely justified in their own terms. Even more importantly the social and political consequences of the division of labor, especially in regard to civic character and education, simply cannot be justified in those terms. Instead, the opposite appears to be the case: To the extent that the division of labor diminishes the civic and ethical character of the citizenry it stands condemned.

Cato's brutal last response serves to highlight the specific heuristic challenges both Smith and Cicero faced. Cato's interlocutor commences the discussion by asking the wrong question, he starts from *profit* and from this concern the final proposed course inevitably emerges. In the final inquiry "What about money lending?" Cato's interrogator is implicitly asking whether routes to prosperity can be disconnected from the substance of character. To which Cato's response, from the perspective of virtue, is that such a disconnect renders any course possible and of course therefore potentially profitable. Smith worries that this rupture may come to constitute the *sine qua non* of the new economy. He fears forms of commerce which disentangle outcomes from habit, custom, and character. This disengagement perhaps explains why Smith's specific proposals for civic education are so woefully inadequate. As long as the ethical and educational groundwork is primarily concerned with preservation and prosperity rather than citizen character Smith's measures may temporarily ameliorate but none can completely forestall the decline of civic virtue.

7

The Future of Character and Education

Character is destiny. In this typically brief but atypically clear epigram Heraclitus illuminates the relationship between the composition and the conduct of both individuals and societies. The epigram's brevity conceals its subtlety. The passage first denies then reaffirms a fatal account of the universe. Not until Nietzsche's "God is dead" do we encounter another sentence so layered with meaning and simultaneously so starkly self-vitiating. Heraclitus appears at first to emancipate but then, instantly, returns to a world in which all is foreordained. Freedom remains an impossibility, only the source of our fate has changed. Often invoked in biographies the epigram stands in as an explanation of the conduct of great men and women, leaders, statesmen, and soldiers. But this use, while compelling as a literary device, conceals Heraclitus' essential insight. Biographers necessarily focus on what can be known, they search out and drag into daylight informative aspects of their subject's character, but the work of biographical dissection destroys the deep, pre-rational integrity of character that bestows upon it that unique quality of fate.

Heraclitus' epigram alludes to just these ways that actions, emotions, and opinions come to us, as if unbidden, from deep within. He suggests that the impulses and actions that we previously assigned to the gods, the Homeric fear or anger that moved among us, were rooted not in the supernatural but the extra-rational. For Heraclitus and for us, large parts of our character remain, like the will of imagined gods, fate-filled in their inscrutability.

What Heraclitus understood as character Edmund Burke called prejudice. Burke believed that the extra-rational, those parts of our identity that are neither composed of nor conducted in the full light of reason nonetheless inform the lion's share of our actions. Moreover, Burke understood that character-driven destiny was not merely individual, that the extra-rational guided not just the fate of statesmen but the destiny of whole societies. Contemplating the inevitable failure of the revolution of Reason unfolding in France, Burke insisted that ordinary men were not philosophers, their share of reason not great, their future depended not on the perspicacity of their deliberations but the quality of their characters.

> You see, Sir, that in this enlightened age I am bold enough to confess, that we are generally men of untaught feelings; that instead of casting away all our old prejudices, we cherish them to a very considerable degree, and, to take more shame to ourselves, we cherish them because they are prejudices; and the longer they have lasted, and the more generally they have prevailed, the more we cherish them. We are afraid to put men to live and trade each on his own private stock of reason; because we suspect that this stock in each man is small, and that the individuals would do better to avail themselves of the general bank and capital of nations, and of ages.[1]

Burke counted on those prejudices, those beliefs held but not perfectly understood, that we have been tracing from Plato's true opinions all the way up to Smith's notion of that which occurs to us first. Burke errs only in describing the ordinary citizen as a creature of "untaught feelings."

---

[1] Edmund Burke, *Reflections on the Revolution in France* (Indianapolis: Liberty Fund, 1999), 182.

Again, from *Republic* to *The Wealth of Nations* I have been enquiring into the myriad ways in which we teach those very feelings, that extra-rational aspect of civic character. While the authors I've considered debate the character and portion of reason the ordinary citizen possesses, none debate the necessity that this other portion, the passions, prejudices, and interests must be taught and taught carefully.

It is perhaps in grief that the emotions that we most mistakenly regard as untaught come to the fore. We are often surprised by grief, if not in its all too inevitable appearance, then in its unexpected expression. On the thankfully rare occasions when that grief is national in scope, we have the rare opportunity to witness the civic aspects of feeling on most poignant display. Our social responses, the small civic acts that a political tragedy prompts with their inchoate grammars of gestural politics, instinctively draw upon subterranean streams of civic virtue. These displays speak volumes about the state of citizenship. For example, in 1968 as Robert F. Kennedy's casket passed through town after town on its way from New York to Arlington crowds gathered by the side of the tracks. Men, women, and children stood at stations, rail crossings, in fields, and urban back lots waiting for the train to pass. Captured in hours of film taken from the train the images speak to a well learned, deep sense of civic duty and even piety. Among the quiet crowds standing atop a railway switchbox were two boys in baseball uniforms quietly saluting, a group of nuns with heads bowed on a train platform, a family clearly come up from the beach standing, stock still with their hands at their sides. These scenes and others like them repeated hundreds of times along those tracks testify to the positive power of Burke's untaught feelings. They provide evidence, from Pericles Funeral Oration to the stillness at Appomattox, that at critical moments our politics are founded and refounded on the civic virtue of the ordinary citizen. The virtue of the ordinary citizen, as in the central political metaphor of Plato's *Laws,* remains the timber upon which the ship of state is borne forward.

And then there is Amanda Lowe. In the spring of 2012 Ms. Lowe, a pregnant, unemployed, and racist citizen of Manchester, assaulted a total stranger, a fellow Briton of South Asian descent, as he returned home from work.[2] Two elements of the attack stand out. First and most striking, as Ms. Lowe and her boyfriend deserted their young children to assault their victim crowds stood by and did nothing. In the CCTV footage that captured the incident and led to Ms. Lowe's swift conviction the victim's fellow citizens, some literally within arm's reach and far outnumbering his assailants looked on as he was kicked, pummeled and stomped upon. Of course, such attacks and incidents are not new, nor is the response of the bystanders. First really discussed at length in the tragic case of Kitty Genovese, the inaction of these passive citizens is often attributed to a human response unhelpfully called bystander effect. Here is an example of, if anything, the very opposite of Burke's untaught feelings. Bystander effect, in its crudest rendering, means little more than the calculation, on the part of the bystander, that someone else, *anybody else* really, will do something. Bystander effect, in its calculative aspect, amounts to a nightmarish modern reappearance of Platonic *logismos*. These actors, in a near perfect perversion of the Platonic citizen, take opinions about security, self-interest and the state and manipulate them into a crude rationale for inaction.

But the Lowe case tells us not merely about the decline of virtue in a single community. The Lowe case points above all to a fundamental change retreat from the cultivation of civic virtue on the part of the state. It is telling that Ms. Lowe's trial and conviction proceeded with such speed because the attack was caught on closed circuit television. This was not a fortunate happenstance. Ms. Lowe was caught on camera because in modern Britain cameras are everywhere. Britain has roughly one security camera for every thirty-two citizens.[3] These cameras can now be found in town squares, shopping malls, soccer stadiums, schools, and even children's change rooms.[4] Understandably the first response of those alarmed by the increasing intrusion of the state into the lives of citizens is to invoke the language of Orwell and Big Brother. This is surely fair, but it misses the point. The British state relies on CCTV because it can no longer rely on the civic virtue of its ordinary citizens. The growth

---

[2] http://www.bbc.co.uk/news/uk-england-manchester-20104542.
[3] http://www.dailymail.co.uk/news/article-1362493/One-CCTV-camera-32-people-Big-Brother-Britain.html.
[4] http://www.guardian.co.uk/world/2012/sep/11/cctv-cameras-school-changing-rooms.

of the security state, Socrates' retelling of the myth of the Ring of Gyges in *Republic*.

What is equally clear is that supervision is no substitute for civic virtue. A simple statistic: the number of reported burglaries in Britain in 1900 was 3812, in 2000? 1.1 million.[5] At the same time Britain became an almost unimaginably more prosperous country, both the number of people living in poverty and the character of that poverty improved exponentially over the twentieth century. Neither police nor prosperity is a sufficient substitute for character. Clearly, we need to get back into the business of cultivating character. All of the institutions in society which explicitly or implicitly shape the character of citizens, which cultivate habits of ordinary and civic virtue, which plant the seeds of a sense of order, and which pass on beliefs about collective life need to be reinvigorated, and none of these more than liberal education.

Recovering the Lost Legacy of Liberal Learning and Civic Virtue

The most important task for defenders of liberal and civic education today is recovery. As with Cicero's recreated forum, the frame of liberal education, like the frame of any important civic institution, must be filled with meaning, significance, and substance if it is to endure. To the extent that liberal education has lost ground to its contemporary critics I would suggest that loss is a consequence not of the strength of those critiques but the shallow understanding and emptying out of the traditional grounds of liberal education, of the historical and philosophical understanding of the enterprise and its intended.

In part this tendency is a consequence of the deep rejection of history that is a regrettable characteristic of this moment in liberal modernity. It is a peculiar conviction of our culture, one farthest advanced among "educationalists," that the latest word is invariably the last. In the philosophy of education this malady emerges in part because of a regrettable confluence of a crudely egalitarian misreading of Rousseau's naturalism

---

[5] http://www.nationalarchives.gov.uk/education/candp/crime/g10/g10cs4.htm.

and an equally unsophisticated quasi-Lockean sensationalism. These are transformed by their conjunction into a political as well as a pedagogic principle. The teacher suddenly and perversely finds himself as forbidden as ever was Emile[6] to refer to authority to justify pedagogy. Eric Voegelin captures this phenomenon nicely as it concerns the classical heritage, but his remarks are surely as valid for Smith, Rousseau, and Locke today.

> Liberals speak of free research in the sense of liberation from 'authorities', that is, not only from revelation and dogmatism, but also from classical philosophy, the rejection of which becomes a point of honour.[7]

Defenders of modern liberal education fail to distinguish between empty appeals to authority and the presence of a compelling account of both the means and necessity of liberal education. In rejecting the tradition of liberal education, they equally reject the tradition of liberal citizenship. This willful amnesia renders modern defenders of liberal education ill-prepared to meet the utilitarian and cultural critiques of education.

The single most regrettable aspect of the shallow modern understanding of the liberal lessons for virtue has been the lamentable tendency to uncritically cede to critics the fundamental ground of liberal education.[8] Forgetting the fundamental relationship between liberal education, character, and citizenship today's educators are all too often forced to defend liberal education on the grounds and terms of its opponents. Nowhere is this more pervasively or pathetically practiced than in the attempts to justify liberal education in terms of its economic benefits. In so arguing these ersatz defenders claim what is manifestly false, that a technological education and a liberal education aim at the same goal: a productive and prosperous economy and an advantageous location within it for the pupil. This concession necessitates the even less plausible argument that a liberal education, as contrasted with say an actuarial education, is equally liable to generate economic success. Having ceded

---

[6] Rousseau, *Emile*, 119.
[7] Eric Voegelin, "Liberalism and its History," *The Review of Politics* 36 (1974): 515.
[8] Of course there is also, as mentioned in the introduction, a growing list of excellent defenses of liberal education on its own terms, most prominent among these being Allan Bloom's *The Closing of the American Mind* and Christopher Lasch's *The Culture of Narcissism*.

the high ground without a struggle liberal education then fights a losing and implausible battle for the low. The response of the five philosophers I've treated and the stark testimony of the twentieth century is equally clear: the fact of prosperity is an equally poor indicator for both the quality of character and the quality of education.

The situation is similarly bleak for those who would defend liberal education against the cultural critique by offering a civilizational "pearl of great price" argument. This argument defends liberal education as simply an education in the Western Tradition, as if such an entity could be definitively known and rendered defensible within a lifetime let alone within the years of schooling howsoever defined. Moreover, this approach invariably forces the proponent of this shallow definition of liberal education to engage in a debate, ultimately irresolvable, in comparative cultural analysis. Sadly, the tradition traced in the chapters above is relevant to this debate, especially in its more virulent campus incarnations, only to the extent that its emergence establishes the decline of liberal education. By confusing the particularities of curriculum with the purpose of liberal education, confusing erudition with education, these proponents unwittingly conflate the necessary curricular choices with firm principles of pedagogy and estimates of cultural worth. Every student of liberal education completes his tutelage knowing less than all there is to know, either across modes of human thought and expression or across cultures. Civic education must always fail if we believe only deep cultural familiarity breeds tolerance among a multicultural citizenry. Liberal education's true object is liberality, no civic virtue better promotes tolerance or protects diversity. No pupil can be taught all of human culture and difference, but he can be taught an openness to his fellow citizen, a willingness to hear him and weigh fairly his opinions. This is the peculiar civic genius of the division drawn between the philosophic and the civic pupil and education. Citizenship does not demand that we be philosophers, it demands that we be virtuous.

Both the utilitarian and the multicultural critiques and their ill-prepared liberal opponents share in common a fundamental misapprehension of the twin foundational premises of liberal education. Liberal education is premised on a profound connection between education and human nature and a concomitant belief in the intractable and ahistorical character of that nature. This contention is as definitive for education as it is for politics and it is the fundamental source of the connection between both. Both the technological and the cultural critique of liberal education fail to recognize this connection and as such they fail to recognize the necessity of educating character. To educate for citizenship is to educate a particular kind of beings, for a fundamental fact of their existence: political life.

In important ways the displacement of an effective and robust liberal education with an ineffective multicultural or technological education presents the greatest challenge to civic virtue, citizenship and political community. This transformation is particularly perilous in our time as a result of the tragic double movement in citizenship. This movement, wherein citizenship is expanded at the same time as its significance is impoverished, appears at first to leave less at stake in the education of citizens. The temptation to consider the impoverishment of citizenship as similarly diminishing the consequences of its miseducation implies a fundamental forgetting of human nature, education, and their respective relations to the political. It rests on a mistaken belief, rejected by each member of my philosophic quintet, that the philosophic component of liberal education can be separated and protected from the civic element. That the education of a natural intellectual aristocracy can somehow continue in the absence of the parallel education of the ordinary citizen. Alisdair MacIntyre succumbs to this regrettable confusion and temptation at the end of his famous and otherwise compelling polemic *After Virtue*.

> What matters at this stage is the construction of local forms of community within which civility and the intellectual and moral life can be sustained through the new dark ages which are already upon us.[9]

MacIntyre and others erroneously conclude that such philosophic communities can be constructed without simultaneously constructing their civic components. Two thousand years ago, from the shade of *De Oratore's* plane tree, Cicero recognized that, dark ages or no, there is no

---

[9] Alisdair MacIntyre, *After Virtue* (Notre Dame: Notre Dame University Press, 1981), 263.

longer a place free from the influence of others and no community sufficiently outside the city walls. The deep connection between the civic and philosophic in education reflects just this deep and inextricable connection between the two in politics. The recovery and continued survival of one depends upon the recovery and continued survival of the other. From Plato through Cicero, to Locke, Rousseau and Smith, the concern for the civic education of the ordinary was based neither on simple beneficence nor on cold-blooded assessments of advantage. It was based instead on a full understanding of the impossibility of separating the one education from the other, the one community from the other.

Plato first recognized that the ascent to the philosophic begins in the civic, to eventually consider justice one must initially consider the city. Civic education is further philosophically justified by the necessity of a certain kind of citizen and polity to the possibility of philosophy. Rather more bluntly, civic education guarantees the peaceable pursuit of philosophy. There is a third critical justification for the education of the non-philosophic, civic education is an education offered in place of another and not as an alternative to no education at all. Civic education mitigates another more corrosive and unceasing education. Plato repeatedly refers to both the danger of an imprudent education in dialectic and the more subtly and therefore more effectively corrosive education of the sophistical city. Cicero echoes Plato's concern. More than the negligent education in empty rhetoric of the forum Cicero fears the education in luxury and ostentation taught constantly by Rome's growing opulence. In John Locke the terrors of boarding school are easily telescoped out to include the corrupting influence of public prejudice. Rousseau offers, in his description of the decline of the Noble Savage and in his indictment of the comfortable nihilism of the Bourgeois, a similar account of the corrupting education offered by polite society. Finally, Smith offers a compelling account of the brutalizing effects on intellect and character of work and life in the emerging mills of Blakean cities. In briefly canvassing these already adumbrated positions I seek to draw out the element of necessity that first and most obviously appeared, between education and politics, in Classical Athens. The liberal and civic education I have attempted to describe is not merely aimed at realizing the ascent to citizenship but at preventing the descent into degaded forms of human existence. Finally liberal civic education is premised on the belief that the fullest realization of citizenship, in its dual meaning as virtue and institution, is both what is required and what is intended for the civic student. A truly liberal civic education becomes a *concern* and like the lexical duality of citizenship it too takes on dual significance. It is both a deeply felt engagement and an essential institution to defend.

Selected Bibliography

Aarslef, Hans. "The State of Nature and the Nature of Man in Locke." In *John Locke: Problems and Perspectives*, ed. John Yolton. Cambridge: Cambridge University Press, 1969.

Augustine. *City of God in Political Writings*. Trans. M.W. Tkacz and D. Kries. Indianapolis: Hackett Publishing, 1994.

Barlow, J.J. "The Education of Statemen in *De Republica*." *Polity* 19 (1987): 353–374.

Barlow, J.J. "The Fox and the Lion: Machiavelli Relies to Cicero." *History of Political Thought* 20 (1999): 627–645.

Benardete, Seth. *Plato's Laws*. Chicago: University of Chicago Press, 2000.

Bloom, Allan. "Interpretative Essay." In *The Republic of Plato*. Trans. Allan Bloom. United States: Basic Books, 1991.

Bloom, Allan. *Love and Friendship*. New York: Simon & Schuster, 1993.

Bloom, Allan. "Rousseau's Critique of Liberal Constitutionalism." In *The Legacy of Rousseau*, eds. Clifford Orwin and Nathan Tarcov. Chicago: University of Chicago Press, 1997.

Bobonovich, C. "Persuasion, Compulsion and Freedom in Plato's Laws." *Classical Quarterly* 41 (1991): 157–179.

Selected Bibliography

Boegehold, Alan L. "Perikles Citizenship Law of 451/0 B.C." In *Athenian Identity and Civic Ideology*, eds. Alan L. Boegehold and Adele C. Scafuro. Baltimore: The Johns Hopkins Press, 1994.

Bonner, Stanley F. *Education in Ancient Rome*. London: Metheun & Co, 1977.

Burchell, David. "MacIntyre, Cicero and Moral Personality." *History of Political Thought* 19 (1998): 101–118.

Chambliss, J.J. "Reason, Conduct, and Revelation in the Educational Theory of Locke, Watts, and Burgh." *Educational Theory* 26 (Fall 1976): 372–387.

Cicero. *De Oratore*, 2 volumes. Trans. E.W. Sutton. Cambridge: Harvard University Press, 1942.

Cicero. *Tusculan Disputations*. Trans. J.E. King. Cambridge: Harvard University Press, 1943.

Cicero. *Orator*. Trans. H.M. Hubbell. Cambridge: Harvard University Press, 1962.

Cicero. *De Finibus*. Trans. H. Rackham. Cambridge: Harvard University Press, 1967.

Cicero. *De Officiis*. Trans. and eds. M. Griffin and E.M. Atkins. New York: Cambridge University Press, 1991.

Cicero. *On the Commonwealth and On the Laws*. Trans. James Zetzel. New York: Cambridge University Press, 1999.

Connor, Robert W. "The Problem of Civic Identity." In *Athenian Identity and Civic Ideology*, eds. Alan L. Boegehold and Adele C. Scafuro. Baltimore: The Johns Hopkins Press, 1994.

Craig, Leon. *The War Lover*. Toronto: University of Toronto Press, 1994.

Cropsey, Joseph. *Polity and Economy: An Interpretation of the Principles of Adam Smith*. The Hague: M. Nijhoff, 1957.

Cropsey, Joseph. *Political Philosophy and the Issues of Politics*. Chicago: University of Chicago Press, 1977.

Cropsey, Joseph. "Adam Smith and Political Philosophy." In *Essays on Adam Smith*, eds. A.S. Skinner and T. Wilson. Oxford: Clarendon Press, 1975.

Dankert, C.E. "Adam Smith, Educator." *Dalhousie Review* 47 (1967): 13–27.

Darling, John. "Rousseau as Progressive Instrumentalist." *Journal of Philosophy of Education* 27 (1993): 27–38.

DiLorenzo, Raymond. "The Critique of Socrates in Cicero's *De Oratore*: *Ornatus* and the Nature of Wisdom." *Philosophy and Rhetoric* 11 (1978): 246–261.

Dunn, John. *The Political Thought of John Locke*. Cambridge: Cambridge University Press, 1969.

Ferrary, Jean-Louis. "The Stateman and the Law in the Political Philosophy of Cicero." In *Justice and Generosity*, ed. Andre Laks. New York: Cambridge University Press, 1995.

Frede, Dorothea. "Constitution and Citizenship: Peripatetic Influences on Cicero's Political Conception in the *De Re Publica*." In *Cicero's Knowledge of the Peripatos*, eds. William W. Fortenbaugh and Peter Steinmetz. New York: Brunswick Transaction Books, 1989.

Frost, Frank J. "Aspects of Early Athenian Citizenship." In *Athenian Identity and Civic Ideology*, eds. Alan Boegehold and Adele C. Scafuro. Baltimore: The Johns Hopkins Press, 1994.

Fuhrmann, Manfred. *Cicero and the Roman Republic*. Trans. W.E. Yuill. Oxford: Blackwell Publishers, 1990.

Grube, G.M.A. *The Greek and Roman Critics*. Toronto: University of Toronto Press, 1965.

Gwynn, Aubrey. *Roman Education from Cicero to Quintillian*. 2nd ed. New York: Russell & Russell, 1964.

Hanley, Ryan. *Adam Smith and the Character of Virtue*. Cambridge: Cambridge University Press, 2009.

Hathaway, R.F. "Cicero's Socratic View of History." *Journal of the History of Ideas* 29 (1968): 3–12.

Hegel, G.W.F. *Phenomenology of Spirit*. Trans. A.V. Miller. Oxford: Oxford University Press, 1977.

Hont, Istvan and Ignatieff, Michael. "Needs and Justice in the *Wealth of Nations*: An Introductory Essay." In *Wealth and Virtue*, eds. Hont and Ignatieff. Cambridge: Cambridge University Press, 1985.

Hope, V.M. *Virtue By Consensus*. Oxford: Clarendon Press, 1989.

Horowitz, Maryanne C. "The Stoic Synthesis of Natural Law in Man: Four Themes." *Journal of the History of Ideas* 35 (1974): 3–16.

Horwitz, Robert. "John Locke and the Preservation of Liberty." *American Political Science Reviewer* 6: 325–353.

Johnson, Curtis. "The 'Craft' of Plato's Philosopher-Rulers." In *Politikos*, ed. Leslie G. Rubin. Pittsburgh: Duquesne University Press, 1992.

Kellow, Geoffrey. "Things Familiar to the Mind: Heuristic Style and Elliptical Citation in *The Wealth of Nations*." *History of the Human Sciences* 24 (2011): 1–18.

Klosko, George. "Demotike Arete in the Republic." *History of Political Thought* 3 (1982): 363–381.

Laslett, Peter. Introduction to *Two Treatises of Government*, John Locke, ed. Peter Laslett. Cambridge: Cambridge University Press, 1994.

Lijphart, Arendt. "Unequal Participation: Democracy's Unresolved Dilemma" (1997). *American Political Science Review* 91 (1): 1–14.

Locke, John. "Board of Trade Papers." In *The Life of John Locke*, ed. Fox Bourne, 2 Volumes. London: Henry S. King & Co., 1876.

Locke, John. *Reasonableness of Christianity*, ed. L.T. Ramsey. London: Adam & Charles Black, 1958.

Locke, John. *On the Conduct of Understanding*, ed. Francis W. Garforth. New York: Teachers College Press, 1966.

Locke, John. *Some Thoughts Concerning Education*. In *The Education Writings of John Locke*, ed. James Axtell. Cambridge: Cambridge University Press, 1968.

Locke, John. "Concerning Reading and Study." In *Educational Writings of John Locke*, ed. James Axtell. Cambridge: Cambridge University Press, 1968.

Locke, John. *An Essay Concerning Human Understanding*, ed. Peter H. Nidditch. Oxford: Oxford University Press, 1975.

Locke, John. *Letter Concerning Toleration*. Indianapolis: Hackett Publishing, 1983.

Locke, John. *Two Treatises of Government*, ed. Peter Laslett. Cambridge: Cambridge University Press, 1994.

Long, A.A. "Cicero's Politics." In *Justice and Generosity*, ed. Andre Laks. Cambridge: Cambridge University Press. 1995.

MacIntyre, Alisdair. *After Virtue*. Notre Dame: University of Notre Dame Press, 1981.

Macpherson, C.B. "The Social Bearing of Locke's Political Theory." *The Western Political Quarterly* 7, no. 1 (1954): 1–22.

Manville, Phillip Brook. *The Origins of Citizenship in Ancient Athens*. Princeton: Princeton University Press, 1990.

Marrou, H.I. *A History of Education in Antiquity*. Trans. George Lamb. London: Sheed and Ward, 1956.

Masters, Roger. *The Political Philosophy of Rousseau*. Princeton: Princeton University Press, 1968.

Megill, A.D. "Theory and Experience in Adam Smith." *Journal of the History of Ideas* 36 (1975): 79–94.

Melzer, Arthur. *The Natural Goodness of Man*. Chicago: University of Chicago Press, 1990.

Milton, John. *Areopagitica and of Education*, ed. George H. Sabine. Arlington Heights: Harlan Davidson, 1951.

Mitchell, T.N. "Cicero on the Moral Crisis of the Late Republic." *Hermathena* 136 (1984): 21–41.

Morrow, Glenn. *Plato's Cretan City*. Princeton: Princeton University Press, 1966.

Morrow, Glenn. *The Ethical and Economic Theories of Adam Smith*. New York: Augustus Kelley Publishers, 1969.

Nederman, Cary J. "War, Peace and Republican Virtue: Patriotism and the Neglected Legacy of Cicero." In *Instilling Ethics*, ed. Norma Thompson. Lanham, Massachusetts: Rowman and Littlefield, 2000.

Nettleship, R.L. *The Theory of Education in Plato's Republic*. Oxford: Oxford University Press, 1935.

Newell, W.R. *Ruling Passion*. Lanham, Maryland: Rowman and Littlefield, 2000.

Nicgorski, Walter. "Cicero's Focus: From the Best Regime to the Model Statesman." *Political Theory* 19 (1991): 230–251.

Nichols, Mary. "Rousseau's Novel Education in the *Emile*." *Political Theory* 13 (1985): 535–558.

Nussbaum, Martha. "Duties of Justice, Duties of Material Aid: Cicero's Problematical Legacy." *Journal of Poltical Philosophy* 8 (2000): 176–206.

Oksenberg Rorty, Amelie. "Plato's Counsel on Education." *Philosophy* 73 (1998): 157–178.

Oksenberg Rorty, Amelie. "Rousseau's Educational Experiments." In *Philosophers on Education*, ed. Amelie Oksenberg Rorty. London: Routledge, 1998.

Owen, David. "History and Curriculum in Rousseau's *Emile*." *Educational Theory* 32 (1982): 117–130.

Pangle, Thomas. "Interpretive Essay." In *The Laws of Plato*. Trans. T. Pangle. Chicago: University of Chicago Press, 1979.

Pangle, Thomas. *The Spirit of Modern Republicanism*. Chicago: University of Chicago Press, 1988.

Pangle, Lorraine and Pangle, Thomas. *The Learning of Liberty*. Lawrence: University of Kansas Press, 1993.

Parry, Geraint. "*Emile*: Learning to be Men, Women and Citizens." In *Cambridge Companion to Rousseau*, ed. Patrick Riley. Cambridge: Cambridge University Press, 2001.

Peters, R.S. *Essays on Educators*. London: Allen & Unwin, 1981.

Phillipson, Nicholas. "Adam Smith as Civic Moralist." In *Wealth and Virtue*, eds. Istvan Hont and Michael Ignatieff. Cambridge: Cambridge University Press, 1985.

Plamenatz, John. "Rousseau: The Education of Emile." *The Proceedings of the Philosophy of Education Society of Great Britain* (1972): 176–192.

Plato. *Gorgias*. Trans. W.C. Helmbold. Indianapolis: Library of the Liberal Arts, 1952.
Plato. *Cleitophon*. Trans. Clifford Orwin. In *The Roots of Political Philosophy*, ed. Thomas Pangle. Ithaca: Cornell University Press, 1988.
Plato. *The Laws of Plato*. Trans. Thomas Pangle. Chicago: University of Chicago Press, 1988.
Plato. *The Republic of Plato*. Trans. Allan Bloom. New York: Basic Books, 1991.
Plato. *Euthydemus*. Trans. W.H.D. Rouse. In *Plato Collected Dialogues*, eds. Edith Hamilton and Huntington Cairns. 16th ed. Princeton: Princeton University Press, 1996.
Plato. *Sophist*. Trans. F.M. Cornford. In *Plato Collected Dialogues*, eds. Edith Hamilton and Huntington Cairns, 16th ed. Princeton: Princeton University Press, 1996.
Post, David M. "Jeffersonian Revisions of Locke." *Journal of the History of Ideas* 47 (1986): 147–157.
Raafluab, Kurt. "Perceptions of Democracy in Fifth-Century Athens." In *Aspects of Athenian Democracy*, ed. W. Robert Connor. Copenhagen: Museum Tusculanum Press, 1990.
Raphael, D.D. "The Impartial Spectator." In *Essays on Adam Smith*, eds. A.S. Skinner and T. Wilson. Oxford: Clarendon Press, 1975.
Rawson, Elizabeth. *Cicero A Portrait*. London: Penguin Books, 1975.
Remer, Gary. "Political Oratory and Conversation." *Political Theory* 27 (1999): 39–64.
Rosen, Stanley. *Plato's Statesman*. New Haven: Yale University Press, 1995.
Rousseau, Jean Jacques. *The Government of Poland*. Trans. Willmoore Kendall. Indianapolis: Library of the Library of the Liberal Arts, 1972.
Rousseau, Jean Jacques. *Emile*. Trans. Allan Bloom. New York: HarperCollins, 1979.
Rousseau, Jean Jacques. "Discourse on the Origin of Inequality." In *The Basic Political Writings*. Trans. Donald A. Cress. Indianapolis: Hackett Publishing Company, 1987.
Rousseau, Jean Jacques. "Discourse on Political Economy." In *The Basic Political Writings*. Trans. Donald A. Cress. Indianapolis: Hackett Publishing Company, 1987.
Rousseau, Jean Jacques. "On the Social Contract or Principles of Political Right." In *The Basic Political Writings*. Trans. Donald Cress. Indianapolis: Hackett Publishing, 1987.
Salter, John. "Adam Smith on Feudalism, Commerce and Slavery." *History of Political Thought* 13 (1992): 219–241.

Scolnicov, Samuel. *Plato's Metaphysics of Education.* London: Routledge, 1988.
Shklar, Judith. *Men and Citizens.* Cambridge: Cambridge University Press, 1969.
Simon, Julia. "Natural Freedom and Moral Autonomy: Emile as Parent, Teacher and Citizen." *History of Political Thought* 36 (1995): 21–36.
Smith, Adam. eds. R.H. Cambell and A.S. Skinner. *An Inquiry Into the Nature Oxford and Causes of the Wealth of Nations.* Indianapolis: Liberty Fund, 1981.
Smith, Adam. eds. A.L. Macfie and D.D. Raphael. *The Theory of Moral Sentiments.* Indianapolis: Liberty Fund, 1984.
Spellman, W.M. *John Locke and the Problem of Depravity.* Oxford: Clarendon Press, 1988.
Strauss, Barry S. "Oikos and Polis." In *Aspects of Athenian Democracy*, ed. W. Robert Connor. Copenhagen: Museum Tusculanum Press, 1990.
Strauss, Leo. *Natural Right and History.* Chicago: University of Chicago Press, 1953.
Strauss, Leo. *The City and Man.* Chicago: University of Chicago Press, 1964.
Strauss, Leo. *Liberalism Ancient and Modern.* New York: Basic Books, 1968.
Strauss, Leo. *The Argument and the Action of Plato's Laws.* Chicago: University of Chicago Press, 1975.
Strauss, Leo. *What Is Political Philosophy?* Chicago: University of Chicago Press, 1988.
Strauss, Leo. *Persecution and the Art of Writing.* Chicago: University of Chicago Press, 1992.
Strong, Tracy. *Jean-Jacques Rousseau, The Politics of the Ordinary.* London: Sage Publications, 1994.
Tarcov, Nathan. *Locke's Education for Liberty.* Chicago: University of Chicago Press, 1984.
Teloh, Henry. *Socratic Education in Plato's Early Dialogues.* South Bend, Indiana: University of Notre Dame Press, 1986.
Thucydides. *History of the Pelopennesion War.* Trans. Rex Warner. London: Penguin Books, 1972.
Tully, James. "Governing Conduct." In *Conscience and Casuistry in Early Modern Europe*, ed. Edmund Leites. Cambridge: Cambridge University Press, 1988.
Uyl, Douglas J. Den and Charles Griswold Jr, Charles. "Adam Smith on Friendship and Love." *Review of Metaphysics* 49 (1996): 609–637.
Voegelin, Eric. *Plato.* Baton Rouge: Louisiana State University Press, 1966.

Voegelin, Eric. "Liberalism and Its History." *Review of Politics* 36 (1974): 520–540.
Waczek, Norbert. "Two Concepts of Morality: A Distinction of Adam Smith's Ethics and Its Stoic Origin." *Journal of the History of Ideas* 45 (1984): 591–606.
Ward, Lee. *John Locke and Modern Life*. Cambridge: Cambridge University Press, 2010.
Wills, Garry. *Inventing America*. New York: Doubleday & Company, 1978.
Winch, Donald. *Adam Smith's Politics*. Cambridge: Cambridge University Press, 1978.
Yolton, John. *John Locke and Education*. New York: Random House, 1971.
Zuckert, Michael. "Fools and Knaves: Reflections on Locke's Theory of Philosophical Discourse." *Review of Politics* 36 (1974): 544–564.
Zuckert, Michael. *The Natural Rights Republic*. Notre Dame: University of Notre Dame Press, 1996.

Index

A

Afranius 78
Agora 15
Antigone 16
Aporia 12, 214
Appomattox 221
Ares 126
Aristophanes 18–20
Athens 3, 13–18, 31, 66, 69, 77, 80, 81, 86
Autochthony 17, 27, 74, 75

B

Baedecker's 182
Bloom, Allan 3, 4, 35, 36, 149
Burke, Edmund 220–222

C

Caecilius 78
Calculation (*logismos*) 50
Canada 107
Canadians 1
Cato 71, 91, 215, 216
CCTV 222
Christianity 96, 158
Churchill, Winston 107
Cicero
   Antonius, M. 81
   Caesar 73, 89, 99, 103
   Caesarism 73, 103
   Cassii 72
   Catulus, Q. Lutatius 81
   Claudii 72
   Crassus, L. Licenius 80
   grammaticus 79, 92
   inchoata intelligentia 99, 106, 159, 196

King Ancus 75
Laelius, Gaius 73, 88, 89
Laws (De Legibus) 78, 96, 100
Letters to Atticus 66
Marius 81
mos maiorum 90, 91, 94, 100, 105
On Duties (De Officiis) 66
On Oratory (De Oratore) 76, 81–83, 85, 86, 92, 93, 100, 104, 126, 226
On the Ends of Good and Evil (De Finibus) 78, 87, 97
Orator 72, 75
Philus, Lucius 88
Pompey 89
pontiffs 86–88
praelectio 79, 80
Quinctii 72
Republic (De Re Publica) 58, 66, 69–71, 73, 75, 76, 84, 88–90, 93, 99–101, 104–106
Sabine women 75
Scipii 73, 74, 105
Scipio, P. Cornelius 73, 91
Sulla 81
Tarquinius, Lucius 75
Tubero, Quintus 88, 93, 95, 104, 105
Tusculan Disputations 68, 77
Twelve Tables 71
Vopiscus, Stabo 81
Cicero, Marcus 68, 70, 89, 90, 103, 105, 106
Cicero, Quintus 89, 90, 103
Citizenship 2–4, 6, 7, 13, 14, 17, 37, 40, 51, 57, 75, 99, 111, 134, 143, 146, 159, 189, 198, 199, 221, 224–228

The Clouds 18, 19, 88
Commercialism 176
Connor, W. Robert 17
Constant, Benjamin 126
Constitutions 43, 59, 71, 110, 148
Corinth 69
Crete 10–12
Cultural relativism 7
Customs 2, 5, 25, 75, 90, 92, 95, 109, 117–119, 123, 129, 131–135, 137, 141, 146, 199, 216

D

Dance 45, 46
Democracy 2, 3, 20, 182
Democrats 26, 37
Diaresis 23, 32, 43, 51, 64, 97, 125
DiLorenzo, Raymond 83
Doctors 1, 52–55, 57, 99
Duty 2, 15, 16, 83–86, 88, 91, 93, 95, 101–103, 105, 109, 140, 143, 152–156, 175, 177, 179–181, 185, 215, 221

E

Education of A Christian Prince (Erasmus) 136
Emulation 95, 100, 106
Ennius 78, 90
Epistemology 13, 112, 113
Erasmus 115, 135, 196
Eros 62, 155

F

Fodors 182

Forum 91, 92, 94, 95, 100, 103, 109, 223, 227
Funeral Oration 2, 14, 17, 18, 221

G

Genovese, Kitty 222
Gitlin, Todd 4
Good breeding 134, 144, 145
Groundwork of the Metaphysics of Morals 156
Gymnastics 37, 44–46

H

Habit 5, 64, 96, 101, 126, 129–138, 141–143, 146, 167–169, 199, 204, 210, 213, 216, 223
Habituation 43, 44, 47, 51, 52, 131, 142, 145, 161, 167, 168
Hera 126
Heraclitus 219, 220
History of the Peloponnesian War 14
Homer 58, 78
Honor 95, 100, 102, 173, 182
Horace 68, 77
Hunting 60–63, 125

I

Imitation 93, 146
Inclination 118, 124, 125, 131, 139, 142, 146, 152–157, 161, 174, 175, 179, 180, 182, 183, 185, 198
Innate principles 143
Intelligence 22, 32, 58

J

Jean-Jacques (Emile) 167, 177–181, 185

K

Kant, Immanuel 156
Kennedy, Robert F. 221
Keynes, John Maynard 188
King jr., Martin Luther 9

L

Labour theory of value 120
Lasch, Christopher 4
Letter from Birmingham Jail 9
Literacy 173, 198
Locke, John
  A Letter Concerning Toleration 110, 111
  An Essay Concerning Human Understanding 114
  boarding schools 134, 135, 164, 227
  Board of Trade Papers 130, 132, 133
  good breeding 143–145
  Macpherson, C.B. 127, 128, 137
  natural law 120
  poor laws 132, 133
  private education 111
  public education 110
  The Reasonableness of Christianity 126, 136
  Tabula Rasa 113–116, 120
  Two Treatises of Government 110, 111, 117, 195
  Virginia 128
Lowe, Amanda 221, 222

M

Machiavelli 103, 109, 121, 196
MacIntyre, Alisdair 226
Medicine 53
Menander 78
Milton, John 108, 109, 111, 114, 115, 135, 136, 140
Multiculturalism 7
Music 32, 37, 41, 45, 132
My Early Life (Churchill) 107

N

Neo-Platonism 85
Newell, W.R. 25, 26, 30
Nietzsche 150, 183, 219
Nomos 45, 58, 163
Numa 86, 87
Nussbaum, Martha 4, 83

O

Ontology 6, 13, 50, 112, 113, 121
Opinion 29, 35, 36, 51–53, 96, 113, 157, 180, 200, 220, 222, 225
Oratory 68, 71, 76, 83, 84, 86, 93, 94, 100, 104, 151
Orwell, George 222

P

Pericles 2, 14–18, 109, 221
Philo-hellenism 67
Piraeus 22
Plato
  Adeimantus 39, 40
  Athenian Stranger 10–12, 43–47, 51, 52, 55–64, 98, 185

Callicles 83
Callipolis 27, 31–34, 36, 37, 40–42, 50, 58, 60, 70
Cephalus 22, 24–26, 36
The Cleitophon 20, 21
The Euthydemus 23
Glaukon (Glaucon) 27, 39, 40
The Gorgias 83, 99
guardians 35, 41
hoplites 15
Kleinias 10, 11, 45, 51, 55, 58, 59, 61, 62, 141, 186
The Laws 10–13, 27, 30, 31, 38, 39, 42–48, 50–52, 55–58, 60–64, 66, 72, 86, 100, 125, 200, 205
logismos 50, 137, 222
logos 50
Megillos 10, 11, 43, 47, 48, 51, 55, 58, 61, 62, 141, 186
Myth of the Cave 9, 27, 28
Noble Lie 26–28, 31, 50, 98, 168
paideia 30, 67, 100
Phaedrus 60, 81, 82, 126
Piracy 63
puppetry 47, 48
The Republic 2, 9–13, 21, 22, 24, 26, 31, 32, 34, 35, 39, 41–48, 50, 51, 55, 56, 60, 61, 64, 66, 70, 93, 98, 99, 151, 163, 168, 185
Ring of Gyges 223
The Statesman 38
Sumphonia 44, 51
Thrasymachus 21, 22, 25, 26, 36, 40–42
true knowledge (*gnosis*) 30
true opinion (*dike*) 30

Platonism 12, 13, 21–27, 29, 37, 40, 54, 56, 58, 64, 66, 67, 70, 82, 84, 85, 93, 97, 98, 125, 151, 200, 222
Poverty 15, 132, 133, 223
Pre-Socratics 86
The Prince (Machiavelli) 103
Propadeutics 39
Pseudo-Xenophon 15, 16
Public education 110, 211

Q

Quintilian 76

R

Reading 12, 64, 69, 79, 81, 92, 96, 97, 103, 114, 115, 117, 119, 135, 136, 149, 172, 173, 183, 187, 189, 198, 216
Religion 133, 177
Rhetoric 69, 82, 93–95, 103, 227
Rhythm 32, 45, 46, 79, 80, 82, 163
Roman Republic 66, 67, 108
Roman Senate 67
Rome 66, 68–74, 77, 80–83, 86, 90, 91, 93, 94, 98, 100, 102, 105, 227
Roosevelt, Franklin D. 147
Rosen, Stanley 23, 38
Rote learning 5, 51
Rousseau, Jean-Jacques
  Amour de Soi-Meme 200
  Amour Propre 159, 174, 179, 181, 184
  bildungsroman 157
  bourgeois 1, 152, 153, 160, 176, 186, 227

Clarens 176
The Constitution of Poland 153
dependence 167, 169, 170, 173, 186
Emile 128, 149, 150, 152–154, 157–167, 169, 171–179, 181–184, 186, 207, 224
fatherland 158, 171
Jean-Jacques (Emile's Teacher) 177
Julie, Ou La Nouvelle Heloise 176
natural man 150, 152, 156, 175
necessity 5, 152, 157, 166, 169–177, 181, 184, 186, 227
neotany 156
On the Social Contract 156, 172, 182
prophylaxis 157, 161
Second Discourse 150, 159, 175, 200
self-sufficiency 172, 177, 181
sensationalism 224
Sophie 178–185

S

Smith, Adam
  child labor 197, 198, 215
  division of labor 114, 192–194, 196–199, 209, 216
  economics 187–189, 192–194, 196, 197, 212–216
  impartiality 204, 205, 208–210
  impartial spectator 204–206, 212
  militia 211–213
  pin-making 197
  political economy 189, 191, 192, 213
  propriety 199–201, 205, 206

Romanticism 212
Scottish Enlightenment 189, 212
sympathetic imagination 207, 209
sympathy 188, 206, 207, 209, 210
Theory of Moral Sentiments 188–190, 192, 194, 196, 199, 200, 209, 212–214
Wealth of Nations 114, 188–192, 196, 197, 199, 200, 209, 213–216, 221
Socialization 29, 203, 209
Socrates 11, 12, 18–30, 33, 35–41, 55, 57, 60, 66, 70, 77, 81, 83, 84, 86–88, 93, 97, 151, 223
Solon 58
Sophists 18, 21, 29, 31, 34, 41
Sophocles 16
Sparta 69
Sport 63
Stanhope, Philip (Lord Chesterfield) 114
Strauss, Leo 3, 12, 20, 43, 44, 67, 96, 109, 120

Terence 78, 80, 81
Themistocles 94
Thetes 15
Thinkery 19
Thucydides 14–18

Urbanism 221
Utilitarianism 6, 7, 29, 189, 224, 225

Virgil 76, 215
Voegelin, Eric 28, 29, 224
Voter fatigue 1, 2

Weaving 38, 72, 143
Western Canon 5

Zeno 201